TERRORISM, BETRAYAL & RESILIENCE

ADST-DACOR Diplomats and Diplomacy Series

SERIES EDITOR

Margery Boichel Thompson

Since 1776, extraordinary men and women have represented the United States abroad under widely varying circumstances. What they did and how and why they did it remain little known to their compatriots. In 1995 the Association for Diplomatic Studies and Training (ADST) and DACOR, an organization of foreign affairs professionals, created the Diplomats and Diplomacy book series to increase public knowledge and appreciation of the professionalism of American diplomats and their involvement in world history. The disturbing aftermath of the August 1998 bombings of Embassy/Nairobi and Embassy/Dar es Salaam forms the dramatic core of Ambassador Prudence Bushnell's "tale of terror and resilience." It is the sixty-fifth volume in the series.

TERRORISM, BETRAYAL & RESILIENCE

MY STORY OF THE 1998 U.S. EMBASSY BOMBINGS

PRUDENCE BUSHNELL

AN ADST-DACOR DIPLOMATS AND DIPLOMACY BOOK

Potomac Books

An imprint of the University of Nebraska Press

Part of chapter 12 was originally published in *Foreign Service Journal* (January–February 2017).

Library of Congress Cataloging-in-Publication Data

Names: Bushnell, Prudence, 1946–, author.
Title: Terrorism, betrayal, and resilience: my story of the 1998 U.S. Embassy bombings / Prudence Bushnell.
Other titles: ADST-DACOR diplomats and diplomacy series.
Description: Lincoln: University of Nebraska Press, 2018.
| Series: ADST-DACOR diplomats and diplomacy series |
Includes bibliographical references and index.
Identifiers: LCCN 2018008993
ISBN 9781640121010 (cloth: alk. paper)
ISBN 9781640121324 (epub)
ISBN 9781640121331 (mobi)
ISBN 9781640121348 (pdf)
Subjects: LCSH: United States Embassy Bombing, Nairobi, Kenya, 1998. | Jihad. | Women ambassadors— United States—Biography. | Ambassadors—United States—Biography. | Leadership. | Leadership in women. | Terrorism—Prevention.
Classification: LCC HV6433.K4 B87 2018 |
DDC 363.325096762509049—dc23
LC record available at https://lccn.loc.gov/2018008993

Set in Scala OT by E. Cuddy.

This book is dedicated to the people whose lives were lost on August 7, 1998, in Nairobi, Kenya, and Dar es Salaam, Tanzania

CONTENTS

ILLUSTRATIONS

PREFACE

This is an account of the "war on terror" and my life. The book begins with the al-Qaeda attacks on the U.S. embassies in Kenya and Tanzania on August 7, 1998, and ends in the fall of 2017. This is my personal perspective.

Most books about al-Qaeda and the war on terrorism highlight the perpetrators. This one starts with the story of survivors and how we found resilience as a Kenyan and American community. Most books about al-Qaeda and the war on terrorism are written by men; I am a woman. Most books about the war on terrorism focus on tactics; I focus on leadership.

I cannot separate the story of August 7—what happened and how—from my own because we were both products of foreign policies made in Washington with little thought of long-term impacts, much less of the people implementing them overseas. I grew up in a Foreign Service family among the ruins of World War II in Germany and France and the consequences of the Cold War in Pakistan and Iran. When I returned for college in the United States in the mid-1960s, policy discussions about race and war were taking place in the streets, and I had to figure out where I fit into this country of mine. In the 1970s policies and attitudes about women made me a feminist, and a court-imposed affirmative action program in the Department of State brought me into the Foreign Service in my own right in the early 1980s.

In 1998, when the bombs went off in Kenya and Tanzania, Congress was in recess. The White House, along with the entire country, was focused on the "Monica Lewinsky scandal" and efforts to impeach President Bill Clinton. Congress held no hearings about the bombings, the national security community held no after-action reviews, and the mandatory Accountability Review Board focused on narrow security issues. Then on September 11, 2001, al-Qaeda attacked the U.S. homeland and the East Africa bombings became little more than a footnote.

Investigations into the 9/11 attacks revealed just how much parts of our law enforcement and intelligence communities had known about al-Qaeda since 1996, two years before we were blown up in Nairobi and Dar es Salaam. I wanted to know how these bombings could have happened, given the scrutiny bin Laden and his cell in Nairobi were getting from special groups in the National Security Council, the FBI, the CIA, and the NSA.

I also wanted to tell the story of our community and what it was like to work in an embassy struggling toward normalcy after a life-changing attack. For all of the treasure and lives consumed by the war on terror, the targets and survivors receive little attention. As terrorist threats and our conflicts with "jihadists" continue through a fourth presidency, I highlight lessons that prevented our government from safeguarding its diplomatic facilities in contrast to our community's resilience and leadership that enabled good people to prevail. We can be wounded, angry, happy, sorry, sad, scared, and hopeful and still carry on.

I tell the story in three parts. Part 1 is a personal chronicle of the bombing and its aftermath that includes a narrative of my own life. I move back in time to share what it was like beginning life as a "third culture" kid in the Foreign Service and moving through patriarchal cultures and the State Department hierarchy to become an ambassador. As a girl growing up in the 1950s, it was inconceivable that I could become a leader, much less one who excelled in disasters. My only role model was Joan of Arc, and I was well aware of what happened to her when she put on a pair of pants and led men. But I did become a leader, intentionally, and the bombing in Nairobi was a test of leadership the likes of which I never imagined. More important to the nation, it was the act of a war in which the United States had no idea it was engaged.

Part 2 reviews the formation of jihadist groups, including those supported by the United States when it worked to make Afghanistan "Russia's Vietnam." It lays out three competing forces—al-Qaeda, the U.S. law enforcement and intelligence communities, and my embassy—all careening down parallel tracks to the fateful day of August 7, 1998.

Part 3 offers the leadership lessons I acquired and an assessment of results after fighting the war on terrorism for almost twenty years, four presidencies, trillions of dollars, and millions of civilians dead, injured, and displaced.

ACKNOWLEDGMENTS

Those who were killed deserve to be recorded in history, and those whose lives were forever changed by the al-Qaeda attacks on August 7, 1998, deserve to know what happened and how. Richard Buckley, aka Top Spouse and Don Ricardo, stood by my side, researched the facts, and stayed on my back until the book was finished. Betty Douglass Sparkman supported me, and Rheta Grimsley-Johnson taught me. Margery Thompson and the Association for Diplomatic Studies and Training put the narrative into the hands of Potomac Books, and the University of Nebraska Press agreed to put it on record. John McConnico provided his Pulitzer Prize–winning cover photograph. Thank you. This is your book, too.

1

WHAT HAPPENED?

1

THE BOMBING

August 7, 1998: Nairobi, Midmorning

The building swayed; a teacup began rattling; shards of glass and ceiling tile sprayed the area. One thought swirled dreamily around my brain as every muscle in my body clenched in revolt. "I am going to die." I was on the top floor of a high-rise office building that I knew was going to collapse.

Moments earlier, it had been just another Friday morning. Another day, another meeting. I was, after all, the U.S. ambassador to Kenya, and ambassadors meet a lot. This one concerned the upcoming U.S. trade delegation that Secretary of Commerce William Daley would be leading. An advance team was already in town helping with the preparations. Two Commerce Department colleagues had joined me for the meeting taking place on the twenty-first floor of the Cooperative Bank Building in downtown Nairobi next to the embassy chancery, which housed many of the U.S. government staff in Kenya. Like most meetings with ministers, it had begun with a press briefing and photo op, followed by a cup of tea to settle in. The tea had been served.

An explosion from the street below drew us to the window. I was the last to get up, and I had moved only a few feet from the couch I was sharing with Commerce Minister Joseph Kamotho when a loud wave of freight-train force hurled me back across the room. Everything dimmed. Shadowy figures silently moved past me. Then nothing. I woke to find myself alone. Where had everyone gone? The man lying face down on the other side of the room was surely dead, I thought, and in a second we would both be plunging down multiple stories of concrete. I would not be the first U.S. ambassador to die in the line of duty with her boots on, or in my case, Ferragamo shoes—but, oh my God . . .

The shaking stopped. The teacup went silent. The man across the room raised his head just as my Commerce Department colleague rushed into view. "Ambassador, hurry, quick, we need to get out of here."

We made our way through the smoky debris and deathly calm into the hallway, checking for other survivors as we went. The man on the other side of the room had disappeared. A woman rushed past us and vanished. The atmosphere was hazy, or maybe it was me. I felt like Alice at the bottom of the rabbit hole. Out of nowhere, the elevator operator who had escorted us into the minister's office appeared.

"Sorry, so sorry," he muttered, wringing his hands as if he himself had caused the explosion. He showed us to a stairwell, its access barred by the heavy exit door blown off its hinges. I hiked up the skirt of my dress-for-success business suit and climbed up and over, careful not to lose my footing on the slippery steel. My colleague, my purse slung across his chest, stepped over a pool of blood to join me. The minister and others who had attended the meeting were nowhere in sight; they must have already left.

We met only a few people coming out of the top floors, dazed and silent. As we descended, we joined a parade of slowly moving, shocked and bloodied Kenyans, crushed together and morphing into a multiheaded reptile calmly slithering down steps and over doors. "Keep your feet on the ground," I told myself. "Focus! Hand on railing, feet on the stairs." I was desperate to keep at least that much control. Now and then someone would cry, "Karibu," the Swahili word for "Welcome," to the people who joined us. A woman's body materialized from above us, and we ever so gently passed her to the people below us. Dead? Unconscious? I had no idea. Another woman sang a Christian hymn. We continued down. Someone began to pray. Blood dripped steadily onto my hair and my arm. Was that my blood? Was it getting into the open cut on my arm? Survival instincts banished idle thoughts: "Keep a grip on the railing and your feet on the floor!" Down we went.

Idle thoughts returned. Then we stopped. "This must be some horrible event. Wasn't a teachers' strike going on? Bank strike? We're in a bank building, yes? Just have to get out of here, and all will be well." I focused on that: "All will be well. Keep your feet on the floor!"

"Fire, fire! Hurry, hurry, hurry!" a man yelled in panic. We were at a dead standstill, smoke washing over us. No one moved.

"I'm going to die." This time I knew it. "At least I will be asphyxiated, not burned to death." The thought consoled me until impulse intervened again. "Think straight." We had been descending stairs for so long. Surely, we were close to the bottom! Get out of the building, and we will be fine. Our medical unit was in the basement of the chancery, separated from this death trap by only a small parking lot. Once in the embassy, we would be fine. All will be well. Stay focused.

The slow-motion descent resumed, and we soon saw light and felt air. We had made it. A frightened-looking Kenyan soldier hurried us down the few remaining stairs and out of the building.

I stumbled out, astounded to see thousands of people restrained by men in uniforms across the street staring at the bloody parade of people emerging with us. My colleague looked around and hissed, "Quick, Ambassador, put your head down; there's press." Who knows what made him think that? "I think I saw it in a movie," he said months later. The journalists in attendance at the minister's pre-meeting press conference had reached the street just minutes before the explosion. Many had stayed to record the carnage. I bowed my head, stemming the blood from a gash in my lower lip, and took a few steps forward. I saw the sidewalk littered with glass shards, twisted metal, and puddles of blood. Another step and I came upon the charred remains of what had once been a human being. I felt my head jerk up.

The parking lot we had walked through earlier that morning had disappeared, replaced by hell. Flames rose from burning vehicles as smoke billowed into the building from which we had just exited. Nearby, a large mound of concrete guided my sight into the remains of the rear of our chancery—much of the back wall had dissolved into shattered rock. A few yards away, our neighboring seven-story office building had turned into an even larger hill of smashed concrete precariously supporting hundreds of people digging frantically through the piles of stone debris with bare hands to find anyone buried under the rubble.

In the middle of the usually busy street next to us, a city bus smoldered, most of its incinerated passengers still in their seats. It had stopped for the red light on the corner. The schoolboys in another bus had been taken to a hospital to have shattered glass dug out from their eyes, faces, and upper torsos. Ahead of us, outside the fence of the chancery, an angry-looking American civilian I did not know stood duty, his suit covered by a flak jacket and a weapon in his hand.

Then came shouts. "There she is! Quick, get her out of here. Get her out of here!" Someone grabbed my free arm, rushed us past the front of the chancery, and pushed us into the back of a garishly painted safari jeep I recognized as belonging to an embassy colleague. Another Commerce colleague was in the backseat trying to staunch the blood pouring down his face. The embassy's senior Kenyan security officer jumped into the front seat. Someone banged loudly on the back, yelling, "Go! Go! Go!"

We shot forward, almost running over a woman who had stepped out from the mass of humanity on either side of us. I was jolted out of my dream state.

"Stop!" I ordered the driver. "We are going to take this slowly." Okay. Now where were we going? I did not want a hospital overflowing with emergencies when my colleagues needed attention now. A hotel? Why not? The luxury spots that catered to tourists might just have a resident or visiting doctor. I must have been thinking out loud because my companions agreed to the idea, and one volunteered: "I'm staying at the Serena Hotel. We can go there."

I do not remember the drive. I do remember my colleague once again reminding me to cover my face as we entered the hotel. I took one look at him and thought, forget it. I wanted to see what was ahead. So, bloodied but unbowed, we three Americans scurried through the luxurious lobby past astonished tourists, photo-equipped for a safari. Once in the hotel room, we miraculously located both a doctor and a nurse, who took one look at the wounds of my colleagues and raced off to find an ambulance. As for me, I was scratched, cut, and filthy, but most of the blood on me belonged to other people.

I cleaned up as best I could and started pacing. From the clunky, embassy-issued handheld radio on the bedside table came staccato conversations interrupting terse commands from the chancery grounds. It did not occur to me to interrupt. I was too focused on trying to piece together what in the world was happening. Clearly we were experiencing a catastrophe, but beyond that I had a whole lot to find out. Then I heard a familiar voice: Duncan Musyoka, my driver and the operator of the State Department–issued, fully armored, right-hand-drive burgundy Cadillac with red-orange diplomatic license plates. A former military driver, Duncan had quick instincts and common sense, and he was still alive. I broke into the radio chatter to tell him where to pick me up. The people listening to the embassy radio net learned that their ambassador was still alive. It was hardly a dramatic intervention, but I was working on my to-do list.

The pre-cellular Nairobi phone system—erratic in normal times—was for the moment working, so I could phone my husband, Richard Buckley, to ask that he contact Mom and Dad and stay away from the downtown area. Army veteran, civil rights lawyer, husband of many years, and currently Top Spouse, Richard knew about coping with crises. That done, I was free to pace, waiting for the doctor to reappear and clear me for duty. The wait gave me the chance to continue the mental checklist of things to be done.

I had been in Nairobi two years, serving my first ambassadorship after three years in the State Department's Africa Bureau (AF), where I had earned my disaster stripes. I had managed the transnational policies portfolio for forty-six sub-Saharan countries. Transnational issues included democracy, development and conflict resolution, prevention, reality, and aftermath. I was a go-to person for kidnappings, political anarchy, embassy evacuations, and, in 1994, the genocide in Rwanda. What I had learned from American missionaries escaping a Hutu militia helped in the rescue of an American Peace Corps volunteer in Central African Republic. The Africa Bureau team had taken care of a head of state overturned in a coup d'état who sought asylum on a U.S. Navy ship. Communicating via a radio station, we had negotiated the release of a diabetic American. Not one American citizen had died on my watch, and I was proud.

This was different.

Time slowed and expanded against a backdrop of urgency as my to-do list got longer. The doctor returned to declare my vital signs okay and my split lip something that could wait to be stitched. Stunned but uninjured coworkers from another part of downtown met me in the lobby and drove me to the suburban office building that housed the U.S. Agency for International Development (USAID), now the only large chunk of office real estate the U.S. government had left. Now high on adrenalin, I bounded up the stairs to find the control center I knew someone would have cobbled together. Sure enough, Linda Howard and Sheila Wilson, Foreign Service office managers who ran my life by day, already had started organizing. Neither of us knew the other had survived until we threw ourselves into one another's arms, and I asked for a steno pad. I simply had to get the to-do list out of my brain!

I do not know into whose hands I thrust our embassy telephone book. "Get teams and find every person in this book," I ordered. Volunteer bomb-response teams formed of Kenyans and Americans from various U.S. government agencies searched hospitals, neighborhoods, and morgues until we accounted for all of our people. It would take days.

A Kenyan colleague described the chaos we were facing at ground zero:

Around 10:30 I was right in front of my office. After talking to this lady, then I was—I went back to my office, was trying to send an email, and then I heard the first explosion. It came like a tremor. And I don't know, I thought it was something outside the embassy. So, somebody asked, what was that? Then I said, I think it's a bomb.

Then people were rushing to the window. Then I thought about locking my office before I could also join them. So, I was heading towards the open area, which was on the Budget section, to see what people were going to see. And on my way, there was a computer room, which was a sealed room. On my way there, just reaching the corner, that's when the second deadly explosion came.

I didn't know where I was . . . the ceiling came on me. I was thrown down. The house was dark. It was dusty. It was smoky. Choking because the duct smoke somehow choked me, and I could not open my eyes. I could see nothing. Then I went down. I was thrown down. Then the bodies were burying me. Then I heard people cry and some of them were—I could hear, I could get their voices and could know, that's so-and-so's voice, but I could not open my eyes.

I could not breathe. I could not do anything. Though I prayed. I said a prayer, about three seconds, that, Lord, just take my soul. Then I remembered, I fumbled for my I.D. because I remembered my dad and my brothers loved me so much that I would want them to see my body. And so, I was looking for a form of identification where if I'm found, they would get an I.D. It didn't occur to me that an I.D. would burn if the house burns.

I started crawling after that when I could feel like I was alive. I started crawling because I was choking. I started moving towards a place I could get fresh air. Then all of a sudden, I felt a breeze come from a direction. I didn't want to open my eyes. I didn't want to breathe. I started crawling towards that place. I didn't know where it was. Then after reaching that place, I realized there was a cold breeze coming from outside. So, I started moving towards that side. It was the window that had been blown. So, as I moved, and I wanted to like keep moving, I realized that I was at the edge. Then I slept there for some time. I was shaking. When I opened my eyes, I saw the garden, a green garden. I said, where am I? As I was moving toward the window, I could feel people's—could feel bodies of the dead people.

After that, then I realized that I was looking for an I.D., I could not get it, I would like my dad to see my body, so I have to jump, to die outside. So, I looked at where I was going to jump. It was far, and I closed my eyes because I didn't know where I was going to die. I wanted my body to be found by my dad. So, I just closed my eyes and then jumped through the window. I was not conscious for some time. When I raised my head, I realized that I did not die.[1]

Like other survivors who had crawled through smoke and dust, debris and bodies, George Mimba joined those who organized themselves into rescue teams to go back into the building to help others. We had no 911, no fire and rescue, no emergency and police assistance. We were on our own.

August 7, 1998, Nairobi, Afternoon

The area around the chancery was chaos. At what was a seven-story office building next door, Ufundi House, hundreds of people were clawing through the rubble with bare hands to locate survivors. As an American colleague later reported:

Meanwhile, a crowd of perhaps 10,000 had quickly formed in front of the embassy. Most, shocked, were just gazing; many others wanted to help, while scores of looters started to swarm into the building through its gaping holes. With the surviving embassy marines—one was dead, another wounded—and a few Army servicemen who were on temporary duty at the embassy, we set up a security perimeter around the building. Part of the crowd, however, suddenly surged forward. They had spotted an embassy guard who had made it from the back of the building to the front and was trapped behind the security fence that fronted the building. His clothes in shreds, his face and body a welter of bloody gashes, he gripped the bars of the fence gate, wailing pathetically.

The surging crowd threatened to sweep our cordon away; had that happened, we would have been engulfed in a sea of humanity, and any attempt at an organized rescue would have been futile. A couple of us stepped toward the lead group of angry young men, urging them to let us continue our jobs. Others meanwhile scrambled to find the key to the gate. Feigning calm, we argued with the front line of the crowd. Glancing over my shoulder, I understood why our words carried such weight and the mob stopped: A marine and a soldier stood three feet behind us, their faces a mask of grim determination, their weapons leveled. We found the key and rescued the guard.[2]

The marines had been off duty, waiting in a van for Cpl. Jessie "Nathan" Aliganga to cash a check and begin weekend festivities, when the bomb went off. Their training kicked in as they grabbed their gear and faced down the growing crowds, and I was very proud of them. The view from the Kenyan side was different, as I would soon learn.

The control room was almost set up by the time I got there, with a large table in the middle for the twenty-four-hour crisis team Linda and Sheila were organizing, and meager communications equipment had been plugged into outlets along the wall: two satellite phones, one photo copier, and a few handheld radios tuned in to the one embassy channel. Someone using the phone yelled that other U.S. embassies in the region had been attacked. Ethiopia? Uganda? No, Tanzania. Our embassy in Dar es Salaam, five hundred miles southeast along the East African coast, had been bombed just minutes after Nairobi, the casualty count yet unknown. This was not something local; these were terrorist attacks, and we were the target.

I made one of the small adjacent rooms my office, but remained in the control room to direct volunteer traffic until we sorted ourselves out. People with medical skills rushed downtown, and USAID drivers formed an emergency motor pool. A senior executive took care of the burst water main, while a contract engineer risked his life to keep electrical wires from reaching rising water and generator fuel in the chancery basement. Position descriptions meant nothing; personal leadership, everything.

I was on the radio with someone at ground zero when a colleague in the control room called out, "Ambassador, Susan Rice is on the phone."

The assistant secretary for African affairs at the State Department, Susan Rice, had formerly served in the National Security Council on peacekeeping and African issues. We had gotten to know one another well, and we shared respect and affection, if not agreement on policies.

"Pru," she exclaimed, "are you okay? What's going on? I had no idea your embassy was so close to the street!"

"Susan," I replied angrily, "I wrote you and the f—ing secretary of state all about it!" Susan was the one person with whom I could use such words. Profanity was a wonderful stress release, but I usually held back. Not this time. I was suddenly really, really angry.

I had in fact written a personal letter to Secretary of State Madeleine Albright because two years of efforts to draw attention to the security vulnerabilities of our embassy had provoked complaints of "nagging" and accusations of being "obsessed" but offered no positive response. Like all other U.S. ambassadors, I had received a machine-signed letter from the president of the United States underscoring my responsibility for the security of all Americans in Kenya (except those under military command). I took it seriously enough to go outside of the chain of command to address Albright directly. She had not answered the letter, but Undersecretary for Management Bonnie Cohen did reply to a letter I sent her. Her note advised me that there was no money to relocate from our dangerous downtown location (a senior State Department official had waived the requirement to have at least one hundred feet of offset from a public street), and we were considered at only "medium threat" of a terrorist attack. That letter had arrived two months before the truck bomb.

I had barely gotten the words "secretary of . . ." out of my mouth when someone behind me interrupted. "Ambassador, the Secretary of State is on the line." I told Susan I would call her back and hurried to the other phone.

Madeleine Albright and I had met on a trip we had taken through conflict-ridden African countries when she was U.S. ambassador to the United Nations. The trip had included a stop in Rwanda, where we visited the mass grave of people I remembered trying to save. Now we were dealing with American and Kenyan bodies, not Tutsi and Hutu.

Like Rice, Albright commented that she had had no idea the embassy was in such a vulnerable spot. "Madame Secretary, I wrote you a letter," I said grimly.

There was long silence. "I never got it," she replied.

There was no point in arguing and not much to say after that, so I got back to work.

Finally, in midafternoon, ground zero was under enough control to allow our team to regroup in my new office at the USAID building. Most of the senior team had been in the weekly Friday staff meeting in my real office when the bomb went off and had made it out alive—all except the head of our consular operations, Julian Bartley. No one had seen him since early morning. Where was he?

We pieced together what information we had: A truck with two men had driven into the rear parking lot and tried to get into our underground parking garage. The Kenyan contract security guard had stopped it. One of the perpetrators had thrown a grenade, and some gunshots were fired, giving the guard time to run, desperately calling the marines on his radio as he fled. Seconds later, the truck had exploded.

In my office, someone's radio crackled. "We've just found the body of ****," the voice announced. "Do not relay the names over the net, understood?" snapped our regional security officer (RSO).

One-third of our American colleagues had arrived less than a month ago, and he was one of the most recent. As I listened to the exchange, I recognized that a part of my brain had been checking people I had seen against a mental list. Better to keep focused on the to-do list. Then I thought about Julian again. He was African American; white skinned Americans were easy to identify in this African city, but Julian could be mistaken for Kenyan. Where was he? I resumed working down the to-do list:

Bring out the dead and find suitable ways to take care of the bodies (the morgues were overflowing).

Find the missing and locate sniffer dogs to help search for survivors at the embassy and the Ufundi House next door.

Tend to the wounded and secure assistance for overwhelmed local medical facilities.

Inform families of the status of their loved ones. Keep people informed with steady radio net broadcasts, although most people in Nairobi were watching events live on television and probably knew as much as we did.

Organize for the hundreds of people headed our way.

Manage Washington.

Deal with the media.

Someone said that the State Department rescue team was not coming as planned because of airplane problems. A few minutes after that, another report alerted us that the Fairfax County rescue squad with the sniffer dogs would also be late because of mechanical problems with their plane. I was getting a headache.

"Ambassador," someone yelled, "the president wants to talk to you."

I waited for him to come on the line, thinking about what I would say. Bill Clinton picked up: "Pru." I could visualize the briefing: "She calls herself 'Pru.'"

"How are you?" he asked.

"Mr. President," I replied, "my heart is bursting with sadness at what happened and glowing with pride at the way our people are responding." Corny, maybe, but it was the best I could come up with at the time.

"Pru," he continued, "I want you to secure the perimeter!"

What? Really? I could hardly believe my ears. Where was the famous "I feel your pain"? We could have used a little of that.

"Ye-es," I answered hesitantly, thinking, why is he talking about this? "Mr. President, we're still bringing out bodies."

"Oh . . . well . . . okay. But as soon as you can, secure the perimeter and . . . hold on a second . . . and you need to secure the perimeter of the building next door, too."

"But, Mr. President," I argued, "they are digging out bodies there, too, from the rubble."

"Oh, okay. But as soon as possible, secure the perimeter!" he ordered.

Wow, I thought. What a help. I should have told him that the bloody perimeter was already secured by a few good U.S. marines with help from a British military training team, but it did not occur to me. I was far too dumbstruck by the instruction. Was no one reading the list of growing casualties, including two of our six-member marine detachment? Why in the world were we being harassed to keep giving the same information to different people in Washington if they were not passing it on? Who the hell was in charge back there? As to securing the perimeter, what an irony! That was what I had been trying to do for the previous two years.

We hung up without further conversation.

At the corner of Moi and Haile Selassie Avenues, the area around the former chancery and the Ufundi House was now secured by Kenyan security forces; marine guards remained on the perimeter of the embassy. Thousands of wounded had walked or been carried by Good Samaritans to Nairobi's now-strained medical facilities. The attention had shifted to creating makeshift emergency units throughout the city and picking up the bodies of the dead. The toll would not end until it reached 213 dead—46 were killed in our chancery—and 5,000 wounded. A local businessman had donated a piece of construction equipment that was being hauled into place to begin removing the concrete pieces of the Ufundi House rubble. A team of Israelis with sniffer dogs were on their way to locate survivors.

At the USAID control room, we were keeping a list of the dead and injured. They had found the body of Julian's son, Jay, who was one of our summer interns. Nearby, outside the cashier's office, were the remains of everyone waiting in line to cash a check before the weekend began, but still no Julian. He had not appeared for the staff meeting in my office, perhaps stopping to greet people or tell one of his endless array of good (and bad) jokes. It was not like Julian to miss a staff meeting. Where was he?

Julian had arrived with his wife, Sue, and Jay the same summer that Richard and I moved to Kenya. As our consul general, he was responsible for the services provided to the substantial resident and tourist American communities in Kenya. He had directed efforts to find a lost college student who had wandered away from her group for days on Mount Kenya and so impressed her that she vowed to join the Foreign Service. Her sister, whom

I met years later, actually did. Julian also directed our visa operations. I happened into the consular section one morning as a church group of gospel singers waited for their tourist visa interviews. With a twinkle in his eye, he asked the group to demonstrate their talent for the ambassador, and the waiting room filled with song—and yes, they got their visas. Julian had accumulated a network of friends that reached to the top of Kenyan officialdom and beyond.

Eventually I ran out of tissues to staunch the bleeding lip and left the control room in competent hands to get stitched up. Before leaving, I made an announcement on the embassy radio. I knew that everyone in the community was glued to their sets, and we had been sending out information as we could, but I wanted people to hear this message from me personally. "We're going to get through this, and we're going to get through this together."

Duncan and I drove to my residence in silence. He had been on an errand outside of the area when the bomb went off and, unscarred, looked a lot better in his trim gray suit than I did in my blood-spattered green one. He soberly radioed the guards the words "two mikes" so they would have the gates open and ready for us to enter in exactly two minutes. We swung into the circular driveway surrounded by tropical greenery and stopped under the awning that led to the front door of the white stucco house. It had been the talk of the neighborhood when it was built by a doctor in the mid-1930s, and it had served as the British East Africa military headquarters during World War II before the United States purchased it as an official residence. Surrounded by five lush acres that included a swimming pool and tennis court, the house was unassuming and very pleasant. It was home.

Behind us the gates opened again, and Richard drove in with a close neighbor. They had been following events through the live broadcasts from ground zero from the moment that the bomb went off, watching the uncensored horror all day. Quick hugs, and I raced upstairs to change into slacks and a long-sleeved red T-shirt. I thought it might hide any blood stains missed in the cursory clean-up earlier that day. My neighbor insisted on accompanying me to the Nairobi Children's Hospital next door, where a doctor was waiting to stich up my split lip. A large and formidable matron greeted us and led us into an examining room, where a young physician waited.

I climbed onto the gurney and took my shoes off. "Did you wash your hands?" my friend demanded as the doctor put on gloves, and she rubbed my bare, cold feet. When it came to formidable, she was a good match for the matron. "Pru," my friend continued, "I'll make an appointment with my plastic surgeon first thing tomorrow." (Really? I thought. Not sure I'll have time.) As she talked, the matron hovered solicitously behind the youthful doctor. "Is that thread as thin as you can get?" "Let me see the needle; is it the right one?" The doctor ignored the women and the scrutiny, sewing me up with a steady hand. A few minutes later, Duncan dropped my friend off and drove me back to the USAID building, again in silence. His brown face was beginning to look as weary and ashen as mine.

By 10:00 p.m. I was exhausted and becoming numb as the list of casualties grew. We could now account for the Americans who were in the chancery when it blew, but not Julian. One of our wounded American colleagues had been mistaken for Kenyan and found herself in a small clinic with a needle poised to go into her arm when she regained consciousness. With extraordinary presence of mind, she had asked to be transferred to the hospital that the embassy used. Is that what had happened to Julian? Was he unconscious in an unknown medical facility?

By now, Julian's friends in the Kenyan military had joined the search efforts. Our bomb-response teams were still combing through morgues and clinics for Kenyan co-workers. Finding them was the priority among an extensive list of objectives I reviewed with the night shift in the control room before announcing, "I'm going home to cry and then get some rest. I would like everyone in this room who is not part of the night shift to do the same. See you tomorrow morning."

I know, I know. Leaders do not say they are going to cry, but I did so deliberately. I wanted people to have permission. The stiff-upper-lip, real-men-don't-cry, feelings-are-for-sissies State Department culture invites burnout. I knew this from months of leading the weary Washington task force in 1994 that was stuck with a policy of nonintervention in Rwanda as almost a million people were slaughtered in one hundred days of genocide. I needed people to take care of themselves now. The work we had to do was overwhelming. Anyway, women can get away with saying they are going to cry, and we all certainly had reason.

Actually, I did not cry that night. I did not even take a shower; I was far too tired. Instead, I lay on my bed with strangers' blood still clotting my hair and listened to the soothing voice of a local radio broadcaster advising listeners how they could help. She gave a call-in number for all employees of the U.S. embassy; the search for our missing continued. My eyes went to the bedside table and this week's *Nairobi Roar,* our community newsletter. The front page declared this to be Friendship Week. A thought popped into my head: "My life is never going to be the same."

2

THE PAST AS PROLOGUE

1948–1965: Germany, France, Pakistan, Iran, and the United States

How did I land in the middle of this existential drama? It was not as though U.S. ambassador was a common occupation for American women. We were less than 15 percent of the ambassadorial core, and most of us were in parts of the developing world like sub-Saharan Africa. Until the 1970s, it was customary for a female Foreign Service officer to resign upon marriage, and most of those who stayed went into the administrative and consular career tracks, rather than the more prestigious political and economic policy reporting. The single Foreign Service women who came into our home for Thanksgiving and Christmas when I was growing up influenced me as career role models, but not in ways that would persuade me to join the Service. I saw the way my father and other bosses treated them, like high-paid servants, and I wanted no part of it. Dad changed his ways, compliments of the women's movement, his wife, and two daughters, as did the State Department. But when I was a girl, the Foreign Service had no appeal.

Our family had lived overseas most of my first nineteen years. In 1948, my mother, Bernice Duflo Bushnell, who called herself "Dufie," swore to her dying day she was never a risk-taker. Yet, in 1948, she climbed onto a troop carrier headed for Germany with two toddlers and a mother-in-law she disliked. They shared a love for my father, Gerry Bushnell, a civilian with the occupation forces, and they were headed for Berlin, then the epicenter of the Cold War between the United States and the Soviet Union. I was eighteen months old; my sister Susan was three years old.

We arrived when the U.S. military was flying 300,000 flights over a sixteen-month period to supply food and fuel to 6,000 Allied troops and every German citizen in the French, British, and American sectors of Berlin. Russians had cut off road and rail access to Berlin in a pique over a new currency enacted in the western part of the country. The U.S. response was to fly over the problem rather than shoot through it. Someone approved the policy to keep American civilians in place and bring in their wives and children. The wives did what expatriate women do everywhere: they organized. The American Women's Club hosted orphans, helped widows, and published a cookbook, *Operation Vittles*, in 1949. The book began with photos of children gazing expectantly into the sky for incoming airplanes; it ended with children's drawings of happy people enjoying Hershey bars. In between were recipes accompanied by the name of each contributor and an anecdote.

One described particularly well the reality Susan and I experienced in Berlin. "Everyone knows the first stock in trade of the German black market is the cigarette," wrote one contributor. "So it was with considerable shock that one mother heard her little three-year-old sweetly ask her for two. On inquiry, she wanted the cigarettes for "the nice man who cleans our mouse cage at school."[1]

We were special in a good way and raised to be kindly to Germans who served us in desolation after losing two world wars. We spent the next six years moving in and out of Berlin and Frankfurt until West Germany chose Bonn as its capital city. I watched with young American eyes as my urban environments changed from rubble and bombed-out buildings in Berlin to cranes and cement mixers in Bonn, where American military and civilian families segregated themselves into spanking new housing complexes.

Mother did the house-hunting. From Berlin, she flew on empty planes heading back to Frankfurt for more goods, dutifully wearing slacks under her skirt as directed in case she had to parachute into Russian territory. Flight crews ordered everyone to check for passports, travel orders, and parachutes, and . . . ah . . . mothers could take one child should a jump be necessary. Dufie would pick "an apple-cheeked soldier" to ask for help that fortunately was never required. By 1953 Germany was on the mend, the dollar was still king, and the Bushnells were traveling the highways in a 1952 Chevrolet convertible, Dad at the wheel and Mom reading from the guidebook.

They made a good pair. Dufie was smart and immensely well organized; Gerry was charming and intellectually curious. He would announce that government travel orders had arrived, and she would do the rest. Both brought to the family a sense of humor and good central New York values, including commitment to public service. I listened to adult conversations about the Holocaust. "How could Germans not have known?" I heard them ask. As refugees from various parts of Germany and Central Europe came and went as domestic staff, I learned never to judge people by their position or circumstances. "There but for the grace of God go we," Mom instructed us. We were lucky. We were American. Our symbols of power and wealth accompanied us through our clothes, our vehicle, and our dollars.

Susan and I went to American schools, so we had no German friends but lots of German minders, women who helped Mom with the chores and with us. No one was hostile, but we were not a part of their world, either, a fact made clear one Sunday in a Catholic church. Susan and I sat through Mass on hard wooden benches on a cold, cobbled stone floor listening to a foreign language and checking things out. The only piece of warmth or interest I could find were curtained boxes along the side.

"What's behind the curtain?" I asked our maid after Mass.

"God," she said.

"God? What does he do?"

"We talk to him," she explained.

"Can I go talk to him?" I asked with the excitement of a six-year-old in proximity to God.

"No," she said. "You're not Catholic."

"Oh." I had nothing else to say.

We returned to the United States in 1954 with the addition of a brother, Peter. Susan and I moved three times and attended four schools before Dad announced that we were going to France two years later. The United States had become a world power, we were fighting communism, and we needed more diplomats than the 1,300 officers currently on the payroll. Gerry was among those who brought the numbers up to 4,000 through the lateral-entry Wriston program, controversial because entrants did not compete through the Foreign Service exam. Gerry was promptly assigned to Europe. I was nine years old and not amused. We were moving again.

Never mind that we did not speak French; Susan and I were plunked into a small private girls' school within walking distance of our house in suburban Paris. We walked past a German-built concrete gun emplacement called a pillbox and lived in a large stone villa that had been taken over by the Germans in the war for its hilltop view. The French Resistance had killed a colonel in our sunroom. World War II was still close. American movies spun love stories and heroics, and *The Diary of Anne Frank* brought the Holocaust into many lives, including my own. I connected; she was my age, she lived in Europe, and she was "different."

For the next four years, Susan and I represented the face of the United States to an all-French cast of teachers and students. The French girls, like our German caretakers, were never overtly hostile, but they did not invite us into their homes or make particular efforts to befriend us. The school's headmistress banned American clothes and "surpreeese parteeees," as she called them in letters to parents at the beginning of each school year. We were taken to task for "rock 'n' roll" (pronounced with Gallic contempt) and at having been baptized Protestant. "At least you are not Jewish," our Religious and Moral Instruction teacher would tell us. "You will go to purgatory while they . . ." She left the rest unspoken. When Arkansas governor Orval Faubus tried to prevent African American children from desegregating a Little Rock elementary school in 1957, we were also accused of being racist. "Right," I thought. "And you're so kind to Algerians." I was far too intimidated to express resentment, so I entertained the thought with my mouth shut.

"Nice little girl. Very conscientious," my teachers reported to my parents. When we did speak, Susan and I—put in the same grade for four years—used increasingly fluent French, which we discarded at the gate of our large front garden. At home, it was

all about movie magazines, Frankie Avalon and Annette Funi-
cello, and the American songs that Radio Luxemburg played for
an hour every night.

The villa had huge windows, marble floors, coal heat, and a
perpetual chill. Paris winters were cold, rainy, and grim. Mom,
Susan, and I agreed years later that this was our most difficult
post. Dufie was forty-three when she gave birth to brother Jonathan. She had two pubescent girls, a five-year-old boy, an infant,
and a husband to take care of in a distant and lonely Paris suburb. When congressional delegations came to town, she put on
her good clothes and a smile to accompany them to the night-
clubs they demanded to see before returning home to assert that
the Foreign Service budget should be cut because the pinstriped
crowd did nothing but push cookies.

Susan and I were left alone to amuse ourselves by what would
today be called "free range parents." Our range extended to Paris:
to the American church on Sundays for a dose of teen social life
and nondenominational ethics, and to museums on Thursdays,
when schools were out and students got discount prices. We went
skiing during winter breaks, and during home leave to the States,
we cleaved to *American Bandstand*.

Four years in France guaranteed a hardship post as a next assignment, and we moved directly from Paris to Karachi, Pakistan, in
1960. The population and poverty were overwhelming. Thirteen
years after "partition," when Pakistan separated from India to create a Muslim state, Karachi, its port city capital, was still choking
with refugees and bitterness. In retrospect, however, 1960–63
were halcyon years for both Pakistan and the United States.

We had John and Jackie Kennedy, a glamorous democracy, an
upscale way of life, and an enviable culture. Pakistani boys lined
up to square dance with us at the Pakistan-American Society, and
I thought how wonderful it was that they so enjoyed the American style of "swinging your partner." It never occurred to me
that the allure may have been something else. In the bubble of
Americana created by our mothers around the Karachi American
School, we danced to 45 rpm records and discussed the merits of
democracy over communism. A high school of fewer than eighty

students supported glee club, debate club, drama club, square dance club, newspaper, yearbook, and various intervarsity sports clubs—all thanks to our mothers. Dufie, with a degree in music, was handed the job of eighth grade science teacher within days of arrival, and she hunched over the *Encyclopedia Britannica* for a year. Our mothers were determined to educate us scholastically and culturally, never mind the foreign context.

The school was international, and I was introduced to Islam through Pakistani classmates and Mrs. Edison's History and Culture of the Sub-Continent. A classmate fainted in school during her first attempt at Ramadan fasting and returned the next day with instructions from her father, a doctor, to eat because she was still too young to start fasting. "What a tolerant religion," I thought, remembering French classmates threatened with hell and slapped in the face for forgetting their catechism. While heavily veiled women in burkas walked carefully along Karachi streets, their view of the world narrowed to what they could discern through a small piece of meshed cotton, the girls and women I knew showed their faces, personalities, and intellect.

Pakistan, we were told, was not ready for democracy, but our fathers would fix that soon. And yes, President Ayub Khan was a dictator, but he was a "benign dictator" and, more important, "our" dictator. While the world was dangerous, what with nuclear weapons, the Berlin Wall, and all, it was also simple. The United States was good, and so were foreign leaders who supported our side. For their efforts, we provided development, defense, military training and equipment, and a blind eye to domestic politics.

It never occurred to any of us teenagers that our square dance exhibits in Quetta or Swat Valley might offend some in the audience. We saw the tolerant side of Sunni Islam under a secular government that allowed women in classes with men. It was a sign of the times that no one was paying attention to Islamist intellectuals gaining adherents to their calls to replace western-style governments with Islamist-based theocracies. We would have been truly shocked to hear a returning Muslim student describe the United States as "a collection of casinos, supermarkets, and whorehouses linked together by endless highways passing through nowhere."[2]

Dad was transferred to Tehran as I was going into my senior year of high school and Susan departed for college. The Foreign Service eventually stopped wrenching teenage dependents from their high school flock because distraught adolescents like me made life painful for the entire family. I was without Susan for the first time in my life while my brothers, Peter and Jonathan, had their own lives. There is nary a photo from that year in which I am smiling. As unhappy and self-absorbed as I was, however, I had enough awareness of our surroundings to recognize how very different this Muslim country was from Pakistan. It had an imperial dictator, Shah Reza Pahlavi, not a military one; it practiced Shia tenets of Islam, not Sunni; and the people carried the mantle of a proud and ancient Persian empire, very different from the pioneer citizens of a newly fabricated nation.

Tehran under the shah was modern, French-leaning, and sophisticated. With fair skin, dark hair, and brown eyes, I looked Persian, spoke poor street Farsi and good French, and negotiated with taxi drivers and everyone else with lessons I had learned from Pakistani bazaars. At the Tehran American School, I adjusted, made friends with other newcomers, and graduated in 1964. Susan came to Tehran for the summer. Together with two American male friends we took a road trip to Persepolis, Isfahan, and Shiraz, avoiding the hostile looks we received from innkeepers. By the time Mom and Dad sent us off to college in Auburn, New York, via Israel and Jordan, Susan and I were experienced travelers. The tears in their eyes as they said good-bye reflected the emotion of a life passage and not concern that they were sending their seventeen- and nineteen-year-old daughters to travel alone through the Middle East. Dad's colleagues at resident embassies would keep a distant watch over us.

Comfortable as a foreigner in other lands, I was unprepared for the climate, isolation, and culture of the small, rural women's college in central New York. I ended up in the infirmary, and Dad came from Tehran to get me. We returned via the State Department in Washington where a man behind a desk wagged his finger at me and said I had better behave in Tehran or my father's career would be ruined. The Department did not like spending money rescuing ill-adjusted teenagers. It was an awkward retreat to the embassy community, and I froze in horror when I had to greet Dad's boss soon after returning. Ambassador Julius Holmes approached us with a smile on his face, held out his hand, and said warmly, "Welcome home." What a difference an ambassador can make!

I taught English to Iranian men at the Iran-America Society and worked in the American embassy commissary as I worried over what to do with my life. The gap year took me outside the bubble of the American military and civilian community. I learned from Iranians, not Americans, about the 1954 U.S.-UK orchestrated coup d'état, when a democratically elected prime minister was booted out of power and the shah reinstated so that Iranian oil fields would remain in private (American and British) hands. The Iranians I met generally liked Americans and displayed a profound sense of loss when President Kennedy was assassinated in 1963. However, their mistrust both of the United States and of their own government seeped through many conversations—often in whispers beneath public smiles, even in private homes.

I got my first real job. I was an eighteen-year-old supervisor of the liquor and sundries sections at the American embassy commissary, enduring sighs and nasty looks from the older Iranian man, Ali, forced to work for a woman and a young one at that. Our job was to keep track of inventory so that fewer bottles of American liquor—Johnnie Walker Black in particular—ended up in the rug bazaars. The shah's entourage made up a sizeable proportion of hefty consumers, and I kept serious track. One day I proudly advised a particularly arrogant member of the imperial inner circle to please get to the back of the line because he was now on American soil and that it is how we did things. My Iranian colleagues were horrified, but I knew I would get away with it. I was an American!

1965–1981: Bethesda MD

Mom and Dad ended their last overseas tour in 1965, and the family moved to the Washington DC suburbs. Susan was already in college, and I had found a place at Western College for Women

THE PAST AS PROLOGUE

in Oxford, Ohio. Dufie in particular looked forward to a new way of life. She had given birth in two foreign countries and raised four children in two more. Like other Foreign Service wives, she was evaluated on Dad's annual performance appraisal for work she was not paid to perform. She felt undervalued by a service that boasted about getting "two for one," and she was ready to come back to the United States, find a job, and conduct her life in English. Gerry was resigned; as much as he would have loved to stay overseas, he recognized the impact on his family.

As for me, I just wanted to figure out how things worked. I was aware of the differences between Shia and Sunni Muslims, wise in the ways of international travel, and clueless about how to make a long-distance phone call. In 1965 my country was in turmoil, and I had no idea where I fit. Was I part of the problem or part of the solution? What did I think about Vietnam? Would I be loyal to my marine friends from Tehran if I joined the peace activists? Did I favor Dr. Martin Luther King Jr. or Malcolm X? For two years I struggled with these questions from the cloistered vantage of a midwestern women's college and transferred to the University of Maryland to get a real education. Much of it did not come from classes.

The land of the free had denied civil rights to a significant percentage of citizens, women included, and the home of the brave was torn apart by domestic violence over the war in Vietnam. On the nightly news I saw political assassinations that should have happened in other countries, not ours. My country, I realized, had flaws and deep divides. But it also had the rule of law that allowed me to participate in demonstrations for peace and marches for economic dignity and civil rights. Popular bumper stickers read, "My country: Love it or leave it." I loved it and had no intention of leaving ever again.

At first I stayed within my comfort zone. With a degree in French literature, I landed a job as a bilingual secretary at the embassy of Morocco and then chief (!) secretary at the department of Spanish and Portuguese at my alma mater. I married a man I had known at the Karachi American School, and we divorced within three years. I did better at work: I had Mom's organizational abilities and Dad's people skills to make me a good secretary. When I reached the peak of my secretarial career track at age twenty-three, I launched myself. I answered an ad under the *Washington Post*'s "Female Help" section for a travel coordinator job at the national legal services training program, run out of a grant to the Catholic University's law school. It changed my life.

A small office of eight people, including Richard Buckley, whom I would later marry, trained attorneys around the country in basic and specialized aspects of the laws affecting their low-income clients. As part of the War on Poverty, the program received funds to address civil legal problems of poor people. Over the next four years, 1972–76, I graduated from coordinating logistics and administration to designing and eventually delivering management training. In the process, I discarded the secretarial demeanor for a more assertive one and got another education.

As I traveled around my country working with hotel staffs, lawyers, political activists, and legal services clients, I grew into an American citizen. I realized I had been taught that clients, most of them women and all of them low-income, were supposed to be helpless and grateful. Not the whites, blacks, Spanish-speaking, American Indians, and migrants I met. They pushed boundaries. I was in awe of people like Annie Smart, community organizer and mother of twelve, who presided over the Louisiana Welfare Rights Association with such effectiveness that she ended up getting 4.6 percent of the popular vote in 1974 running against Senator Russell Long for the U.S. Senate. Women like Annie Smart were running meetings, creating strategies, organizing, and influencing. I learned management skills from my day job and leadership skills from black women.

Watergate kept all of us agog and left us grateful for a functioning democracy when President Richard Nixon left office in disgrace and in peace. His successor, Gerald Ford, was unsuccessful in persuading the American people to elect him in his own right, so Jimmy Carter replaced him in 1976. By then, the training grant had ended, and I decided to put down roots and truly become American in Albany, New York.

Why there? New York State was the only area I knew outside of DC, and Gerry and Dufie had retired to Cooperstown, where he ran the school board and she ran the League of Women Voters. The U.S. economy was in recession, and I was told by an employment counselor, "There are no jobs in New York State." I had already been without work for a year and discovered to my amazement that I met the criteria of "hardcore unemployed," thereby becoming eligible for the federally funded Comprehensive Employment and Training Assistance Act. If an organization agreed to train or employ the worker, the government would pay the nominal salary for a period of time. I connected with the Public Executive Training Program at the State University of New York at Albany and trained state government employees. I borrowed money from my parents and went to night school at Russell Sage College for a master's in public administration.

Two winters and one degree later, I left for warmer climes and Richard Buckley, by now my life partner, who was directing the Dallas Legal Services Program in Texas. It was not an easy decision. He was twelve years my senior with five children. He also truly loved me and was the first man to actively promote my abilities. And I loved him.

It was not easy to find work in Dallas. I was "not huggy enough" when I interviewed for the job as director of a women's center at a local college and, according to the man who interviewed me for a federal government job, my skirts should have had longer slits. So I set myself up in business as a training consultant and became an expert in the developmental cycles of American men, their midlife crises, and burnout.

NASA had a problem in Houston—its senior engineers, who had put us on the moon in the Apollo program, were bored with the concept of a space shuttle and too young to retire. The organization had a lot invested in those men, and they, in turn, had responsibilities for mortgages and college tuitions. What to do? I was hired to help them explore who they were as human beings, not just engineers, and devise strategies to overcome burnout. I steeped myself in research on adult development—male development, actually—and used astronaut Buzz Aldrin's autobiography as a case study. I was thirty-two, and the participants were in their fifties, but most did not seem to mind. One did. A misogynist made it his business to humiliate me through sexist remarks and a scathing evaluation. I ignored his sarcasm and rolling eyes, kept my dignity, and lived to talk about it the next day. It was an important lesson to me.

An ironic confluence of events in 1979 pushed Richard and me back to the East Coast. The U.S. embassy in Tehran had been attacked and U.S. diplomats taken hostage. The shah of Iran had been exiled from his country and replaced by a Shiite cleric, Ayatollah Khomeini, who was showing the world that the United States could be brought to heel if you were not afraid to violate diplomatic treaties and human rights. I had worked in that embassy, and the life experience I had put behind me became real again as I saw familiar places. On the radio, Secretary of State Edmund Muskie was talking not just about Iran but also about a new midlevel Foreign Service entry program for women and minorities, the result of a decade-long class action lawsuit. Richard and I decided to go for it. I applied and was accepted into the administrative career track, just like Gerry.

In 1979 on Christmas Eve, the Russians invaded Afghanistan. President Carter began a covert war against the Soviet Union, funding Afghan warlords, who called themselves "mujahedeen," or freedom fighters, to wage war against the Communists. The word went out across the Muslim world as Carter's initiative was vastly expanded by President Ronald Reagan. The call for *jihad*, the holy struggle, attracted Muslim men everywhere. By 1981 I was in the Foreign Service and unaware of the impact that policy would have on my life and my country.

1980–1993: United States, Senegal, India

My family was flabbergasted when I joined the Foreign Service. First, it was still "pale, male, and Yale," which is why an affirmative action program was needed to bring diversity into midlevel ranks. Second, it was a lifestyle from which my sister, Susan, and I had gladly walked away as soon as we returned to the United States. Susan married and raised two children in Bucks County,

Pennsylvania, as a community college professor, while I traveled as a management trainer, always within U.S. borders.

"You won't last five years; you're too rebellious," Dufie predicted. She was wrong by twenty years, but she had me pegged in one respect. I had seethed under authoritarian treatment as a child and had grown into a feminist. I still resented the fact that I had been denied access to credit following my early 1970s divorce despite years of uninterrupted work, because I was not "head of household." I returned to the name Bushnell, got a bank account and a car loan, which I immediately paid off, and turned a corner. How would I fit with the conservative Foreign Service culture? Mother had her doubts. Dad had this: "Change career tracks. You'll never get anywhere as an administrative officer; become a political officer." I was, however, specifically hired for management work, which I enjoyed because of the autonomy it provided. The culture had not changed much from Gerry's time. One competed to enter through a difficult exam process, competed for a good assignment every two to three years, competed for rewards, and competed for promotion in a process that rank-ordered each candidate and recommended a certain percentage for "selection out." The stakes are high. If you fail to be promoted within a certain number of years, you are fired. In this context, individual achievement trumps teamwork, and getting ahead of the other guy trumps everything. People like me who were parachuting from outside without the full Foreign Service exam process elicited attitudes from ambivalence to hostility: "These women are the first to launch class-action lawsuits claiming discrimination as a vehicle to win court-ordered promotions or plum assignments. Give them a wide berth; otherwise, find a fine surgeon to extricate the daggers and high-heel marks from your back and to reaffix your testicles."[3]

I did not need French-language training to prepare for our first assignment to Dakar, Senegal, and I made myself available for temporary work in the Africa Bureau organizing the congressionally mandated human rights reports, a very particular prism through which to learn about sub-Saharan Africa. In 1982 Richard Buckley and I moved to Dakar. The former capital of French

West Africa, it juts out into the Atlantic Ocean as the western-most point of the continent. Through the centuries, thousands of people had walked through the Door of No Return from the pink stucco slave house on Gorée Island to the ships that took them west to the Americas or north to Europe. I saw the United States through entirely different eyes. As general services officer and head of shipping and customs, my job was to make sure the supplies, household effects, mail, diplomatic pouches, and holiday presents transiting the port of Dakar arrived on time at embassies in Mali, Mauritania, The Gambia, and Guinea-Bissau. I also headed up the budget and fiscal office, and I promptly hired a good bookkeeper.

This was my chance to practice the management skills I had been teaching—but in French, with people of a different culture, around a substantive area I knew little about. The skills paid off, and the techniques worked. We produced results through goal setting, regular staff meetings, feedback, teamwork, and sometimes fun. In return, my French/American/Senegalese team taught me the cultures and courtesies of West African people while stressed-out Americans fretting over incoming or outgoing household effects gave me practice in people skills. After a year, I was pushed up into a supervisory role and received a Foreign Service promotion before I received Foreign Service tenure. That was rare.

Within the first month of our arrival in 1982, Richard was offered a job at USAID. A few days later, a group of women spouses appeared on our veranda thoroughly put out that he had gotten in days the kind of work they had been unsuccessful in securing after years at post. Had the embassy gone out of its way to find a job for a male spouse? Most certainly. Richard's first and only male spouse predecessor had departed post early, leaving a bitter memory. Foreign Service "wives" were no longer a part of the employee's evaluation or expected to make sandwiches for the Fourth of July reception, but they still had little opportunity for employment.

I was handed a chance to be noticed by the ambassador, who gave me a task completely outside of my job description: over-see the French-language program during a pilot project to bring every American government employee at post up to a Washington-designated level of language proficiency. Every U.S. government employee had to learn a certain degree of French. The pilot failed, but I did not. I was bumped up to supervisory general services officer, the head of infrastructure services—motor pool to communications, plumbing to real estate—while Richard was hired as one of the first male community liaison officers (CLO) in the world. The community and ombudsman work that Dufie and other wives had done for free as I grew up was now a paid job. Richard put spouse employment at the top of his priority list as CLO.

In 1984 I was promoted and assigned to the consulate general in Bombay (now Mumbai) as head of administration. I was the first woman administrative officer, and more than one Indian man noticed. "I can't believe the United States of America would send a *woman* to do this work," one said contemptuously to my face. I negotiated constantly with realtors and suppliers, learning that nothing is fixed until the ink is dry. I supervised security upgrades to the consulate, a former maharaja's palace, gleaming white next to the Indian Ocean after our embassy in Beirut was blown up by a pro-Iranian suicide bomber who detonated a vanload of explosives at the front of the building, killing sixty-three people. Had the building been set back one hundred feet, the bomb's impact would have been vastly diminished. It was a no-brainer, therefore, to change regulations to require such a setback. It was also apparent that resources would be needed to upgrade overseas diplomatic facilities in other areas.

Our consulate in Bombay had a protective wall around it, but the Burma-teak wood gates needed replacing, and the palace itself required structural changes. It was a pleasure to work with security colleagues to maintain the architecture as we hardened the structure. Meanwhile, the crowds protesting outside the walls about one or another of our transgressions gave proof to the need for these upgrades. As post security officer, I was the one my boss would send to hear grievances and accept petitions. "They will see that you are such a nice lady, and you will be perfectly safe," he would assure me, handing me my talking points.

Twice I was given the chance to practice policy and diplomacy.

I was in charge the day Prime Minister Indira Gandhi was assassinated and the issue became when to lower our flag to half-staff. Angry crowds in front demanded immediate action, while the Indian protocol office insisted we wait. We waited. Upon his return, the consul general, who had broken his arm, asked me to accompany him to a government building to sign the official condolence book before the Russian consul general had the chance. A rare Indian woman official spotted me among hundreds of men and put me at the head of the queue, so I was soon making my way to the table on which the condolence book awaited a U.S. signature, television cameras rolling behind it. Before long I was shoulder to shoulder with the Russian consul general. He was bigger, but I was determined, leaning into him every time he tried to push me to the side. We got to the book, and the cameras kept rolling. Would he shove such a nice woman aside or yield? He stepped aside. I signed my name for country and democracy.

The next time I was in charge, the world's biggest industrial accident took place at a Union Carbide plant in Bhopal, affecting 500,000 people. The American board chairman arrived in India eager to show concern. I strongly advised him that India was not the United States, and now was not the time to show up at a disaster site with little but an apology. He ignored my advice, went to the site, and was promptly arrested, likely for his own protection. Such was the mark I made for common sense. Richard, meanwhile, was serving as principal of an American elementary school, arguing with British teachers over curriculum and correct spelling: "color" or "colour"?

By 1986, four years overseas had made us both ready to return to Washington and the Foreign Service Institute, the department's schoolhouse. As director of executive development, my challenge was to create a midlevel management training program appropriate for all career tracks in the Foreign Service in order to satisfy a congressional mandate. Instead we decided to focus on leadership.

To learn what the practice of leadership looked like in the Foreign Service and the State Department context, my colleagues and I went in pairs to ask career leaders what precisely they did when they thought they were exercising leadership effectively. Teamwork was necessary, they said, along with advocacy, listening, problem solving, influencing, and setting goals. And, we were warned, it is almost impossible to do that plus manage policy in the Washington arena. "It damned near killed me," said Roz Ridgway, one of our most respected senior officers. Mary Ryan, another admired leader, advised me to seek a job as deputy chief of mission for my next assignment.

DCM? Me? I was in the management track, and the top jobs went to political or economic policy wonks. On the other hand, I was competitive in spirit and experienced in the practice of most of the executive skills we were training others to practice.

I asked my colleague Judith Kaufmann and her husband, George Moose, heading off to Senegal as spouse and ambassador, if I could practice my pitch about why I, a lowly administrative type, would make a good DCM. George agreed to hear me out in the State Department cafeteria. Then he offered me the job as his DCM in Senegal. My former Senegalese teammates were proud and welcoming.

The view was different from the number two perch. Instead of ground-up, it was top-down, and instead of providing services, I was managing State Department sections and coordinating with the other agencies. The State component handled diplomatic relationships and political and economic reporting. It delivered a range of services to in-country Americans and visa services for host-country citizens, and it also provided housekeeping services for other agencies. That was it. The U.S. government's other activities in Senegal were carried out by a dozen other agencies. Ambassador Moose and his successor, Katherine Shirley, had no say in other agencies' personnel, budgets, goal setting, or assignment systems. They did have power to lead, to convene agency heads, to establish mission objectives, and, if necessary, to send people home with a "no confidence" cable. As the number two, I had as much power as my boss delegated. George and Kathy were generous.

At first, every time George left me in charge as chargé d'affaires, one agency head or another would feel compelled to try to diminish me. One, an older man who far outranked me, moved my job down the organizational chart he had prepared for visiting VIPS. I gave him the choice of changing the chart or listening to me wonder aloud to his visitors why years of service had not taught him about how a mission runs. Another man asked in senior staff meeting that I authorize a male subordinate to represent the absent George at an all-male wine club because I was . . . well, that was obvious. Instead I invited him to an offline discussion about representing the U.S. government in organizations that discriminated against women.

The most memorable encounter was with an agency head whose attitude toward Ambassador Shirley I found both disrespectful and contagious among the men he supervised. I asked the man to speak to the subordinate whose behavior I was criticizing and decided, while I was at it, to end the conversation on my own behalf.

"Do not ever call me a 'pretty young thing' again," I instructed.

"I have never called you pretty!" he retorted.

Good one, I had to admit. We got along just fine after that.

What I lacked in experience in conducting diplomacy and reporting events, I made up in my "you can do this" self-talk every morning. I watched George and Kathy carefully and studied visiting officials to learn what they were doing and how they were doing it. The Senegalese helped, too. They had been dealing with outsiders and Europeans for four hundred years. They showed me the value of courtesy and the advantages of listening to understand. They gave me insights into Islam and taught me to negotiate with far more humor than I had learned in the streets of Karachi and Tehran. They seldom used the word "no," even if that was their bottom line. Maintaining the relationship was paramount even in disagreement. Dialogue was important. We did, in fact, have a lot to talk about because Senegal was a strong partner in regional peacekeeping, international organizations, and Islamic states.

Dakar was an easy place to visit—Gerry and Dufie were among the first—and we hosted two of Richard's children as well as many friends. My job was the 24/7 kind, however, so I learned to enjoy myself in bursts. An airplane crash with Americans aboard, a coup d'état in a neighboring country, the death of a mission family member—any of these crisis events could and did take precedence. My job was to manage them.

We left Senegal in 1992 for Washington. I was surprised and genuinely thrilled to be asked to serve as ambassador to Rwanda. Wow! Someone had noticed me. Life was good. I was accepted into the Senior Seminar, a nine-month program for select members of the military service and civilian national security agencies deemed to have good prospects at higher levels. I also spent months filling out reams of paper for clearances, meeting this or that requirement for the White House and Senate, and making every aspect of my life public in preparation for an appointment as U.S. ambassador. In late December I learned that the medical office had denied Richard a clearance to go to post because of inadequate hospital facilities in the capital, Kigali. I faced the most difficult choice of my career: to say no to the ambassadorship and accept that I might never be asked again; to say yes and separate from Richard; or to put his health at risk by having him accompany me as a private citizen. I spent a sleepless night balancing career ambitions against other aspects of my life. I withdrew my name, and we stayed in Washington.

A few weeks later, in January 1993, President Clinton assumed office. George Moose became assistant secretary of state for African affairs and invited me to become one of his deputy assistant secretaries (DAS). I would handle all transnational policies, from democracy, disease, and conflict to environment, refugees, and women, in forty-six sub-Saharan countries. I said yes, and spent at least a third of the next three years traveling around refugee camps, conflict zones, capital cities, and rural areas of Africa. In Washington I managed our meager resources, our management and regional policy offices, and an assortment of crises. "Disaster DAS," a colleague branded me.

I was as far out of my comfort zone as I had been the first few months as DCM in Dakar. I was the only member of George's team who had not served as ambassador. I quickly saw that my position had given me a place at the table, but it did not guarantee that I would be heard. I had to start managing myself differently. I learned never to walk into a meeting, especially a policy meeting, without knowing ahead of time what I wanted to get out of it and who I had as allies. I found that the more intentional I was, the more proactive I became and the more fun I had. I also cultivated credibility, a particular tone and demeanor—always assertive and confident and, if speaking in anger, focused, calm, and low in pitch. I never ended a declarative sentence as if it were a question, and I avoided at all costs self-diminishing statements like "You may disagree, but . . ." or "I'm not an expert . . ." After some internal debate as to whether it would taint my pure soul, I decided that interrupting was also fair game. Heaven knows it was done to me often enough. I learned the gesture to ask for silence and got practice in continuing what I had to say when someone interrupted. I found the words "Let me finish" easy to articulate. Boastful stories and self-aggrandizement? I could do that, too. The "nice little girl; very conscientious" from the French school was creating a new persona.

1993–1996: Washington DC

I worked as deputy assistant secretary for three years in the Africa Bureau. Mostly I managed crises. The most life-altering of all was the 1994 Rwanda genocide.

I was acting assistant secretary of the Africa Bureau on April 6, 1994, when the plane carrying the presidents of Rwanda and Burundi was shot out of the skies over the capital, Kigali. Within hours of the plane crash, radical Hutu militias erected barricades around the city to capture and slaughter Tutsi compatriots. Targeted assassinations of political leaders Hutu and Tutsi continued, and within a few days the civil war had reignited. Our concern centered on the Americans, and by the end of two weeks, we had evacuated all embassy personnel and families, along with other American citizens and foreign diplomats who chose to leave. To ensure their safety as they made the dangerous trek overland, we agreed not to include any Rwandan citizens, including U.S. government employees and colleagues. They were left to their fate, and some died as a result. Once the Americans were out, the White House lost interest. The National Security Council ordered our ambassador to the United Nations, Madeleine Albright, to propose the withdrawal of all UN peacekeepers from the chaos and violence. There was no longer any peace to keep, the argument went.

More than 800,000 people were slaughtered in the next hundred days, most of them Tutsi killed by gangs and neighbors with machetes and small weapons. Ultimately, the largely Tutsi Rwanda Patriotic Front vanquished the Hutu military. The victims had won. The perpetrators, including the government, fled by the hundreds of thousands across the borders into refugee camps on a live volcano in Eastern Zaire (now called Eastern Congo). A cholera epidemic broke out, and the United States finally and ironically decided to intervene by sending help. We were slow in doing the same for the genocide victims and victors, who remained in Rwanda. The new government inherited a country littered with corpses, a busted economy, no treasury, and a suspicious international community.

I saw an aspect of policy making that I had not known existed: how to manage a crisis by deciding not to decide. The White House could not adopt a formal policy of "genocide bystander" because that would have looked bad. We would not commit to any alternative because Americans still remembered the soldiers who had died in Somalia in 1993. Instead, the NSC's head of global issues, Richard Clarke, called meetings and made work.

Every day my colleagues and I huddled around a large table in a secure room holding video conferences with people from other agencies. Now that all but a few peacekeepers had been removed, Defense Department representatives gave every reason why the United States should not use troops, technology, resources, or the bully pulpit to intervene. Could we not at least jam the hate radios calling people into the streets to kill? I kept asking.

Jamming radios was against international law, one study said. Jamming radios was too expensive, another stated. Jamming radios would not work because other frequencies could be found, still another report noted. The Defense Department had no more radio jamming equipment, we were told. The weeks of fruitless discussion finally ended with these words: "Pru, radios don't kill people, people kill people." I told my Defense colleague that I would quote him.

We were doing nothing to stop the killing, so I took it upon myself to call Rwandan military figures perpetrating the genocide to let them know we were watching and to advise that they would be held personally accountable for their deeds. The 2 a.m. phone calls were among the most bizarre conversations I have ever had:

"You need to stop the killing of civilians," I would say.

"Ah, Madame, we are fighting a terrible war and have no resources to control spontaneous uprisings."

"But you do have the ability to put an end to the hate radio."

"But, Madame, we are a democracy, and we believe in freedom of the press."

Experiencing genocide, even from a distance, seared my soul. U.S. national interest had trumped moral imperative. No one could claim that keeping American citizens, treasure, and resources out of harm's way was bad management. We had indeed managed the crisis and in so doing abdicated leadership that could have saved hundreds of thousands of people. My Defense Department colleagues mocked me for my pathetic efforts, but I was spared the level of regret President Clinton, UN ambassador Madeleine Albright, and national security advisor Tony Lake voiced once they were long out of office. At least I had tried to do something.

Getting out of Washington was always a pleasure, and I did so as often as I could. Usually my purpose was to tell murderous warlords like Charles Taylor to stop killing. They hated hearing that from a woman, especially a petite, uppity white woman. The other issues I promoted—democracy, women's rights, and addressing HIV/AIDS—took me to cities and villages where I learned about the impact of community for good and evil, the power of resilience, and the acceptance of death.

The three-year assignment of grueling Washington days and harried trips across Africa ended with the opportunity to serve as chief of mission in Nairobi. I immediately accepted the assignment. Kenya's president, Daniel arap Moi, was in disrepute for having rigged elections, and the Washington interagency consensus held that nothing good could be accomplished while he was in office. The U.S. mission, the largest in sub-Sahara, involved nineteen U.S. government agencies, many with regional responsibilities, and suffered from low morale—this had always been so, I was told; it was just one of those posts. I could do what I wanted, and no one would care.

Richard and I cared. We wrote our leadership agenda and put "raise community morale" and "focus on teamwork and shared goals" at the top. I crafted my entry strategy to include a request that I be called "Madame Ambassador" or "Ambassador" in public because I was a short woman and did not need to be further diminished. While Richard volunteered in the embassy community, I worked with interagency groups that created delicious objectives like stemming corruption and promoting transparent and fair presidential elections. I began sending cables of concern about the location of our chancery building, which was on one of Nairobi's busiest corners and across from the railroad station, with none of the physical setback requirements to safeguard security.

Another local vulnerability came with my gender. Two of the previous three ambassadors had been women, and the third had been a combative male who liked to go *mano a mano* with Moi. It took me months to see Moi privately and longer to build a personal relationship. That said, we were living a mile high, close to the equator, in a white stucco home on five acres outside of a city that had two international airports and a huge diplomatic community, including a United Nations office. We had lots to be happy about.

In November 1996 Richard and I decided to celebrate. The ambassador's residence, built in the 1930s, had served as the headquarters of the British East Africa Army command until the U.S. government purchased it in 1946. It had been American for fifty years, and so had I. Richard and I hosted a Boomer Bash for everyone in the mission born in 1946. We rocked around the clock, twisted the night away, and practiced the Macarena for good measure. What a good posting this was going to be!

3

THE RESPONSE

August 8, 1998: Nairobi

I sat in the bathtub, bandaged hands aloft, as Top Spouse washed strangers' blood from my hair. I was on automatic, one step at a time. The control room was in good hands, and I could have a normal breakfast before I climbed into the burgundy Cadillac with orange-red plates so Duncan could take us to ground zero. I needed to see it for myself. As he drove us down the winding roads that took us to our now eerily quiet corner of the city's center, he said solemnly, "God has a plan for us, Ambassador. We are still alive." Duncan was by nature a quiet, serious man who excelled in finding me among herds of diplomats after official events in time to get in front of the traffic jams that official processions created. He had not talked about God before, but then his colleagues had not been blown up before. Had he been with them, he would have been blown to smithereens as well.

A group calling itself the Islamic Army for the Liberation of Holy Places had barely waited for the documents and papers exploding from the U.S. embassy to hit the ground before taking responsibility for the attacks. We would soon learn its other name: al-Qaeda. Duncan maneuvered the Cadillac into the cordoned area near the blast site. Our marines were still standing guard with assistance from the British military trainers. "Perimeter secured, Mr. President," I thought. There was no telling when the plane carrying reinforcements would arrive.

Duncan parked next to the surprisingly clean sidewalk in front of a singed, wounded version of the brown concrete lunchbox of a building that had housed more than a dozen U.S. government agencies. USAID colleagues had sent as many supplies as they could muster, and our chief security engineer was putting them to good use inside the tent he was using as an office. Nearby, the Cooperative Bank Building, which I had twice believed would hold my remains, loomed ominously over the huge piles of rubble and dead cars. Its windows, like all others in a five-block area, had been blown out. Next door, a team from the Israeli Defense Forces climbed around chunks of concrete with sniffer dogs to locate the thirty to forty people estimated to be buried alive under the Ufundi House. My security engineer colleague handed me a hard hat. On the front of it, he had put the gold consular seal of the United States with the typed title "Ambassador" pasted underneath. We walked up the few steps from the sidewalk into the remains of extraordinary violence. The offices closest to the explosion bulged with rubble—concrete, file cabinets, desks, computers, calendars, furniture, papers, bits of clothes, dangling wires, pieces of ceiling, large shards of glass, and huge piles of stuff. The smell of death was everywhere.

The bomb had swept through the building and returned in the opposite direction, my colleague explained, turning broken glass into missiles and leaving a crater ten feet wide in the rear parking lot. He spoke softly as he gave me the guided tour of death through our motor pool, personnel, shipping, budget, political and commercial offices, and down a corridor to the embassy's cashier.

"The folks waiting in line to cash checks died here. . . . Over there, you can see where someone was flung against the wall. . . . Be careful where you step. . . . No, we don't know the extent of structural damage, but it looks pretty bad." The briefing gave me a good sense of what had happened inside. Lurid media photos and live television coverage had only captured the damage outside.

I finished the tour and took from the car a large bouquet of roses sent in sympathy by Sally Kosgei, the permanent secretary of the Ministry of Foreign Affairs and my closest connection in the Kenyan government. I put them on the front steps to mark the grave that had been our workplace. I had complained about those steps and the proximity of our building to the street in God knows how many cables. Now they led to remains of the dead. I was sickened and angry.

The control room at the USAID building was buzzing and organized. It was Saturday, but everyone had shown up. People were used to taking charge, thank heaven, because we had some good managers among our senior ranks, especially at AID. Some people still looked in shock; others came on crutches and in bandages. Volunteers were forming groups to pay calls on the families of the known dead. Where was Julian? We still had no word. Another group was creating funeral committees to prepare for the immediate burials, customary under Muslim and other Kenyan traditions. The bomb response teams continued the gruesome search for the missing among overflowing morgues. Our human resources staff dashed off travel orders for people who were to be evacuated, as our security people handled the demands of hundreds of FBI agents soon to arrive to begin the investigation. Drivers from USAID and what remained of our motor pool staff were already ferrying visitors from the airport to hotels. Communications and IT teams had begun cobbling equipment together; local and international phone service was still intermittent. The budget and fiscal offices dealt with the necessary authorization requests for the money we would be hemorrhaging. The minutia was incredible, and the loss we felt from the deaths of colleagues weighed heavily. By now we had counted their numbers, and every one of the forty-five employees who had died left a hole in our community. Had leadership not emerged from the survivors, we would have closed down. Instead, we bustled grimly. Leadership, I noticed, still had nothing to do with position and everything to do with character and personal skills.

Multiple demands flew my way. Kenyan president Daniel arap Moi had convened all ambassadors to State House, while a military medical evacuation plane was on its way to pick up our most seriously wounded. We were not sure everyone would make it, and I had one chance to say good-bye. Which would it be? State House or the hospital? A thought entered my brain, the advice a former boss and mentor had given me when he sent congratulations for my appointment as ambassador. "Take care of your people, and the rest will take care of itself." I went to the Nairobi hospital and delegated State House to someone else.

The pace there was busy and controlled, but I could see that the people were starting to wear out. So were their medical supplies. I hoped that the U.S. military medical personnel and provisions would arrive soon. Determined to retain composure, I moved from bed to bed of embassy staff encased in bandages. Who was I to fall apart? I had my health, limbs, and family almost intact. The least I could do was to measure up to the dignity of my wounded colleagues. We said our good-byes, hoping everyone would survive. They did.

I visited the Kenyan minister of commerce next. He had been sitting right next to me twenty-four hours earlier. Now he greeted me heartily from a hospital bed with forty stitches in his head.

By the time I returned to the control room, I had learned the obvious: the international media was in town demanding attention. The State Department's public affairs people must clear interviews with the U.S. press—local media does not matter—and they had given the go-ahead. The journalists appeared as interested in my stitched lip as anything that came out of my mouth, and I was too busy to care about either.

By midafternoon, I was more than busy; I was mad.

"Can you hear the anger in my voice?" I asked a former colleague from Nairobi now on the department's Crisis Task Force in Washington. I had long ago adapted to the narrow parameters of acceptable behavior imposed on angry women by male-dominated organizations. I had learned to channel negative energy into a tone of focused calm. I used the F-word seldom and with intention. Whether he recognized the tone without the intense eye contact I cultivated, I am not sure, but he said the right thing. Yes. He could hear the anger.

Yet another flight was screwed up. The medical evacuation plane, already late in arriving, had landed without a backup crew or any supplies. The reason? We had not specified they would be needed, so it was our fault, said our military colleagues on the Washington end. The injured and our medical team, which had been working nonstop for twenty-four hours to keep them alive, now would have to wait on the required fifteen-hour crew rest. With little hope for a waiver, I nonetheless climbed the chain of command at the Defense Department, listening to an assortment of reasons why it was not their fault that the crew had arrived unprepared. Thankfully, no one died.

I also used the same calm, don't-mess-with-me voice with the FBI a while later. They wanted to keep our dead American colleagues in Nairobi for another two weeks in order to perform autopsies there. That meant their families would return stateside without them. No way was I asking shattered families to leave loved ones behind. I was ready to take on FBI director Louis Freeh if I had to. I did not. The bodies would be released.

Secretary Albright called to advise me of her intention to pay an official condolence visit. Really? The rescuers still had not arrived, and the greatest number of casualties had come from the very sections needed to staff high-level visits like this one. I told her that we could not handle it, and she seemed to understand. Her entourage did not and made no pretense of hiding their displeasure with me when they arrived a week or so later.

The most difficult part of the day came with the calls on family members of deceased and missing colleagues. One of our newly arrived colleagues was leaving immediately with his two daughters. His Foreign Service officer spouse had not felt well Friday morning, but, like so many of us who worry about first impressions, she came to work anyway. Now she was dead.

We still had not found Julian Bartley, although many were looking. He was a member of Nairobi's Rotary Club, a golfer, and a chronic networker. One of his best friends was a three-star general in the Kenyan military who vowed to find him. Sue Bartley remained quiet, calm, and dignified though it all. She was a twenty-seven-year veteran spouse, having served in the Dominican Republic, Colombia, Spain, Israel, and Korea before coming to Kenya. Like my mother, she had raised children, Edith and Jay, in multiple cultures as her husband rose to senior levels. Their son, Jay, had graduated from the International School of Kenya (ISK) and stayed with his parents to attend the United States

International University in Nairobi. He also had volunteered as ISK's basketball coach. When the high school lost one of its most beloved teachers to a deadly carjacking a few months earlier, Jay was one of the people whom traumatized students sought for counsel. In that way, he was like his father. Sue already knew Jay was gone. She garnered hope for Julian's well-being with a ferocity that broke my heart.

Duncan drove me home, again in silence. Usually we would listen to a tape of music I provided; not that day. I made it through the arched front door into the tiled entry hall, closed the door quickly, and sobbed.

August 9–14, 1998: Nairobi

Just as we were beginning to think we had established a semblance of order, chaos erupted. Our most seriously wounded colleagues had finally been evacuated, forty hours after the bombing, and we were making headway in accounting for our dead and missing. Then on Sunday, August 9, the rescuers arrived, hordes, all within a few hours. Suddenly we were dealing with a Marine Corps support team, a State Department foreign emergency support team (FEST), the Fairfax County Urban Search and Rescue Squad, a USAID team from the Office of Disaster Assistance, an Air Force planeload of support personnel, and hundreds of FBI agents. None of them appeared to have arrived with logistics or administrative support personnel, and each of them had a different set of expectations and needs.

As confusion grew, one of my senior teammates offered to resign after his efforts to control the newcomers failed; another offered to blow his top. That was it. I stomped into the control room and asked someone to call attention. Top Spouse happened to be present, and in his best military voice—the one he saved for special occasions—he bellowed, "Ten-shun!" The room fell quiet, and I took over with the imperious command the situation warranted. "Take a good look at me," I announced. "I am the chief of mission here. Nothing, I mean nothing, happens at this post unless I say so. And if I'm not here, this is my deputy, and nothing happens unless he says so. Is that perfectly clear to everyone?"

I told folks to get organized into working teams, and when ready, they could see Linda to set up meetings with me. In the meantime, the Nairobi teams would carry on. I left them to it. I also insisted that the following weekend, everyone on the Nairobi side stand down to allow our colleagues to do what they came to do—help.

Julian's body was found in one of the city's overcrowded morgues. That made twelve dead American colleagues who would leave in coffins on a mortuary flight the next day. Their families would immediately follow on commercial airlines. It was unacceptable to me that we might say our good-byes without the Foreign Service rituals that accompany arrivals and departures.

I decided on a memorial at our residence. Unfortunately, everyone was so busy, and not even Top Spouse was available. I decided I would start the prep work myself. It was Sunday, and our household staff had weekends off, which left Duncan and me. What had I been thinking?

"Duncan, find the coffee maker, and I will find the tablecloths," I instructed as we rushed into the empty house.

"Where, Ambassador?" he queried.

How did I know? I never made the coffee. Top Spouse had long ago assumed full responsibility for managing the household and official functions.

"Never mind," I answered. "You find a tablecloth, and I will look for the coffee maker."

"Where, Ambassador?"

Was this really beyond our capabilities? A voice came from the front door. "Can I help?"

Community to the rescue! Linda must have alerted them—she knew where my strengths lay. Soon others joined us, and in remarkably short order, chairs were set up theater-style on the large veranda overlooking the back garden. Tubs of fresh roses materialized; cookies and coffee turned up on the dining room table, and my lovely neighbor found a pianist and created floral arrangements. News of the late afternoon service spread, and soon an overflow crowd arrived.

In the living room off the veranda, the lead person from Washington briefed family members about the ceremony at Andrews

Air Force Base at which President Clinton would preside as the coffins of their loved ones arrived. One of our widowers would not have enough time to collect his son at college and get to Washington in time. He asked if the ceremony could be postponed a day.

"No. Sorry," was the knee-jerk answer. It made me bristle.

I pushed back. "Why can't arrangements be made to postpone the ceremony for a day? I'm sure the president won't mind, and anyway, it's worth asking." The arrival ceremony was subsequently postponed.

A few minutes later I stood in front of my community to say something about the Americans we had lost, seven women and five men from six U.S. government agencies. Jessie Aliganga. Julian Bartley. Jay Bartley. Jean Dalizu. Molly Hardy. Ken Hobson. Prabhi Kavaler. Arlene Kirk. Louise Martin. Michelle O'Connor. Sherry Olds. "Tom" Shah.

Others followed, remembering our friends and what they meant to us. Some family members spoke, while others listened in heartbreaking silence. Duncan, who was our only Kenyan colleague present, began with this: "I was born a Kenyan, but today I feel I am an American." At the other end of the veranda, the pianist played quietly. We ended in silent prayer. Someone played "Taps." We handed out remembrance roses, and we said good-bye as best we could.

The next morning I stood next to the foreign minister on the tarmac of Jomo Kenyatta International Airport watching flag-draped coffins being lifted into a military aircraft. I wondered as each went by to whom I was saying good-bye and silently sang good ole American Fourth of July songs to keep control.

"You're a grand old flag, you're a high-flying flag and forever in peace . . ." Could that be Julian going by? Which coffin is holding his son, Jay?

"I'm a Yankee Doodle dandy, a Yankee Doodle do or die . . ." Is that Molly Hardy? "A real live nephew of my Uncle Sam . . ." Is that Prabhi? Arlene? "Born on the Fourth of July . . ." And so it went.

We planned our memorial for the thirty-four Kenyan colleagues we lost, the nine women and twenty-five men from three agencies. Chrispin Bonyo. Lawrence Gitau. Hindu Idi. Tony Irungu.

Geoffrey Kalio. Joel Kamau. Lucy Karigi. Francis Kibe. Joe Kiongo. Teresa Warimu Kiongo. Dominic Kithuva. Peter Macharia. Francis Maina. Cecilia Mamboleo. Lydia Mayaka. Catherine Mukeithi. Moses Namayi. Francis Ndungu. Kimeu Nganga. Francis Njunge. Vincent Nyoike. Francis Ochilo. Maurice Okach. Edwin Omori. Lucy Onono. Evans Onsongo. Eric Onyango. Caroline Opati. Josiah Owuor, Rachel Pussy. Farhat Sheikh. Phaedra Vrontamitis. Adams Wamai. Frederick Yafes.

Stoic faces and haunted eyes identified the many family members of the dead. They were so quiet in their grief. As we greeted each other in the residence garden, many offered hugs and whispered words of encouragement. "God is great," they told me, one after another. Kenyans were teaching me the power of faith.

There were individual funerals. American and Kenyans went in mixed pairs to represent the embassy, often going great distances. It took a toll on an already exhausted and traumatized community, and it was the right thing to do. Two hundred and one funerals took place, but as a nation, Kenya mourned the death of Rose Wanjiku most publicly. She had survived under the Ufundi House rubble for more than four days. She became a national symbol of hope, "the Kenyan Rose." When she died, hope turned to anger. Besides the dead, 400 people were severely disabled, and 164 more had acute bone and muscle injuries. Thirty-eight others were blinded and fifteen totally deafened; seventy-five more suffered from severely impaired vision; and forty-nine were living with hearing disabilities.[1] Hundreds of businesses were damaged or destroyed, many of them mom-and-pop enterprises with little or no insurance. All of this happened because Americans had become targets of foreign terrorists. What community would not be furious?

The anger was directed at us. On August 7 our marines had performed as trained with courageous competence. That was what I saw. What Kenyans saw were white men pointing guns at Kenyans coming to help at a moment of crisis. The spirit of *harambee*—mutual support—appeared violated at the time it was needed most. Kenyans could not see the devastation behind the still-sturdy walls of the building. We were accused of hostility, indifference, and racism.

The travel advisory that the U.S. State Department issued, citing the chaos of the bombing and scaring off tourists, made the local headlines, while pundits and politicians lambasted us. I decided to appear on television. The intention was to show that we shared their hurt and anger and to explain why we had acted as we had. The devastation, flooding, and live wires inside the building were blocked from public view but nonetheless made it a death trap. Everyone in the building was escorted out for their own safety and for security, including looters. The word "looter" provoked fury among the political class—all but the Moi government, which remained silent. How dare the U.S. ambassador accuse Kenyans of looting! Never mind that the press had already printed the news. That was different! I spent the next few months confronting the consequences of my words.

We learned that a man named al-Owhali had been arrested in Nairobi and another man had been taken into custody in Karachi, Pakistan. I was too busy to think much about it.

Two days after the television fiasco, I faced a CNN reporter on camera who opened with, "Ambassador, is it true that you sent a letter to Secretary Albright complaining about the security of the embassy before the bombing?"

How in the world would she know that? Never mind. I instinctively obfuscated and moved on. I knew better than to lie. Later that night, which is when colleagues in Washington started their day, the secretary's counselor and the deputy spokesperson told me there had been a leak concerning my letter to the secretary, and they wanted to know my thoughts about what to say.

"CNN already asked me about that on camera this morning," I replied, clearly giving an answer they did not want to hear.

"What? Who approved your appearance on CNN? Why did you say anything?" They sounded very put out. "We'll have to figure out what to do now and call you back."

Was their problem my doing? They sure acted as though it were. I hung up and paced the bedroom, feeling despair and loneliness. I was trying so hard to do things right, to lead as best I could under terrible circumstances, and now I was being taken to task, in that ever-so-subtle way that can drive you crazy, for a leak that had occurred in Washington. Over the previous few days I had wept for others' pain. This time it was all about me.

One of them called back to say things were settled and I had done nothing wrong. The words were welcome, but I recognized that no one had my back in Washington.

In Washington, career people rather than political appointees were chosen to respond to the press. Pat Kennedy, one of the key recipients of my cables as assistant secretary for administration and acting assistant secretary for security, commented, "Bushnell expressed her concerns over the vulnerability of the embassy, requested a security assessment team, and stated her desire to have a new building. In January of 1998, the [State] Department expressed its agreement and shared its understanding for the ambassador's concern and stated that the requested assessment team would be sent in the near future. . . . Unfortunately, we simply lack the money to respond immediately to all the needs of embassy construction. Just like, I guess, a family with limited resources, we need to have a priority ranking of how to spend our money."[2]

The Foreign Service of the United States of America is just like a family with limited resources? Then whose job is it to secure them? Later Tom Pickering, undersecretary for political affairs and number three in the department's hierarchy, noted, "Even had we had the money to operate on Ambassador Bushnell's recommendations—and, I tell you, we sympathized, understood, and supported those recommendations—we would still be in the early phase of construction right now."[3]

In other words, I had voiced concerns a couple of times beginning in late 1997. Those were met with sympathy, but, too bad, there was no money for a new building—and even if there had been, we would still have been in the old one at the time of the bombing. Nicely done; narrow truths. I was learning a lot about managing the message.

That night, President and Mrs. Clinton, along with members of the cabinet and grieving families, received the coffins from Nairobi.

4

THE IMPACT

August 22, 1998: Nairobi

Life was surreal. Our home, generally protected by a brick wall and Kenyan contract security guards, now crawled with Air Force personnel with guns. Armed State Department Diplomatic Security people escorted me to work in an armed convoy, yelling at pedestrians to "Stay back," with Duncan now in the lead car. The yelling did not help our popularity.

The day's paper reflected our then-current reputation through a letter to the editor. "I was also disappointed by the American rescue team who favored their own people. It appeared that Kenyans were not the team's priority. The American rescue team's effort was shameful and disappointing. However, my highest regard goes to the Israeli and French rescue teams who were simply outstanding and true friends of Kenya. Let the Americans know that most Kenyans were saddened by their open discrimination toward local people injured in the bomb blast."[1]

To reach the eight-story apartment-house-turned-USAID-office-turned-temporary-embassy-chancery, we stopped at checkpoints manned by Fleet Antiterrorism Support Team (FAST) marines with sniffer dogs. The building itself was protected with concertina wire and a sniper's nest. The neighborhood was the safest place in Nairobi.

I put a dusty plastic palm tree that had survived the bombing at the front door of the building and a framed poster next to the notoriously slow elevator:

Courage
doesn't always roar.
Sometimes courage is
the little voice at
the end of the day that says,
I will try
again tomorrow.[2]

At the recommendation of our regional psychiatrist and with the help of visiting Army counselors and others, every employee of the U.S. mission was signed up for a "critical incident stress debriefing." Top Spouse, already well known in the community, applied his cheerful energy toward active recruiting, and for a couple of days every room in the residence, including our private quarters, was humming with group discussions. Outside of the USAID building, this was the safest place and a lovely spot. Mixing Kenyans and Americans made for sometimes-stilted conversations, but I would not hear of separate groups. I did limit my own group, however, to my senior team. Some had been out of the country when the bombing occurred, while others had experienced the full force of the explosion and immediate aftermath. I had seen when the rescuers came how quickly we fell into "we" who had survived the unthinkable and "they" who had not, and I could not afford that dynamic among my closest teammates. The people I depended upon, like Michael Marine, our deputy chief of mission who had been in the United States when we were bombed, needed to be with us emotionally and every other way.

Our group, like the others, answered three questions: Where were you when the bomb went off? What did you do? How do you feel now? I had not yet articulated my feelings publicly, and what I heard myself say boiled down to commander's guilt: self-reproaching and painfully sad. It was my responsibility to keep people safe, and I had failed—tried, yes, but failed. I did not weep—I always saved that for later—but I did choke up. By the end of our discussion, every single person on the team made it clear that he had my back, the bombing was not my fault, and we would carry on.

As we said good-bye after the session, one of the military colleagues on my team handed me a softball I knew well, autographed by the first-ever members of a Kenyan softball team. A few weeks earlier, at the invitation of the Peace Corps volunteer who had created that team, I had thrown out the first ball and later been handed it, covered in signatures, as a gift. As my military colleague stumbled through the dust-filled offices, he had come across this. He pressed it into my hand now, saying, "Here's your softball, ma'am. Your ball. Your mission." So, it was.

Refugees from the former chancery set up their workstations cheek by jowl with their hospitable USAID colleagues. The remaining floor space crawled with electrical and computer wires. Supply boxes, computer parts, and other stuff we had rescued littered the hallways. On the eighth floor, which my front-office colleagues and I now shared with the classified communications unit, we were allowed one safe for classified material hugging a load-bearing column. This was a fragile building.

A blessing for Americans was the U.S. military post office. A team had been sent to Nairobi to assess whether we qualified for military postal privileges when the bomb went off. The group had taken it upon itself to turn a part of the USAID underground parking garage into a postal facility in service before the end of the month. We could savor another world far away from the stresses of ours.

The workplace had been bombed, our colleagues were dead and injured along with thousands of Kenyan neighbors, our spirits and friendships were shaken, and hundreds of people descended upon us. Some came to help us reconstruct, starting with consular services, and others to investigate the crime. Foreign Service colleagues from all over the world pitched in to get us back on our feet. We needed them. The VIPs and disaster tourists were starting to show up. The first two were necessary; few were helpful.

First came Secretary Albright. She told me she could no longer put off an official visit, and she was right. Unfortunately, the mood in Nairobi had turned from compassion to anger as the extent of devastating losses to lives, limbs, and livelihoods became apparent. As much as 10 percent of its GDP may have blown up on August 7, and the U.S. government had not offered anything but in-kind contributions and $25,000 in disaster relief funds that I could authorize as ambassador. We had been blown up in the month of August, when Congress was not in session, and at a time when the only domestic issue of political importance was the Monica Lewinsky scandal.

The secretary arrived hours late because her military aircraft had broken down. We had to cancel one-on-one meetings with political opposition leaders, who reacted with fury. Then there were the atmospherics. Everywhere we went, suspicious and alert Diplomatic Security agents surrounded us. Zealous precautions included blocking access to a hospital we visited. A woman had to give birth on the sidewalk outside; she named the baby Madeleine Albright. The secretary's public statements of condolence promised assistance but gave no round numbers or timeline. We were behind a demanding schedule all day.

At some point, the secretary asked me about my onward, or next, assignment. I was taken aback because I had put that issue aside. Before the bombing, Top Spouse, Linda, and I had been stressing over onward assignments. They wanted Central or Latin America, and I—the one who would need to learn professionally adequate Spanish—was resisting. When Albright asked where I wanted to go next, I was unprepared, and out of my mouth came "Guatemala."

"You'd be great for Guatemala," the secretary replied. And that was that. So, I thought, that is how deals are made—it definitely is all about who you know!

It was dark and very late by the time Secretary Albright stood on the back veranda of the residence for a town meeting with the American embassy community seated in the garden swatting bugs. The Mission Award for Heroism she bestowed on the community of beleaguered survivors meant very little to people who wanted assurances that the bombings would galvanize Washington to take better care of its overseas civilian employees.

Top Spouse made sure our promised senior team meeting with the secretary was private, and in the process he created a kerfuffle among the secretary's entourage, who could not bear even two minutes apart from their principal. As they stood in doorways, ears cocked to our conversation, one of my teammates, a victim-turned-survivor-turned-first-responder-turned-crisis-manager and now "just" a Foreign Service officer, voiced grave concerns about continuing security threats. "This will not be the last bombing by al-Qaeda. What can we anticipate from Congress, whose starvation-level funding was the excuse for not providing adequate security overseas?"

"Congress has a short memory," was the secretary's response. It was not what we wanted to hear. The delegation left shortly after the meeting. I think all of us were relieved to check off "condolence visit" from our various post-bombing to-do lists.

Local feedback to the visit was not positive. One opposition political figure summarized reactions this way: "She came and went, leaving the wounds as raw as ever. If anything, the visit . . . appears to have rubbed more salt into the still bleeding wound that the blast inflicted on Kenyans."[3]

The next VIP arrived on August 20. FBI director Louis Freeh wanted to celebrate the success of ongoing investigations with photo ops. Past my bedtime on the eve of our meeting, I received a call from an agent announcing that the director was on his way to see me with urgent news. I jumped into my clothes as his vehicle arrived at the residence.

"Did you know," Freeh asked breathlessly, "that the U.S. government was planning missile strikes against targets in Sudan and Afghanistan?" I invited him into the small study.

"No, I did not," I replied. Washington did not generally share such intimate secrets with their ambassadors. (That part I kept to myself.)

"What are you planning to do?" Freeh asked. He had already commandeered a plane to evacuate his people, he said, and a few seats were left. "Take my advice," he advised. "Select people you want to take those seats—unless the Department of State has made other plans for you."

Whaaaat?? I stopped listening and looked at Freeh incredulously. The guys with the guns were going to leave because missiles would be landing next door, and I was supposed to choose some folks to leave with them? First of all, the Foreign Service does not evacuate unless the threat is imminent, unarmed though we may be. Second, there is a rule called the "no double-standard policy," which expressly prohibits U.S. government officials from hoarding information—much less airplane seats—when the safety and security of all Americans are at stake. Finally, Nairobi was a long way away from Sudan's border, and we were not at risk from collateral damage.

I wished Freeh a bon voyage, confirmed that Washington had no plans for us, and called key teammates to the residence to review likely scenarios. We concluded that, at worst, some hotheads might emerge angry from Friday Mosque prayers and make noise. Al-Qaeda had killed too many Kenyans to attract much public anger from our retaliatory attack, and besides, the embassy was protected by marines. The next day, as missiles flew into a pharmaceutical plant in Sudan and an al-Qaeda training camp in Afghanistan, the department warned U.S. citizens around the world to take care. We closed the embassy and American schools at noon and waited to see what would happen. Not much. A few days later, the FBI returned.

The missile strikes failed to deliver on both accounts. Bin Laden was not dead, and the plant that employed three hundred people produced legitimate drugs. In the U.S. Congress and American media, President Clinton was ridiculed for fabricating acts of war as a means to deflect attention from the investigation into his personal conduct. In Nairobi, we carried on.

September–October 1998: Washington DC, Nairobi

On September 11, 1998, the memorial service for the 224 people who died at al-Qaeda's hands in Tanzania and Kenya opened with a stunning procession up the central aisle of the National Cathedral in Washington DC, as *Fanfare for the Common Man* echoed from all corners. The percussive sound of the kettledrum went through me like the waves of a nearby truck bomb. I jumped, and my cells went into panic mode. I wanted to run. Instead, I sat wondering if any of the other survivors or grieving families present had also just experienced a spark of terror. We looked heartbreakingly disciplined and stoic. The ceremony that ensued was beautiful, the music exquisite, the rhetoric soaring, and the mood prayerful. It was a farce.

A 400-page report had come out that morning, alleging that the president had lied about his relationship with Monica Lewinsky. President and Mrs. Clinton arrived late and left early, merely a phantom presence. The cabinet members arrived on time with their entourages and scurried away as the service ended. Only Jesse Jackson stayed to greet people after the service. I had not realized how accustomed I had become to the courtesies of Africans.

I was angry even before the service had begun when I learned how little money the administration would ask from Congress in its supplemental security budget request. Susan Rice reassured me, "Don't worry, Pru. Madeleine will take care of it." I was doubtful. It was starting to look as though it was not just Congress that had a short memory.

A few days later, I asked the two most senior career colleagues I knew to join me in discreet conversations with the Office of Management and Budget (OMB) and Hill staffers to respectfully make the case for the security of our people and get funding levels increased. My colleagues looked at me in genuine horror. I had just taken a step too far out of the box.

I had already trespassed unspoken rules by agreeing to be featured in *Vanity Fair*'s Hall of Fame and *Glamour*'s Women of the Year. I recognized I was taking risks by putting myself in the spotlight after a horrific event and discussed the possible impact with country team members in Nairobi. Most encouraged me in order to keep our story alive, but one member cautioned that I could create resentment. He might be right, I thought, but the family members of the victims would surely understand my need for validation and appreciate the efforts to educate Americans about the dangers of practicing diplomacy. The resentment I experienced came from senior department colleagues, not from victims or survivors.

As I continued consultations that week, numb alienation replaced the anger I had felt at the memorial. "Have you come to closure yet?" people wanted to know. "Aren't you ready to move on?" "Why haven't you sent in the reports due last week?" Washington colleagues clearly expected a certain range of behavior, and I had the sense we were not measuring up. In our world, we were cobbling together the communications system, fretting over the life insurance benefits to desperately needy Kenyan families, coping with permanently wounded colleagues, and dealing with an unfriendly local press. While American media tittered over President Clinton's sex life, Nairobi papers were listing the needs and losses of thousands of people. As my community and I surveyed the crises ahead, the department declared the crisis closed. We wanted help and attention. Our Washington colleagues had moved on and wondered why we had not.

Six days after the event at the National Cathedral, the State Department's undersecretary for management, Bonnie Cohen, told the Senate Subcommittee on Foreign Operations that "diplomacy can't be conducted on the cheap," and then went on to show them how it could be. In her testimony, Cohen listed the department's structural weaknesses:

> More than 300 vacancies worldwide.
>
> Overworked and insufficiently trained staff.
>
> 12 percent reduction of Diplomatic Security staff in the past 10 years.
>
> 18 new embassies opened in past 13 years, with almost no additional funding.
>
> Near-obsolete communications systems.
>
> A state of building disrepair that would "surprise if not appall" Americans.
>
> No appropriations for capital projects since FY 1995.[4]

With that as a prelude, she asked for money to restore the embassies in Nairobi and Dar es Salaam, increase the number of security personnel and perform some upgrades, provide some assistance to Kenya and Tanzania, and create antiterrorism funds. That is it. The U.S. government enjoyed a budget surplus, but the three hundred vacancies, the appalling state of buildings, the obsolete communications, and the startling vulnerabilities of 80 percent of our embassies did not rate the expenditures.

The administration did request about $30 million in disaster-related assistance funds to help Nairobi citizens and businesses devastated by the attack. It would still be months before we would see the money, and it was far less than the Kenyan government had requested, but at least we could start working. More than 100 buildings and 250 businesses were damaged or destroyed, and among the 5,000 people injured, a large percentage would remain permanently disabled.[5] There was a catch to the funding, however. Not a penny of the money was to go to administrative costs, that is, to support the people now responsible for figuring out how the funds were to be divided, managed, measured, and accounted. That was to be an additional challenge for the Kenyans and Americans who had survived the bombing. The victims of al Qaeda were to be punished with more work by congressional mandate. Although I enjoyed seeing family and reconnecting with friends, I viewed them from a great distance, through a cloud of confusion and huge sadness. My perspective was as narrow as that of a woman in a burqa. It was a relief to get back to Nairobi.

We had become by then a new and fluid community of newcomers, temporary help (TDY'ers, for "temporary duty"), injured people who had returned from American hospitals, and survivors who had remained. On the front page of the August 27 *Nairobi Roar,* Worley "Lee" Reed, our security engineer, summarized our feelings about the people who put their lives aside to assist us.

Documenting Heroes: I have searched for human words to express the thoughts and feelings concerning our recent catastrophe. There are no words that adequately perform the duty. I wish, however, to pass a message to our colleagues who did not directly participate in the old Embassy search and rescue operations.

For the ones who were TDY or on leave during this nightmare, we are thankful for your lives. We are thankful that God, in whatever form you believe in Him, kept you safe from this criminal act. We are thankful that we were not required to carry you from the building. Never ever permit yourself to wish that you could have helped in the search and rescue. We knew each time we entered the building that we may not be coming out alive again. If you had been here to help, you may have been the last victim of this tragedy. God saved you to serve a higher purpose than to add to the death toll of this criminal. We are happy that you are alive. We want you to also share that happiness. . . . On behalf of the people who worked at the bombed Embassy, we honor you for your hard work and efforts. There are many forms of heroes.

While the bombing remained ever present for us, the department had deemed the security threat over, gone, passé, yesterday's news. The protective details had left town, and Duncan and I were back to cruising Nairobi without escort in the burgundy Cadillac with red-orange license plates. At the overcrowded USAID building one morning, a sniffer dog detected a suspicious package, and we were told to take cover in the underground parking garage. As we headed down the stairs I heard someone gasp softly, "Oh, God." The rest of us filed silently down to wait for the all-clear in the dim, dusty subterranean space. At first I thought I should move around and let people see the calm me-in-charge. Not a person wanted to interact. I found the Cadillac and sat in the backseat, silent and alone.

Not long afterward, a colleague in the Africa Bureau called to alert me that the department was planning to remove the Fleet Antiterrorism Support Team marines providing our perimeter security because of . . . funding issues! And anyway, my Washington colleague explained that the experts said we had already been bombed and so would not be targeted again.

Really?? Were these the same experts who had announced we were only at medium risk of a terrorist attack three months before al-Qaeda's attack? I informed my colleagues in a low and calm voice that the day the marines were withdrawn, everyone in Washington would see me on international CNN, tears streaming down my face as I waved good-bye to the brave boys in camouflage fatigues who had protected us. The FAST marines remained. But so did the threat of their removal.

Visitors kept coming, and many wanted a photo op in the "old embassy," as we now called our former workplace. To me the place still reeked of death, but it was important that people from Washington understand what had happened, and there was no more visceral way to show them. When one group innocently asked to have their photo taken against the backdrop of smeared remains of a colleague we had known well, I almost threw up. I learned the next day that all three of us who had escorted that group of VIPs had endured a sleepless night. We decided then and there to close the building to future tours.

We were living betwixt a past that hurt badly, a future that guaranteed nothing, and a present that truly sucked. Did I know before the bombing that you can chart the stages people go through as they respond to disaster and then try to recover? No, but I was sure seeing it unfold. The amazing feats of bravery we had witnessed on August 7 represent the "heroism" stage. The empathy we experienced in the immediate aftermath is the "honeymoon" stage. We were now in the "disillusionment, resentment, and group fragmentation" stage. Great. As the textbook said, we were absorbing our losses and feeling angry over unmet expectations.[6] Washington and the world had moved on. We needed to get our act together.

October 16, 1998: Nairobi

One-third of our senior team had arrived over the summer, some only days before we were bombed, and all of them faced huge challenges best resolved together. So we met on the residence veranda and set our priorities. We put them on the front page of the *Nairobi Roar* under the headline "Where do we go from here?" Each category included an array of actions we had to take concurrently. Here was the priority list: 1. Put people first. 2. Reestablish operational systems and efficiency. 3. Address moves and space issues. 4. Reestablish close ties of friendship with Kenya.

It was my job to reflect the value of putting people first by getting resources and delegating decision making. It was also my job to represent our needs to Washington in ways that would fit the peculiar circumstance of a community that was neither dead nor evacuated nor normal. Not since Beirut 1983 had the State

Department experienced a calamity of this size, and mechanisms to assist beyond the rescue phase did not meet our needs.

We described our battered circumstances in a cable sent to Undersecretary for Political Affairs Tom Pickering, Undersecretary for Management Bonnie Cohen, Director General Skip Gnehm, Assistant Secretary for Administration Pat Kennedy, and Assistant Secretary for Africa Susan Rice.

> On behalf of the country team, I would like to invite you to visit Nairobi to see firsthand the impact of the August 7 bombing on our people, our operations, and our bilateral relations. The difficult and enervating discussions with Washington colleagues over the supplemental budget request, release of ESF [economic support funds], and presence of FAST marines—to name only a few issues—indicate that too few people appreciate just how severely the attack has affected every aspect of our personal and work lives. A brief stop-over could make a difference in demonstration of security and institutional support for efforts to put this mission back together.

No response. For Washington's attention, we were unsuccessfully competing with Iraq weapons inspections, Indian and Pakistani nuclear tests, disorder in the former Yugoslavia, and the Monica Lewinsky scandal.

We did get a visit from the Republican staff members of the Senate Foreign Relations Committee, and we included in their itinerary conversations with community members and teachers to give them an understanding of why putting people first was such an imperative. Let them hear about the child who asked, "Mommy, when you go to work today, are you going to die?" They listened, and what they took away were complaints about the State Department that they were only too happy to exploit once they returned to Washington. I know because I received major blowback from that visit a few weeks later.

Meanwhile, we carried on. "Be kind to yourselves, and be kind to one another" became my public mantra. Community leaders and Top Spouse formed networks around the families who had needed the most support. Our medical team, local counselors, therapists, and teachers offered mental health and other services. Not that many people walked through their doors. Americans feared damage to their security clearances and professional reputations. Kenyans chose family, community, and faith over western-style therapy. At least the opportunities were there. The Marine House, as the barracks for our detachment was called, welcomed newcomers and lots of children to community activities. The residence pool and tennis court were made available to American employees and their families 24/7. The American Women's Association created a Bomb Relief Fund to send child victims to the United States for free eye surgery.

Putting people first meant listening to the Nairobi community, too. We at the U.S. mission were not the only ones experiencing disillusionment. As the inventory of human and material losses was translated into Kenyan shillings, the government asked for $150 million and criticized the Clinton administration's assistance request to Congress, which was less than a third of that.

I was the face of the United States, and people had a lot to say to me. I listened at memorial services, at hospital visits, and at city functions and found that the only person who was not saying much was President Moi. Our conversations before the bombing had been "frank and candid." We saw one another frequently and argued a lot. I once interrupted our conversation to comment that we were fighting again and asked Moi if he was enjoying himself. "Yes," he declared. "I am a democrat!" Now our interactions were stilted and often unpleasant. He announced that his government would have nothing to do with helping us find another site for the chancery. The Clinton administration's icy distance hurt his pride, and the paltry congressional responses to funding requests hurt his public image. He eventually became more respectful as he watched me deal with challenges over the next few months, but our relationship was never the same. Thank goodness for Sally Kosgei, the permanent secretary at the Foreign Ministry, who kept our bilateral issues on track and our relationship ever cordial.

I knew I had to take care of myself if I was going to take charge and take care of others. For the body, I swam laps, got massages, and drank good wine. I wore the brightest suits in my wardrobe because they made me feel better and gave me a chance to show our murderers that this ambassador was still in the pink. For the brain, I began reading Spanish translations of Danielle Steele novels in preparation for Guatemala, a pastime guaranteed to fixate my attention on something other than the endless to-do lists. For the spirit, I meditated, I prayed, I gardened, and I allowed a friend to lure me into a few sessions of Reiki, a healing technique based on the principles of energy and natural healing processes. I would have howled at the moon if someone had told me it would work.

I decided to share the Reiki process with the senior team. After all, isn't that what a leader does—model constructive behavior? I closed one meeting with a cheerful announcement that I had begun Reiki treatments, an alternative form of healing, and would be happy to provide the name should anyone want to try it. No one had a thing to say, although I am pretty sure some eyes rolled. Three men followed up.

"Ambassador," one of them said, "we think it's great that you have found a method of treatment that's working for you, but we're practicing something else."

"Oh?" I was really interested. "What?"

"It's called the RAD method."

"The RAD method?" I was now intrigued. "I've never heard of it. What is it?"

"Repression, alcohol, and denial. And it's working very well for us."

Others coped by working themselves to exhaustion. Some came into my closet office and wept. Fortunately, we began to see results thanks to the help of newcomers and temporarily assigned colleagues, perseverance, and energy. We now had two functioning satellite offices and a newly purchased interim office building bordering the Nairobi National Park wildlife conservation center near the airport. For the newly important requirement of a 100-foot offset, we purchased boulders that would accommodate wild animals and deter wild terrorists. Negotiating boulders with the head of the Kenya Wildlife Service was an "only in the Foreign Service" moment.

On a cool, sunny day in a walled-off area of the gold Athi Plains, two marines in dress blues raised the American flag on the pedestal salvaged from the old embassy. We stood at attention, and I thought of the souls of our neighbors and colleagues imprinted in that flag. I avoided eye contact after the ceremony lest my stiff upper lip relax into unbearable grief. We were going forward, falling apart, picking ourselves up, and trying again tomorrow. At least I was.

Then the Accountability Review Board came to town.

November 1998: Nairobi

The secretary of state must call an Accountability Review Board when a U.S. embassy sustains loss of human life or significant property damage. William J. Crowe, retired admiral and former U.S. ambassador to the United Kingdom, split his board into two groups: one went to Dar es Salaam and the other to Nairobi. I was well aware that the first person held to account would be the chief of mission. U.S. ambassadors are among the few Senate-confirmed government officials who actually have written job responsibilities, including the safety of all Americans in their country of assignment.

I could not wait! Other than the crisis-debriefing sessions in the residence a few days after the bombing, no one in the department or anywhere else had asked me what had happened. The board was mandated to listen, and I was ready to talk. I had sheets of yellow legal paper listing every cable I had sent over two years by subject line and reference number and the responses when there was one. On the eve of my interview, I had also asked my senior team, "Are we sure that we did everything possible to secure the embassy before we were bombed?" When I walked into the lion's den, I wanted not only data but also the armor of a pure heart and a few arrows of righteous indignation in my quiver.

I was called into a dimly lit hotel conference room in which a group of unreadable white faces sat around a large rectangular table. I ignored them all and locked eyes with Admiral Crowe. I recognized leadership when I saw it and trusted that he did, too. I told my story to him.

I had arrived in Nairobi in August 1996, when the State Department's Office of Foreign Buildings was planning to renovate our overcrowded building that violated security requirements for a 100-foot setback from a public thoroughfare. The 100-foot setback requirement was a result of the bombing of the U.S. embassy in Beirut in 1983. But budget cuts had ensured that requirements were waived. I had suggested an assessment of the value of the building and other properties around town with an eye to relocating. "There's no money for assessments," I was told, and anyway, the United States was only leasing the land from the Kenyan government. Would I please move aside and allow long-approved Washington plans to unfold? I did.

I knew from an intelligence briefing before coming to post that a terrorist financier, Osama bin Laden, had an al-Qaeda office in Nairobi and that the United States was monitoring his communications with the aim of disrupting his operations. It sounded reasonable to me. The mile-high city of perpetual spring attracted an array of dubious characters: Somali warlords, the Sudanese People's Liberation Army leaders, Ugandan Lord's Resistance Army rebels, Rwandan Hutus who had helped perpetrate the genocide, and Rwandan Tutsis who had fled it. Al-Qaeda was just one more.

Throughout 1997, crime worsened and political demonstrations grew, so we perfected our emergency action systems, charged our countrywide warden network with disseminating information, practiced embassy radio alerts, and held town meetings. We considered relocating the medical unit, decided against it, and successfully moved a few of the agencies out of the chancery to other locations. Meanwhile, we focused on a considerable policy agenda that included assistance for free and fair presidential elections at the end of the year.

Things began to change in August 1997. The members of the Nairobi al-Qaeda cell discovered their phone was tapped. A joint CIA-FBI team arrived and, with Kenyan assistance, raided the home of Wadih el-Hage, the head of the cell and a U.S. citizen. Not long after, el-Hage moved his family to Texas. When he landed in New York, the FBI tried to turn him, but el-Hage refused. That was the end of it as far as I knew.

About a month later, we learned of a plot to bomb the embassy. Al-Haramain, an Islamic charity organization near the Somali border, was discussing how to get the weaponry. I cabled the department advising what we faced and what we were doing about it. No one answered. Indirect word from the Washington intelligence community came with the request that we do nothing yet to allow time to check into al-Haramain's other links. The Kenyan government increased security at the embassy, as I requested. As the host government, Kenya was responsible for the security of resident diplomatic facilities. The bomb threat turned into an assassination threat, then back to bomb. Still no word from Washington. I asked President Moi to dismantle al-Haramain, and he did so, deporting its staff amid considerable media attention and Muslim outrage. I sent yet another cable to the department. I also asked if there was a link between al-Qaeda and al-Haramain, and the answer was no.

In November 1997 I was in Washington for a conference when a man walked into the Nairobi embassy with information about a possible truck bomb. The information was sent to Washington, shopped around to other intelligence services, and declared faulty. The guy was a flake, I was told. In the meantime, during my Washington consultations I was lectured by the Africa Bureau executive director that senior people in management and administration were getting irritated by my "nagging" about embassy security and vulnerability. I was advised to stop sending cables regarding security concerns. I sent another cable soon after I returned to Nairobi, citing the recent warning and highlighting the rising anti-American sentiments among the Muslim community following the takedown of al-Haramain, the increasing political violence leading up to elections, the mugging of one of our largest American employees outside embassy doors, and, yes, the building's continuing vulnerabilities.

In February 1998 Gen. Tony Zinni, the four-star head of the Defense Department's Central Command into whose theater Kenya fell, volunteered to provide a vulnerability assessment team, since the department said it had no money for such purposes. The department declined his offer but did approve money to send a team of experts to suggest some reasonable upgrades.

Two months later I got my annual performance appraisal. For the first time in my seventeen-year career, I was not asked to draft a benign critique to fill up the "Needs improvement" section. Instead, I received a completed one with the notation that I tended to "overload the bureaucratic circuits," a coded reference to my repeated efforts to draw attention to our security posture. That was it. I decided to write a personal note to Secretary of State Albright and another one to Undersecretary for Management Bonnie Cohen. Instead of chastising an ambassador for "overloading circuits" with security concerns, the department's managers could more usefully ask Congress for sufficient funds to keep us safe. In my note to Secretary Albright, I cited the threats and the actions we had taken and noted that "the chancery remains vulnerable, and I remain nervous." I gave the letter to the visiting director general, head of human resources, who promised to hand-deliver it. In his own thank-you letter to me, he wrote the following: "I am concerned, as you are, with the security problems that the Mission faces. I just hope that it does not become too much of an obsession. I found similar security concerns in both Addis Ababa and Pretoria, but neither had problems as severe as yours."[7]

Within a month, the undersecretary for management responded: "I understand that the current chancery office building in Nairobi lacks adequate setback and structural features to resist blast and ballistic forces. However, because of Nairobi's designation as a 'medium' security threat for political violence and the general soundness of the building, its replacement ranks relatively low among the chancery replacement priorities."[8]

Over the summer the threats died down, and so did my cables to Washington. On August 7 we were blown up. I described the consequences and the imperfect rescue efforts. When I finished, some of the people around the table asked about security weaknesses within our control, like pressing the Kenyan government more aggressively for another radio network, but it was hard to top my story. Instead, the group's determination to find someone in Nairobi at fault fell on my colleagues, who were grilled far more intensely than I. It was an excruciating experience to be accused even indirectly of inadequate performance on the small issues when larger ones back in Washington were ignored.

Days before the Accountability Review Board arrived, a New York grand jury indicted bin Laden for long-term conspiracy to attack U.S. facilities overseas and kill American citizens. It mentioned bin Laden's alliances with the governments in Sudan, Iraq, and Iran as well as Hezbollah producers of bombs against U.S. embassies and military facilities in the past. It noted that he recruited Americans and set up humanitarian front organizations to move money, people, and materials around the world. It said he owned land for terrorist training camps, warehouses for explosives, bank accounts under assumed names, and sophisticated communications equipment and weapons. In 1993 al-Qaeda began training Somali tribes to oppose the United Nations' humanitarian efforts in Somalia. In October members of al-Qaeda participated in an attack on U.S. military personnel where eighteen soldiers were killed and seventy-three others were wounded in Mogadishu. That year bin Laden and "others" also tried to develop chemical weapons and obtain nuclear weapons components.[9]

The indictment, issued only three months after the bombings in Nairobi and Dar es Salaam, showed a level of detail that made it clear some people knew a great deal about bin Laden and al-Qaeda. Apparently that did not interest the Accountability Review Boards—or Congress, for that matter.

The Nairobi team looked exhausted at the event Admiral Crowe hosted at the conclusion of the board's work. He had tears in his eyes when he acknowledged how sorry he was for the way we had been treated before and after the bombing, I felt we had earned every word of the apology. It turned out to be the only apology we would ever get.

The Marine Corps birthday ball, the social event of the year, took place a few days later. We had suffered two casualties in our detachment. Cpl. Nathan "Jesse" Aliganga had died on August 7, and Sgt. Daniel Briehl had received a Purple Heart for his injuries and his heroic actions on the same day. This year's ball was going to be particularly poignant. As the president's personal representative, the ambassador is the guest of honor with the job of reading a White House message during the grand opening ceremony.

The marine who came to brief me stood tall in front of my desk in the tiny office I used. I asked what the detachment wanted me to say about Corporal Aliganga. Tears came down his face as he explained that the guys had talked about it and decided it was time to start moving on, so please keep the reference to a minimum. He was not the first man to cry in that small space, and I usually handed over a box of tissues and waited quietly. But I ignored this young man's tears in deference to his dignity. I had learned a lot about grief: I could not take it away from anyone, but I could accompany.

Marine birthday ball pageantry is always splendid. Women at their most elegant and men in ribbon-bedecked uniforms or black ties provide a fitting backdrop to the Marine Corps Color Guard as they present the American and USMC flags. A magnificent cake was rolled in, and it was time for brief remarks before the ceremonial cutting. One piece would go to the oldest marine present and one to the youngest. I said a few words and sat down. The marines remained at attention around the cake. A colleague took the podium to say a few words about Corporal Aliganga. He talked and he talked. He had been close to Jesse and had not smiled since the bombing. A marine at attention, sword in hand, began to sway in front of the cake. On went the talk. The marine swayed again. Our colleague kept talking. The marine started to go down, saved by a quick-acting woman sitting nearby who pulled him backward by the belt. Our colleague continued to talk. When he finally stopped, he said thank you. And then he smiled, a big beautiful smile that we had not seen since August.

He smiled all night long, and so did Top Spouse and I when, duties performed, we got to dance. I had rock 'n' rolled my way through three years in Karachi, two years in Tehran, and a lot of Marine Corps balls. When Donna Summer belted out "I Will Survive," I threw my body around, hands high in the air, shimmied and shivered and wiggled my hips with Osama bin Laden on my mind. Later I danced and mourned until it was time to go. Richard and I had long ago learned to leave the party to the marines before any of them had drunk enough to start asking me to dance. I took the detachment's gift with me. Ambassadors often receive a token present, usually something inexpensive from a catalog. The Nairobi detachment that night gave me a Marine Ka-Bar knife inscribed with my radio call sign, "Albany." I did in fact feel that we had survived combat.

5

THE TURNING POINT

December 1998: Nairobi

We received a holiday card from the White House, lived through another VIP visit, and hosted my parents for Christmas. Those were the highlights of an otherwise difficult month. The card came as a result of the VIP visit we had survived a few months earlier: the U.S. trade delegation led by Secretary of Commerce Bill Daley. That was the trip we had been planning in the office of the Kenyan minister of commerce on August 7. The two Foreign Commercial Service colleagues who had accompanied me had been severely wounded. Inside the embassy, Commerce Department employees Adams Wamai and Moses Namayi had died. Tobias Otieno was badly wounded and blinded, and so was Ellen Bomer, who was in town to help prepare for the Daly visit. She wrote her own tale of August 7 in a gripping book, *Ms. Gloria: A Survivor of Terrorism*. When the visit finally did take place, it represented far more than the actualization of a postponed trip. It was a milestone in how far we had come since the attack and how much we still hurt. We met with still-grieving families, and I had to excuse myself before I cried in pain.

As Daley said his farewells to me, he asked if there was anything I wanted to communicate to President Clinton, whom he was meeting in Tokyo the next day.

"Yes," I snapped. "You can tell him to send a holiday card. We did not get a condolence letter, and it's too late for that now, but it would be great for the community if they knew he cared." Among the cards and letters Top Spouse was putting into a condolence binder, hundreds had come from Americans, Kenyans, and others around the world. Two had come from members of Congress. None had come from the White House.

"What?" cried a member of Daley's delegation, someone from the First Lady's office. "You mean the White House never sent condolences? Oh, my gosh, Hillary will be appalled! Don't worry; we'll take care of it."

They did. We printed the message on the front page of the *Nairobi Roar* on December 30. It read, in part, "All Americans were moved by the manner in which you, your colleagues, and thousands of Kenyans rose to the challenge of rescuing those still alive in the rubble, dealing with the grief of those who lost loved ones, and mobilizing resources to treat the wounded and clear the debris."

There was no mention of perimeter security, and I suspected our country desk officer in the AF bureau had written the letter. But it was not the thought that counted—it was the signature. It represented to the community that the president knew we were still here.

A colleague from the Medical Bureau arrived a few days later to tell me that the Republican staffers who had gotten an earful during their trip to Nairobi had returned to Washington to give an earful to unnamed people in the State Department. Folks at senior levels, my medical friend warned me, were furious that I was "washing our linen in public." In fact, some were beginning to think I had "gone over the edge." As to the cable we sent requesting a visit from specific senior-level people, one of them would be coming, but it was to shake his fist in my face. I do not remember what else he said. Had I been physically assaulted, I could not have felt more shocked and bruised. The director general, our next visitor, was kind and helpful when he came and made life far easier in the future, but that prior episode left a bitter taste.

Four months had passed since we were bombed, and by this time I had long incorporated traditional ambassadorial activities with post-bombing stuff. Pending the arrival of more substantial funds, we made a press event out of every assistance dime we found. I reappeared in the countryside and in the press on issues other than August 7. I talked a lot about trade and avoided the subject of the bombing. I attended diplomatic functions and found a salve in their ordinariness. My diplomatic colleagues provided an emotional safety net, steering clear of bomb-related topics. Those who knew me well had already heard my story, and those who met me subsequently were too polite to ask.

My embassy colleagues were not as shielded. Americans felt the' Nairobi community's resentment, and it stung. As Lee Ann Ross wrote, "We design a disaster relief package for the Kenya victims and argue with Congress to get money. We only have the ambassador's disaster fund to begin with, $25,000. It takes until December to get any more money. Tragic. The Kenyans can't believe that we can't be more responsive. We can't either. Tensions run high. Somehow many see us at fault. It's as if they think we blew ourselves up. We are never viewed as victims."[1]

Kenyan colleagues were even closer to public resentment. By day they struggled to help put our organization back together, and by night they had to listen to their friends and families fiercely criticize us. They also were aware of inequities. Americans got plane tickets to leave the country for rest and recuperation; Kenyans got nothing. Americans had the opportunity to request another assignment, while Kenyans had no choice but to stay. Kenyans once had access to all parts of the USAID building, and now we locked them out of areas that were "classified." It was hard to feel jolly about the season.

One week before Christmas I sat on the residence verandah with our management team discussing how we were going to perform holiday rituals. We had received a worldwide advisory that bin Laden might attack again along with instructions to close down. Coincidentally, in Nairobi we heard about a threat to blow up an American school, and we had three of them in Kenya. We shut down everything from the embassy to the schools.

Time dedicated its December 23 cover story to "The Hunt for Osama" and quoted bin Laden as he spoke about the August 7 bombings. "If the instigation for jihad against the Jews and the Americans in order to liberate [Islamic shrines in Mecca and

Medina] is considered a crime, then let history be a witness that I am a criminal. Our job is to instigate and, by the grace of God, we did that—and certain people responded to this instigation. . . . I am confident that Muslims will be able to end the legend of the so-called superpower that is America."

In Nairobi, we were taking threats very seriously. I looked around at our senior team as we talked about the precautions we would take and wondered silently if we had the wherewithal to sustain another attack. Not for the first time, community came to the rescue. Having closed the embassy, I was now engaged in a repeat performance of my entry-level job in shipping and customs: figuring out how to get holiday packages to the young and old notwithstanding bin Laden's threats. On the enclosed veranda of the residence, we figured out what to do and set our minds upon making the best of the holiday season. The Marine Corps detachment launched its annual Toys for Tots campaign, and people sang holiday songs at the Marine House. Families got their packages.

On Christmas Day, Mom, Dad, Richard, and I carried out a Bushnell tradition that Dufie and Gerry began in Germany: a holiday dinner with community singles. Dad manned the bar, and the rest of us served, because our staff were celebrating with their own families. Soon even the nervous FAST marines began to loosen up. As we cleaned up later, I felt normal for the first time in months. Wonderfully normal.

On December 31 we celebrated another embassy tradition, the New Year's Eve sundowner in the Nairobi National Park. In the shade of an acacia tree a few miles into the park, we clustered around vehicle tailgates, careful not to stray too far into the wild animal preserve. We looked through binoculars at a distant rhino. The Athi Plains radiated dry earth and quiet peace, and we talked softly. We were together, and the year was disappearing. The sun sank behind the Ngong Hills as "Auld Lang Syne" floated our way from a tape deck in someone's car. We hugged one another, pretending we did not see tears. We had survived. So many others had not.

I looked over the acacia-dotted plains toward the Ngong Hills. A curtain of pink cirrus clouds had parted in the middle, displaying a wide shaft of blue, blue sky. I wondered if it was an omen. Would things really get better?

January 1999: Nairobi

A colleague handed me a *New York Times* article by James Risen and Benjamin Weiser with the headline "Before Bombings, Omens and Fears." What followed were jaw-dropping details about incidents that involved me and facts that shocked me. The article was perfectly timed to be printed within twenty-four hours of the official unveiling of the Accountability Review Board's report, and it was far more interesting.

> In the spring of 1998, Prudence Bushnell, the U.S. ambassador to Kenya, sent an emotional letter to Secretary of State Madeleine K. Albright begging for the secretary's personal help.

> Ms. Bushnell, a career diplomat, had been fighting for months for a more secure embassy in the face of mounting terrorist threats and a warning that she was the target of an assassination plot. The department had repeatedly refused to grant her request, citing a lack of money. But that kind of response, she wrote Albright, was "endangering the lives of embassy personnel."

That language came from a cable I had written, not the letter, but who cared. The facts were true enough, and someone was sharing them. The article quoted me and I vaguely remember speaking with one of the authors but I was not aware of the information they now revealed.

The article noted, "The Central Intelligence Agency and the Federal Bureau of Investigation had been amassing increasingly ominous and detailed clues about potential threats in Kenya, officials said." I wondered who these officials were and who had told the reporters about the cables and events leading up to August 7. But I was too astonished by what I was reading to dwell on it. I had no idea that the FBI had known about al-Qaeda and had been tracking bin Laden ever since the investigation into the 1993 World Trade Center bombing. No one had told me the CIA-FBI team had taken Wadih el-Hage's computer and found a letter describing U.S. intelligence efforts to investigate the group, an allusion to the group's role in Somalia in 1993, and a reference to a cache of files that had been removed from el-Hage's house and hidden elsewhere. I had no clue that, according to the article, investigators had begun a "somewhat frantic, concerted effort" to find the files on the theory that an attack was being planned using Kenya as a "jumping off point."

The story underscored the warning we received in November 1997 when the man walked into our embassy to describe how we would be attacked. He was now in jail in connection with the embassy bombing in Tanzania. So our "walk-in" was the real thing, not the fabricator I had been told he was. As to my efforts to alert Washington to our vulnerabilities, "Ms. Bushnell's increasingly insistent demands for a new embassy were so far out of step with the State Department's plans that officials at headquarters were beginning to see her as a nuisance who was obsessed by security, according to an official familiar with the matter."[2]

It stung my ego to be depicted as someone who wrote "emotional" letters "begging for help," perceived as a "nuisance" and "obsessed." I was also annoyed that nowhere did anyone note that I had been right. We were vulnerable and in danger. Far easier to paint the victim as a kook. The news story showed the Washington interagency community for what it can be: ruthless, blameful, and prone to cover-up.

Admiral Crowe's ARB report gently chided the CIA for faulty assumptions and asserted that while there was "strategic" intelligence, none was "tactical." The FBI was not even mentioned. "The Boards did not find reasonable cause to believe that any employee of the United States Government or member of the uniformed services breached his or her duty in connection with the August 7 bombings. However, . . . we believe there was a collective failure by several Administrations and Congresses over the past decade to invest adequate efforts and resources to reduce the vulnerability of U.S. diplomatic missions around the world to terrorist attacks." The report estimated that it would take $14 billion over ten years to secure all of our diplomatic facilities in need. It made recommendations, requested more information sharing, commended the staffs in Nairobi and Dar es Salaam, and closed the books on the matter of the August 7 bombings.[3]

I had developed a startling new depth of anger and sadness. Distractions were essential to my well-being, and I was grateful to be in Kenya, which offered so many of them. Among our friends, Jonah Western and Shirley Strum gave us the best insights into wildlife. He had led the Kenya Wildlife Service, and she had researched a troop of baboons for years. When they invited us to Shirley's research station, we gladly accepted. Jonah flew us in his bush plane, and Shirley met us at the landing strip. "I was hoping for a walking safari, but there is a rogue elephant around," Shirley lamented. Whatever. Later our cozy conversations were interrupted by distant gunshots. Then came a loud knock on the door. So much for being in the middle of nowhere. A Kenyan neighbor warned of bandits, the source of the gunfire, and reassured us they had probably left the area. Okay.

We had a lovely evening. I took my last walk to the outdoor loo a short distance away in the very dark beyond, flashlight in hand. I heard the hiss of a cat and turned the light to find a large, menacing snake rising up on its haunches—or whatever—to get a good frontal look at me. Not sure of the protocol, I backed up slowly and quietly until I could safely and loudly announce to the household that there was a snake in the middle of the path to the privy.

Jonah at first doubted me, then found it and identified it as a puff adder. Very dangerous. Oh, my. I was inspired to write a rhyme: "What do you do on the way to the loo when you find a puff adder hissing, 'How do you do?'"

The next day we had a picnic next to a wild river, passing on the way a dead copperhead. I was beyond rhymes, wondering what to make of such weird and dangerous encounters. Were these omens? No, I concluded, just sources of danger that life can offer beyond acts of terrorism. I found it a consoling thought.

Our residence gardens offered closer and safer distractions. The Kikuyu highlands around Nairobi, a mile high and close to the equator, enjoy two rainy seasons and rich soil. The only time as an ambassador I actually felt "extraordinary and plenipotentiary," as it says in my title, was on my knees in healthy dirt planting or weeding. I had filthy fingernails, and no one talking to or at me. Best of all, I could depend on satisfactory results. Then came the bombing. I lost all interest—pluck a weed, and it will only grow back. It all seemed so meaningless.

I needed to get beyond passive, and I decided to bring my community back together, for my own solace if for no one else's. In a quiet, unused corner of the garden I began work with a Japanese landscape artist to create a commemorative space for those who had died in the chancery. This was the only property left in Nairobi that the United States owned at this point. We designed a water feature rimmed with bricks inscribed with the names of each colleague who had died in the embassy. It would be inaugurated at the Remembrance and Recognition Ceremony.

It was challenging to achieve a pace that moved us forward but not too quickly. Some people needed to recover, and others, to remember. You might as well wish brown eyes blue, I was finding, as wish a person's reaction to trauma different. I thought it would be a good idea to have a formal dedication of the memorial garden that also recognized individual outstanding contributions in the moments after the bombing. Secretary Albright had handed us a group award for heroism, but any subsequent recognition was going to be up to us.

It was a rotten idea. Writing, reviewing, and rewarding individual performance, even though we had long before agreed that there would be no money attached, stirred bad memories and second-guessing about what had happened on August 7. People denied others' accounts and found nominations greatly exaggerated, and one was deemed an outright falsehood. A senior colleague threatened to file a grievance if one award was approved, and Top Spouse said he would do the same about another one. That was not our finest marital hour. The awards committee reconvened, creating more hard feelings, and adjusted its findings. I adjusted the focus of the ceremony from recognition to remembrance.

A few days before the event, we learned that family members of our deceased American colleagues would also be attending. That made it a different event altogether. They would come as a delegation, which meant they would have Washington minders. That always meant more work. Our planning broadened from a focus on local families and employees to the visiting American family members. They, too, had lost their community, and we wanted to be welcoming.

Saturday was another gorgeous day of blue sky and puffy clouds. A large tent gave shade to the community and visitors. Susan Rice, assistant secretary for African affairs, said a few words, and then George Mimba, head of the Foreign Service National Employees Association, got up. "If the bombing was meant to divide Kenyans and Americans, it failed miserably. The people of Kenya and the United States of America have come out more united than before. . . . Looking into the faces of still-grieving family members, when I see them I see our late colleagues. From their faces, I see hope and determination to keep the candle burning."[4]

Then the family members of the dead filed in silent procession around the bricked fountain. Susan and I stood to receive them at the other end, standing near a marine in dress blues and a large wreath. Americans shook hands or hugged. Kenyan family members, the women especially, held me close, whispering, "God be praised" or "God is good." Once again, I admired their faith.

Susan met with family members of State Department employees after the ceremony. They looked angry and sad and let us know why. They listed the department's slights, indifference, and overly bureaucratic reactions to their pain and needs. I had grown accustomed to listening to anger, but theirs was particularly painful to me. Susan was silent and expressionless, listening carefully. That night she and I talked about how the State Department could be restructured to put security and "force protection" on the agenda of the top-level policy people. Nothing changed.

Then, finally, the $37 million in assistance arrived. This was five months and a week after hundreds of businesses, mostly mom-and-pop stores, had been blown up, more than one hundred buildings damaged, and thousands of people injured because they happened to be in the area of the U.S. embassy chancery on August 7. This was not compensation. Members of Congress wanted to make that perfectly clear. No way were we compensating anyone for an al-Qaeda attack. After all, we were the targets, not the perpetrators. This was to help, not to remedy.

Whatever they called it, I was happy to have something other than my words and my presence to show we cared. We paid for medical expenses, surgeries, prostheses, psychological wounds, and follow-up procedures for individuals. We rehabilitated buildings, including the Cooperative Bank Building, purchased a new structure to replace the Ufundi House, and assisted large and small businesses in recouping some of their losses. We provided school fees for orphaned children and funding for crisis response infrastructure. All of the money was funneled through local nongovernmental organizations, and most of it was distributed with full-court press. My smiling face was all over the media.

March–May 1999: Nairobi

Spring arrived. Richard and I would be leaving in a couple of months to begin the annual rotation cycle. I was too busy to think of any departure, however.

"Ambassador, you have a problem." A few of the senior team followed me into my office after a staff meeting. Oh, good, I thought. Just the words I live for.

"Some of the people in this building are stuck," one reported. "They can't get over the bombing, and their attitude is having a very negative effect not just on their staffs but on the others, too." They went on to elaborate. I said nothing.

A few minutes later, the very people about whom they were speaking showed up. "Ambassador, you have a problem." Those words again! "Some of the people in the mission are showing absolutely no regard for the emotional toll the bombing has had on many of our people, and their attitude is having a very negative effect on everyone." They elaborated; I listened.

Frustration had permeated our cheek-to-jowl circumstances, and being kind to one another was a challenge. Claims for physical injuries had been denied—a form from workers' compensation informed me that I could not prove my documented hearing loss was a work-related injury, so too bad. Information about which bureau to go to for what issue was tortuous to find. Kenyan employees had to deal with more work at the same pay without the benefits offered to Americans. The double standards stung. Many would be facing new American supervisors, and everyone who had taken refuge at the USAID building was moving into a vacant building near the airport and game park, far from restaurants, shops, or even a bus stop.

I decided to call in the experts, as great a variety as I could find, a veritable deluge: experts from the Oklahoma City community bombed in 1995, trainers from the Foreign Service Institute, the State Department regional psychiatrist for South Africa, and local counselors. The front page of the *Nairobi Roar* was a menu of counseling and training opportunities.

It was "normal," I learned, for victims of terrorism to feel angry, impatient, stressed, isolated, and beleaguered. Take your pick; it was normal. It was a relief to feel validated. I was not damaged goods. I was normal. What others felt, I did not know. By now I had learned that I could only provide the environment in which people could heal. I could not heal for them.

I felt the community shift. Whether it was the information, the attention, or my imagination, I am not sure. Maybe I was the one shifting with only sixty-some days left, but it did feel as though we were getting back into sync. We still had one important bomb issue to confront, the old embassy. Once it was declared unfit, I was given the decision to have it imploded or chipped into pieces. I went for the latter. I never again wanted anyone to hear the sound of a blast coming from that corner. Of course, people complained, but there you are. Now what would we do with the space it had occupied? We wanted a park. This was hallowed ground commemorating 213 deaths, and we strongly felt it should never be forgotten. We wrote to Washington.

The response was polite and firm. The U.S. government actually did not own the land; we had years remaining on our lease from the Kenyan government. We were not to create a park. We were to return the land. Period. I recognized defeat and announced Washington's instructions at a country team meeting to stunned silence. "You can't do that," someone said. "You can't give back that land to the Kenyan government. You know what will happen. One of Moi's cronies will grab the property and put a high-rise on it, and no one will ever know what took place. You can't do that to the Kenyans."

He was right, and I was vexed that I had to be publicly reminded. This was not about us. While our economic and commercial folks worked with the Kenyan and American business communities to find private money for a foundation, I worked President Moi's cabinet to extract a promise from every minister that he would support my request that the government donate the land for a park. The owners of the Ufundi House property, where the "Kenyan Rose" and too many others had died, contributed their land to make a respectable piece of quiet space on a bustling corner. My only request was that a wall inscribed with the names of those who died be a part of the design. I did not want people forgotten.

That left one last big problem, the security of our colleagues left behind in the USAID building. Once the people from the old embassy departed for other quarters, the FAST marines would be removed. USAID in Washington had no plans or resources for a move. The colleagues who had come to our rescue on August 7, squeezed us into their work space, and helped us take the first steps toward recovery were to be left in a vulnerable and highly visible building without any protection. Nothing I could say—or threaten—would make a difference. I did try.

A few days before departure, Gen. Tony Zinni, head of Central Command, called. "You tell your USAID people that they have between now and the end of the fiscal year to find themselves another place to live. I will keep my marines there on my own nickel till then but not a second more." The sense of relief that permeated the eight floors of that rickety building was palpable. USAID found a new place, and our colleagues stayed safe.

On May 20, 1999, I had less than twenty-four hours before I would forever be the former ambassador to Kenya. Wow. I had had a lifetime of saying good-byes, but not like this.

I had paid my farewell courtesy on President Moi, and although he was in a foul mood, he promised to give the land on which the old embassy stood to a memorial park foundation. Secretary Albright sent a warm cable recognizing my work, which I appreciated. The Kenyan media were kind, which I also appreciated. One pundit entitled his article "Bushnell's Engaging Tour of Duty in Kenya," and another took note of our focus on gender issues, corruption, human rights, HIV/AIDS, environment, and governance. It was a boost to my often-bruised ego that they noticed. More important, it showed that our hard work to repair the Kenya-America friendship was getting results.

The May 20 *Nairobi Roar* commented: "As we reflect on the past, think about the now, and hope for the future, we will always have you in our hearts. No other leadership could have served us so well in pulling us through the last year. We thank you for the privilege of serving and working with you both. We wish you safety in your travels and the best at your next Foreign Service posting."

I was touched. But I wanted more. I wanted a going-away party, and no one was planning one. I was hurt. When I told Linda that I was pining for a "proper" good-bye, she just looked at me.

As Duncan took Top Spouse and me on last-minute errands, I was still feeling mildly sorry for myself. Our final stop was the residence of our DCM, Michael Marine, and his family. Duncan maneuvered the burgundy Cadillac with red-orange license plates onto their narrow driveway. Flanking each side stood the employees of the U.S. mission, smiling and waving. Hundreds of people had conspired to keep this secret. I was awed.

It was not the ten-foot carved wooden giraffe they gave me, nor the songs or the toasts that touched me most; it was the message the community tacitly sent by creating the surprise party in the first place. They cared. "We're okay, and so are you" was the message I took away. "Go in peace; the good people have prevailed." It was the last time the community and I were together. Top Spouse and I said good-bye to Duncan at the airport the following night, and our life in Kenya was history.

6

THE CONSEQUENCES

August–December 1999: Washington DC, Guatemala City

The State Department hosted a grand commemoration on the first anniversary of the East Africa bombings. Some of the easier recommendations from the Accountability Review Boards had been farmed out for implementation, and my colleagues had moved on to Kosovo, East Timor, North Korea, Y2K issues, and President Clinton's impeachment proceedings. A moment was set aside to remember.

Elegantly and carefully staged in the grand Benjamin Franklin Room on the eighth floor of the State Department, the ceremony had uplifting music, high rhetoric, and stilted protocol. Attendance was limited because of space. I was asked to stop sending the names of the people from Nairobi who had been left off the invitation list because I was disrupting the seating arrangement. It felt as if the event were being held for someone other than us. Downstairs in the lobby of the diplomatic entrance, the names of American colleagues lost in the bombing were added to the wall commemorating those who have died on duty. The names of my Kenyan colleagues were on a plaque around the corner from the lobby in an interior courtyard.

No one was happy, but this appeared to be the department's way of showing it cared. Compensation was just one of the issues that did not go away. Efforts and lawsuits by the families of American victims as well as Kenyan survivors crashed into legal walls. Medical issues persisted. Our most seriously wounded colleagues confronted surgeries and medical events that would go on for years; the department created an Office of Casualty Assistance from need and victims' frustrations. Months after the attack, many of the families of victims still had not received autopsy reports or much of anything else of satisfaction. The anger I had witnessed from State Department families in January was still simmering.

The department did organize a "family meeting" in May. But instead of simply focusing on the families of August 7, 1998, they included the military families of the soldiers killed in Mogadishu, Somalia, in 1993. Strange bedfellows brought together by one legal indictment for two different al-Qaeda attacks on Americans, one on a battleground and the other on an urban street corner. Family members of the dead and wounded sat together in a department auditorium listening to a parade of representatives from a variety of U.S. government agencies—from the Internal Revenue Service to the Departments of Labor, Justice, Defense, and State. Rather than feeling assuaged, some of the Nairobi families felt worse, as if they were simply problems to be dealt with and forgotten.

I had other issues to deal with now. I was Guatemala-bound and learning about the consequences of thirty-five years of internal conflict sparked by the U.S.-instigated rebellion in 1954. Decades later, peace accords were finally signed in 1996, strongly supported by the United States, but wartime legacies remained: mistrust, hate, corruption, narcotics, gangs, oligarchs, poverty, and judicial impunity. The challenges were considerable.

I learned that the U.S. embassy in Guatemala City was almost a twin to the old embassy in Nairobi—same vintage, same architecture, same proximity to busy downtown streets, same State Department attitude about relocating: no way; there was no money. The department had asked Congress for only a portion of the funds Admiral Crowe said would be required to make all embassies safe. In response, one U.S. congressman introduced legislation that would force Washington to spend much more. "I don't want the responsibility falling on the Congress so that if something in the future happens, they can say, 'You didn't provide the authorization,'" said Rep. Doug Bereuter (R-NE).[1] The legislation came to naught. As I made the requisite courtesy calls on congressional staffers and members, accompanied by an assigned colleague from State's congressional relations bureau, I was expressly forbidden to mention the word "security." When I did anyway, my political appointee minder interrupted to advise me: "Ambassador, you are not to talk about this."

The senior appointees at State in charge of security and overseas buildings did not appear keen to talk about security either. They met with me jointly, opening the conversation with the words, "Pru, why do you keep choosing embassies that don't have setback?" I took it as a rhetorical question and listened to their proposition: I would not launch complaints, cables, or any reminders of Nairobi for ninety days. They, in the meantime, would initiate efforts to secure the current Guatemala premises satisfactorily, in other words, meeting the State Department's own regulations. We made a deal, and the U.S. government eventually controlled all three streets and all of the buildings around the embassy. Yes, I learned, we can innovate. It just takes political will and the right policies.

Richard and I spent the summer in a small furnished apartment in Arlington, Virginia, with two unhappy cats from Kenya while I worked to attain professional proficiency in Spanish, learn everything I could about Guatemalan history and politics, and stuff down the sorrow and anger that stayed with me. I went to a leading military expert on post-traumatic stress disorder (PTSD), who acknowledged that I met some of the criteria. So now what? I was headed for Guatemala City as the U.S. ambassador. What was I going to do? It wasn't that bad. I would soldier on. The department had made no provision for follow-up attention to bomb survivors. One did not suffer trauma in the Foreign Service; one sucked it up. And we suckers did not complain for fear our careers would suffer from the label "damaged goods." By the time I was to be sworn in as ambassador, my clenched jaw was throbbing in pain, bad enough to send me to the medical unit. The old-fashioned Foreign Service doctor diagnosed it as TMJ, temporomandibular joint disorder, and prescribed an increase in estrogen and a reduction in stress.

It was a relief to move to Guatemala. The issues were compelling, the language was Spanish, and nothing had anything to do with the bombing. I could compartmentalize my brain, although not my cell memory. On my first day of work we drove into the underground parking lot of the embassy—just like the one in the old embassy Duncan used to drive into—and every cell in my body panicked. My heart raced, and I wanted to flee. Fast.

"It is okay; you are fine. It's okay; you're fine. It's okay; you're fine," I repeated until I calmed down and could put a smile on my face. I had Guatemalan and American colleagues from thirteen U.S. government agencies to meet. It was a relief to know that Linda Howard was again going to serve with us as office manager. She understood what others could not.

The embassy had a sizeable representation from the development, law enforcement, and military communities, reflecting the policy issues we faced. The U.S. past in Guatemala was not pretty. We had engineered the coup d'état against a democratically elected president in 1954, the same year we ousted the democratically elected prime minister of Iran. In Iran, the interest was oil. In Guatemala, it was land for the United Fruit Company. The Dulles brothers, who ran the State Department and the CIA, also sat on the board of United Fruit. The land reforms promoted by the new president represented a Communist threat, or so they told Eisenhower. We supported a military takeover of the country and moved in and out of the conflict for decades, supplying and training military and paramilitary operatives who committed atrocities and acts of genocide against the poor and largely rural Mayan communities. With the end of the Cold War came a shift in U.S. policies and an apology from President Clinton for past deeds. A bipartisan Congress committed hundreds of millions of dollars to implement the 1996 Peace Accords. Its reforms were to transform Guatemalan society.

The embassy country team identified four priorities: reinvigorating the stalled peace process, promoting trade and economic development, helping to establish a rule of law, and ensuring assistance and security for all Americans visiting and living in Guatemala. We set milestones for each and went after them. I was a powerful figure as ambassador and an object of interest as only the second woman chief of mission from the United States. The press followed me closely, happy to use my statements about impunity, violence, and labor reforms to stir the political stewpot. American expatriates liked me because I held town meetings around the country. Guatemalan oligarchs were highly suspicious, and the newly elected populist president, Alfonso Portillo, was anxious to curry my favor. His public commitments to the Peace Accords gave us reason to hope, and the country team established ambitious goals.

Richard took a new alias, Don Ricardo, and resumed his functions as Top Spouse. The interviewer for the English-language weekly, *Revue*, wrote this: "*Don Ricardo*, as Ambassador Bushnell's husband has become known in Guatemala, is a strong, warm figure who wears his role of 'the ambassador's spouse' very comfortably. The day I interviewed him, he was about to make his first appearance with the Damas Diplomáticas, who were calling on the new First Lady of Guatemala. He appeared totally unconcerned that he might be the only male *dama*." Actually, he loved it. The residence was another white stucco house built as a private home, but larger and more elegant than the Nairobi residence. This one had a grand entrance with a showcase stairway and a massive chandelier. Instead of a small downstairs study, we had a wood-paneled library with hidden bar. The large veranda opened onto a large, flat, rectangular expanse of green that just begged for improvements. We shared the residence and the garden with armed security guards from the Guatemalan police. The walls that surrounded us had guard towers, and I had nine bodyguards who accompanied me in a convoy every time I left the compound. Otherwise, they were installed in the renovated space of the attached garage. I wanted no part of it. I would be fine without them.

"You want to fire the Guatemalan policemen with the guns who have the keys to our house?" Don Ricardo asked pointedly. The guards stayed, and I adjusted. Armed men roamed the garden, so I took my exercise inside on our new treadmill.

By the end of 1999, Don Ricardo and I had settled in nicely. The never-ending problems of the bombing were on the other side of the world. A new century had arrived. Fireworks and firecrackers exploded everywhere. At midnight, I was snuggled in bed with a pillow over my head to muffle the sounds of explosions that triggered spasms of startle response, a familiar symptom of PTSD.

2000–2002: Guatemala City

Guatemala was tough. The political left and many Mayan communities mistrusted us because of past support for right-wing killers. The political right hated the reforms we supported. Organized crime syndicates in and out of government took issue with our drug interdiction programs, and violent gangs took issue with everyone. I was glad we had kept the bodyguards. I was also glad I had been schooled in the conflicts of the sub-Sahara. I understood macho culture and negotiating with killers. I had dealt with bullies, and I had speeches aplenty about corruption, human rights, and the status of women ready to translate into Spanish. I was familiar with unpopularity, and I had seen large-scale violence and genocide.

We had strong members on the country team who believed we could make a difference, and we created effective strategies to do so. Colleagues also bound up my wounded pride and sent me back into the public arena when the press beat me up for supporting joint military programs against narco-traffickers; for persuading the government to condemn Cuba in the UN Human Rights Commission; for doing business with their democratically elected government, whom the wealthy hated; and for promoting labor and other reforms demanded by my government under the newly elected president, George W. Bush.

Although appointed by the Clinton administration, I now represented Bush. No one could believe that Republicans would actually support changes that touched corporates interests, so the Guatemalan business community decided it must be my idea to make intellectual property rights violations an issue between our two countries. Street vendors demonstrated with expensively printed signs when I noted that Guatemala's current intellectual property rights legislation did not meet international standards, putting at risk Guatemala's participation in the new Caribbean trade initiative.

And it surely was my idea, people said, to invent the Bush administration's policy to insist the Guatemalan government and congress ratify labor agreements signed in 1954—or face removal of trade preferences. Even I was surprised that the Republican White House had issued such instructions, but the howls of protest they provoked among the Guatemalan wealthy business class went way beyond what I had anticipated.

The head of the congress, former dictator Gen. Efraín Ríos Montt, called me La Imprudencia, a label that stuck. I was denounced for violating diplomatic protocol by meeting directly with members of Guatemala's congress; for interfering in domestic affairs; for demanding what surely would mean the economic ruin of the country. Calls to the Guatemalan government to throw me out were followed by letters to the *Wall Street Journal* and to the White House asking for my recall. At the breakfast table every morning, Don Ricardo advised me to "get over it" when I complained of political cartoons and nasty op-eds in the newspapers.

Such was the cost of getting results. In the Guatemalan congress, intellectual property rights legislation was strengthened and a new labor code passed. Judges confronting impunity, union leaders demanding reforms, and human rights activists uncovering abuses received our public support. Assistance programs helped Mayan people, and law enforcement programs deterred drug and human traffickers at least somewhat. At the trial of the murder of Bishop Juan Gerardi, a human rights icon brutally killed in 1998 after he reported evidence that the military had committed 85 percent of the human rights violations during the thirty-five years of conflict, La Imprudencia was in the audience. The press accused me the next day of having influenced the "guilty" verdict.

In August 2001 large groups of demonstrators appeared in front of the embassy with a huge banner that read "Bushnell Go Home" and burned me in effigy. I was astounded by the adrenalin accompanying my fear that someone would be hurt. I could handle verbal assaults and ugly cartoons, but demonstrations produced spikes of stress that left me empty and exhausted. What if something happened to someone? I was sensitive to my body's reactions and signs of PTSD. Flashbacks were scary but rare, and nightmares were infrequent. It was the adrenalin peaks of concern about people's safety and the accompanying waves of sadness that left me hollow. La Imprudencia persevered anyway. I smiled a lot and continued to state our policies in a Spanish that improved with practice.

Don Ricardo and I headed as often as we could to the Mayan highlands for respite. Among the mountains where much of the internal conflict took place and many of our resources landed, we enjoyed the visual delights, artistry, and different cultural worldviews. In Quetzaltenango, Guatemala's second largest city, I commented to the Mayan mayor about the hope I always experienced among indigenous people despite centuries of oppression and today's violence and mistrust.

"That is because everyone knows that one day this country will be Mayan again. They tried to kill us, but we are still here," the mayor said. "It will not happen in my lifetime, and it will not happen in my children's lifetime, but it will happen one day, and my work is to help in the preparation." I admired his perspective and patience.

We used the residence for musical evenings, inviting people who despised one another and many who did not like me. The protocol made it easy on everyone: give greetings in the receiving line, get a drink and finger food, find a café table, and listen to jazz, marimba, opera, or Broadway. The talent was often Guatemalan. Have another drink and then go home. Follow-up could result in a private lunch on the veranda between a human rights advocate and a military official or a discreet meeting among other adversaries. Outreach like this helped redeem my good standing, and so did our sponsored productions of *West Side Story, Once upon an Island*, and *Grease*, with all-Guatemalan casts and off-Broadway producers. There is more than one way to implement policies, and this was by far the most fun.

A year into our Guatemala assignment I was invited to speak at the Oklahoma City National Memorial as part of the opening celebration of their museum and memorial. Did I really want to revisit my experience with an act of terrorism in the detail required to come up with a decent speech? Wasn't it better to just move on like everyone else seemed to have done? On the other hand, a team of Oklahoma City mental health practitioners had made the journey to Nairobi to help when we needed them, and what better audience to hear our story? I decided I did not want to pretend the bombing had never happened.

I had no idea if I would have anything in common with the audience of survivors, first responders, loved ones of those who had died, and members of the community at large. Before a large audience in a city new to me, I described what happened to us on August 7, 1998, and how we had reacted. I ended to a standing ovation, and I learned why later. Our stories connected. When a ton of explosives in the back of a truck blew up the Murrah Federal Building and killed 168 people in 1995 in Oklahoma City, survivors rushed back in to help colleagues. Like us, first responders shared an initial reluctance to cede their place to other rescuers. Many who came to help in the aftermath created more chaos than assistance. The media brought turmoil, and survivors experienced the same frustration with the "Have you found closure?" question. The bombing raised profound questions of meaning and faith, and this demanded resilience from pioneering spirits to journey forward. Surviving family members carried anguish and anger, and some survivors showed evidence of disabling injuries and chronic pain. People felt the same pressure we had to "get on with it," while supervisors and managers faced the similar challenges of reconstructing their operations. Like us, no one appreciated being considered damaged goods. Like us, the community took the lead in healing its wounds.

Of course, there were differences, too. Oklahoma City was the first terrorist event of this dimension on U.S. soil. Congress passed victims' rights legislation and millions of dollars for security upgrades in federal buildings in the United States. As a security precaution, Pennsylvania Avenue and other streets around the White House were permanently closed. Meanwhile, U.S. embassies remained vulnerable overseas. Not mine, however. Washington colleagues engaged in creative thinking: we purchased two buildings adjacent to the embassy and found ways to safeguard the streets. We could remain in an urban area and feel safe.

Al-Qaeda made its way back onto the front page a few months after our trip when, on October 12, 2000, it blew up the uss *Cole*, killing seventeen sailors and injuring thirty-nine more. The fbi and the military briefly investigated, Congress held a hearing, and the media moved on.

In January 2001 I was called to testify in the case of *USA v. Usama bin Laden*. The assistant U.S. attorney for the Southern District of New York, Patrick Fitzgerald, had issued an indictment against twenty-one people for the bombings of Nairobi and Dar es Salaam, and four of them were on trial:

> Wadih el-Hage, the Lebanese American administrative head of the al-Qaeda branch in Nairobi, was charged with perjury. Twice he had lied to a grand jury, both before and after the bombings. Had el-Hage told the truth in 1997, the prosecution alleged, the bombings would never have taken place.
>
> Mohammed Saddiq Odeh, who lived on the coast of Kenya, was charged with participating in mass murder and helping to construct the bombs that went into the trucks in both Nairobi and Dar es Salaam.
>
> Mohamed Rashed Daoud al-Owhali, who hurled the stun grenade outside the embassy in Nairobi just before his companion detonated the truckload of explosives, was also charged with participating in mass murder.
>
> Khalfan Khamis Mohamed was charged with providing the logistical support necessary to carry out the attack on the embassy in Dar es Salaam.

The trial began with a range of conspiracy charges, and the prosecution spent days putting al-Qaeda insiders and other experts on the stand to tell the story. Bin Laden ran an international network of terrorist groups capable of carrying out attacks even in the face of operational failures. He managed al-Qaeda through a *shura* council of advisors, which he headed. He had an international financial system to move money and used state-of-the-art technology to issue orders. He had operated with impunity for five years from Sudan, where the government had given him special privileges. He had interacted with the government of Iran, and its proxy military organization, Hezbollah, had trained al-Qaeda operatives to blow up buildings. Bin Laden had personally chosen the embassy in Nairobi as a target because it was accessible, it housed the U.S. embassy to Sudan, and it was headed by a female ambassador whose death would provoke more media attention.

Bin Laden was connected to the attack on U.S. soldiers in Somalia in 1993, an attempted purchase of chemical weapons in 1994, the bombing of the World Trade Center in 1995, and the bombings of the two U.S. embassies in 1998. Al-Qaeda cells were still operative in Brooklyn, New York; Orlando, Florida; Dallas, Texas; Santa Clara, California; Columbia, Missouri; and Herndon, Virginia.

In a large, frigid file room at the rear of a New York City federal courthouse, the survivors of the East Africa bombings who were summoned as witnesses waited for days for their turn to testify about the attack itself. Most had received only hours' notice to get their lives in order before they were whisked to the bitter cold of the Big Apple. They were provided with donated heavier clothing at the airport by a solicitous Witness Task Force, but gratitude was morphing into frustration as day after day passed in the dreary storeroom. The tension was contagious.

I was lucky. I was only coming from Guatemala, less than a day's trip away, and Richard was with me. I had to wait only three gray days, but it proved to be plenty of time to relive events, absorb lingering anger, and witness the pain many still experienced.

I heard nothing from the State Department until late at night before the morning I was to testify. At first I thought someone had actually remembered and wanted to wish me well as the first witness in this phase of the trial. No, the lawyer was calling to remind me that under no condition was I to reveal classified information in court. I almost threw the phone across the room. By the time I was called to the stand the next day, I was mentally fatigued and physically tense.

Judge Leonard Sand dominated the crowded, wood-paneled courtroom in a black judicial robe. Gray computer monitors, their cables snaking across the floor, almost hid the jury—all but their faces, which looked alert and interested. The four dark-haired, bearded defendants in traditional Muslim garb of neutral shades sat facing the judge, surrounded by lawyers in their traditional garb of dark suits. Everything about the place appeared sober. The jury looked serious, the judge imposing, and the defendants bored. Behind the brown-slatted bar that separated the gallery from the rest of the courtroom, spectators, journalists, and some families of al-Qaeda's victims quietly observed this case of mass murder.

The prosecution and defense attorneys asked me open-ended questions with deference. Then a defense attorney asked about the many antennae on the roof of the old embassy, and Judge Sand snapped, "Don't answer that." The lawyer tried to rephrase the question, and Sand interrupted. "Counsels, in my chamber." Just like on TV.

For the next few minutes and forever, I faced some of our murderers, who were staring intently at their computer monitors. Al-Owhali, who had thrown the grenade that brought so many thousands to their windows, continued to pick his teeth, as he had been doing while I spoke. I was delighted to be dismissed from the stand shortly after the judge returned.

Former colleagues and neighbors from Nairobi followed me as witnesses. George Mimba had found himself buried under bodies, Sammy Nganga under piles of stone rubble. Frank Pressley had lost part of his jaw and a large section of his shoulder. Moses Kinyua and Elijah Mutie Mue would wear disfiguring facial scars forever. Tobias Otieno, Peninah Mutioho, and Caroline Ngugi were blinded. Father John Kiongo Kariuki had seen his brother and niece blown up.

Caroline Gichuru described being blown from her chair and blinded by blood, stumbling toward the daylight that had replaced the concrete exterior wall of her office. Only loud warnings from shocked onlookers stopped her from tumbling into the concrete wreckage two stories below. Marine Sgt. Daniel Briehl testified to falling down an elevator shaft and going to the hospital; he left out the fact that he had returned to the old embassy, ignoring his injuries, to rescue others, an act that won him the Purple Heart.

Horrifying testimonies in and of themselves, they represented only a tiny sample of the stories and injuries that more than 5,000 Kenyans could describe. The last of these witnesses, Dr. Gretchen McCoy, described the bloody chaos outside the embassy and the desperate efforts to help the wounded at a local hospital. The litany of horrors ended when the names of the 224 Kenyans and Tanzanians killed by the bombings were read into the record.

Before I left the courthouse, Patrick Fitzgerald invited Richard and me to meet his boss, Mary Jo White. In her office, the two launched into a strange and abstract apology that "the wall" had prevented them from doing more before the bombing took place. I had no idea what they were talking about and lamely suggested that they review their procedures. Even Richard, a criminal defense and civil rights attorney before Foreign Service days, did not understand.

That night, all of us witnesses were given a special night tour of the Statue of Liberty. The boat ride was icy cold, the view of the Twin Towers and other landmarks crystal clear. It felt extraordinary to share this with other survivors. New York City looked pristine and innocent, untouched by the evil that had changed so many lives so far away. I returned to Guatemala's sunshine with relief.

In August Richard and I flew to Nairobi for the opening of the August 7th Memorial Park on the corner of Moi and Haile Selassie Avenues. Was this really the site of the old embassy chancery—it seemed so green, even peaceful. The brown concrete box that was our workplace was gone, and so was the seven-story Ufundi House next door. The high-rise Cooperative Bank Building that I thought would become my tomb looked the same, only spiffier, with new windows and scrubbed walls courtesy of the U.S. government.

Then I heard a tinny voice screeching hymns into a scratchy microphone on the corner close to the train station. For two years I had heard that same voice from my office every day around noon, and for a second I was transported. The violent fireball had not consumed us; life was normal; I was back in 1998 explaining to the foreign minister that the White House had agreed to a "pull-aside"—a short, informal conversation—between President Moi and President Clinton at an upcoming regional meeting. No, I remembered saying, a pull-aside had nothing to do with a swimming pool; it was Washington-speak for an informal meeting.

Then I was back in the park. It looked good. Walking paths swished around green plots of scrawny plants that would bloom gorgeously once they took root. They led to a large, curved wall on which the names of the dead had been etched next to an inscription: "May the innocent victims of this tragic event rest in the knowledge that it has strengthened our resolve to work for a world in which man is able to live alongside his brother in peace." The park and its small museum seemed modest in comparison with the Oklahoma City memorial, I thought, but that was okay. Our park honored the dead with equal sincerity.

On August 7, 2001, the park was dedicated in front of family members of the dead and five hundred invited guests. On the other side of the entrance turnstiles, thousands of people jostled to get closer to the site, just as they had on the day of the bombing. Dignitaries spoke, and when we finally stopped, the crowds surged forward, snapping off the brand-new turnstiles as they poured through the narrow gate openings, trapping some of the visitors. No one was out of control or necessarily ill-intentioned, but for a moment the crowds appeared as ominous as they had three years earlier. In a private ceremony at the U.S. ambassador's residence, Kenyan colleagues spoke of their remembrances. Like mine they were very real. I was happy that I did not run into anyone who asked if I had come to closure. None of us had. We had had a trial and we had a memorial park, but nothing was over yet.

When we returned to Guatemala, the "Bushnell Go Home" demonstrations were beginning to subside, and we got back to business. On September 11, 2001, we were having breakfast when the phone rang. It was our regional security officer. "Ambassador, turn on the TV," she ordered. "The bastards are doing it to us again." Richard and I shared the horror of the rest of the world as we watched the second plane go into the World Trade Center towers.

The attacks rocked Guatemala. If the United States was not safe, what country was? We had seemed invulnerable, and now . . .

we were not. Cards and flowers poured into the residence and embassy. One man delivered his bouquet personally to our protocol assistant. "Tell the ambassador I was at the demonstration against her. That was work. This is personal. I am very sorry." I went on live radio to discuss in Spanish what I had learned in Kenya about talking to children about disastrous events. It was a linguistic milestone for me.

In the spring of 2002, the country team decided to go after one of the most powerful men in Guatemala, a member of "the Brotherhood," popularly known as the "dark forces." Gen. Ortega Menaldo was the former head of military intelligence and a current Portillo advisor. We suspected him of crimes sufficient to warrant voiding his visa to the United States. We got the evidence, made the case, and secured the department's approval to stamp "VOID" over his U.S. visa. It was headline news. As the government of Alfonso Portillo proved increasingly incompetent and corrupt, we reduced our expectations, and I began speaking more frequently and publicly about government corruption. Over tea on the residence veranda toward the end of my tour, I even confronted President Portillo. I told him that we were aware that his private secretary was considered his bagman. I had to ask my embassy colleague how to say "bagman" in Spanish. Portillo got the message.

"So," he said, "I suppose you think I am stealing?"

"What else can I think, Mr. President?"

He said nothing. Portillo would eventually spend time in a U.S. prison for money laundering and returned to Guatemala in 2015 still a hero to many. For the remainder of my tour, he acted as if I had never spoken.

By the time I left Guatemala, the shift in media coverage left me feeling somewhat redeemed. When Richard and I arrived at Reagan National Airport on our final flight through Atlanta, we found our checked luggage missing. He later received his; I did not. In my suitcase I had packed all of my jewelry, my work clothes, and documents too important to send ahead. It was the first time I had consigned valuables to checked bags, because we were carrying our two Kenyan cats as our hand luggage. I lost an international collection of irreplaceable jewelry and our medical records. Was it retribution for pulling a visa? If so, it was worth it.

2002–2005: Falls Church, Virginia

Don Ricardo turned back into Richard, and I turned back into an ordinary American woman. It was not easy. I had wondered before we left Guatemala what I would miss the most after six years of serving as an ambassador. Certainly not the armed escorts and men with guns stalking my garden; not even the fine house, terrific staff, or fully armored BMW—those came with a price. I missed my persona and the respect it brought. Now, like every other American woman regardless of age, I was called "girl," "gal," or "guy" and treated accordingly. In the State Department, I was not to be called at all. As I sought onward assignments after Guatemala, it became clear how deeply I had annoyed people in management.

"So, Pru wants to return from Glamourland," said a human resources colleague at the start of a conversation about a job. I had forgotten about the photographs in *Vanity Fair* and *Glamour*, but others clearly had not.

"Why did you leak to the media that you had written to the secretary before the bombing?" asked another, evidently never wondering if that the rumor could be false. No one gave me direct feedback, but I felt I had embarrassed the department. I could understand anger when it came from Kenyans; I could not understand the chill when it came from career colleagues. The folks in management were not interested in supporting me, so I did my own job hunting, securing an assignment as dean of the School of Leadership and Management back at the Foreign Service Institute. It was perfect for me. I was back into training with supportive bosses, talented teams, and many leadership lessons.

In 2001 the Council on Foreign Relations and the Center for Strategic and International Studies reported the state of the State Department in a letter to newly inaugurated President George W. Bush: "The apparatus of U.S. foreign policy making and implementation that you have inherited is in a state of serious disrepair. The Department of State suffers from long-term mismanagement, antiquated equipment, and dilapidated and insecure facilities." The memorandum noted:

Dysfunctional human resource policies resulting in workforce shortfalls, including a deficit of nearly 15 percent of Foreign Service officers.

Outdated communications and information management infrastructure, including obsolete classified networks in 92 percent of overseas posts.

Shabby and insecure facilities all over the world that frequently do not meet Occupational Safety and Health Administration (OSHA) standards. Serious overcrowding in nearly 25 percent of all posts, and substandard security in 88 percent of all embassies.

Inadequate authority for ambassadors to coordinate and oversee the other agencies and departments.

Bifurcated policymaking and budget management.

A professional culture predisposed against public outreach and engagement, undermining its public diplomacy effectiveness and its coordination with Congress and other agencies.[2]

Secretary of State Colin Powell vowed to do something about this. The Diplomatic Readiness program he proposed included a massive overseas construction program and a welcome purge of antiquated computers. Powell also made leadership training mandatory for all midlevel and newly promoted senior executives in the Foreign Service and Civil Service.

"My boss should take this course." That was a comment I heard at every grade level, mid to senior. Other favorites: "They won't let us." "We can't do that." "No one understands us." "Congress likes the military better than us." "We have no constituents." And worst of all, "You can't measure diplomacy, so why set goals?" Creating positive change through teams focused on shared goals might work in the field, but in the policy establishment of Washington, the practice of leadership was anathema, no matter how eloquently the secretary waxed. It was not that anyone was against it; it was just not done. And while Secretary Powell urged people not to "be afraid to be the skunk at the picnic," the message had little reinforcement. The Washington policy group planning to invade Iraq was small, secretive, and intolerant of any discussion about the merits of their proposed policies. "Do what you are told" was the order of the day, and everyone was getting in line. At the leadership seminars, speaker after senior career speaker also reminded people that Washington makes policy while the field just implements it, so do what you are told.

On the day that the United States invaded Iraq, I was taken aback to find Secretary Powell's chief of staff, Lawrence Wilkerson, coming to the session of a capstone seminar that dealt with policy dissent. "What are you doing here?" I asked with a smile. "Spying," he cheerfully announced. I led the discussion of the range of options available for respectful dissent—from doing nothing to resigning—using Rwanda as the case study. Wilkerson gave me a passing grade, but I found the episode chilling.

I was just as frustrated by the disinterest in security issues among career colleagues just as our political leaders were declaring a global war on terrorism. At the Leadership and Management School, we conducted the first-ever statistically valid survey of crises confronting overseas employees. It proved the Foreign Service was a dangerous lifestyle. When I briefed the results at senior staff meetings around the department, they would wish me "good luck on your project" as if the dangers overseas had nothing to do with them. Like discussions of leadership, they enjoyed the topic well enough, but they were making policy. Their imperative was to get invited to the high-level meetings on their issues of choice. So good luck on *your* project.

As to the global war on terrorism, I was horrified. My government had chosen to ignore the al-Qaeda attacks in 1998 as too insignificant to review or change much of anything, and now, having failed to protect the homeland, it was going to war with Iraq and Afghanistan. My fellow American citizens and I were to go shopping as fearful, nonparticipant onlookers. Strategically, I saw the advantages of the war metaphor—it simplified our approach; it was politically and emotionally expedient; it permitted emergency measures; and it centralized command and control in the hands of a few. From my experience, it was also going to make the problem worse. The more people we killed in other countries, the more people in other countries would mistrust us, even hate us. To make war against what was a centuries' old political tactic was downright kooky. What does success look like? No one asked me for my opinion, and I kept my mouth shut.

Instead I talked about leadership at every opportunity. I started telling and retelling the story of Nairobi complete with lessons learned. I redesigned the two-week mandatory seminar for ambassadors before they departed for their posts and inserted those lessons. I joined a leadership roundtable of midlevel colleagues brainstorming ways to bring leadership into the Foreign Service culture. I did this for three years.

In 2004 Secretary Condoleezza Rice replaced Colin Powell. Leadership was out; "transformational diplomacy" was in. Another team, another policy priority. We invited one of her inner circle to speak with senior staff at the Foreign Service Institute to define the term, and he responded, "I cannot tell you what transformational diplomacy is, but I can tell you that the Foreign Service can't do it." Oh, great, I thought. It was going to be *that* kind of political appointee crowd.

Time to go, I decided. The fit with the State Department and the Foreign Service was no longer a good one. With immense pride and no tears, I accepted the American flag handed to me at my retirement ceremony, the survivor flag from my office in Nairobi. I gave it to Richard. He beamed.

U.S. government foreign policies had mapped my life for forty years as a child, an adolescent, and later as a Foreign Service officer. From now on, Richard and I alone would determine where we lived, how long we stayed, with whom we would be friends, what we would say, and what we would do with our lives. U.S. foreign policies would no longer dominate—or so I thought. On my last day as a government employee, I found myself clutching tightly to my State Department identity badge before I handed it over to the human resources person. My final act was to ask a security guard to let me out of the building.

2

HOW DID IT HAPPEN?

7

THE PROXY WAR

Now what? What does "retirement" mean to an overachieving woman of a certain age? Where are the role models? I did nothing for three months and almost went crazy. Then I opened a one-woman shop and began giving talks about leadership, crisis management, the Rwanda genocide, the Kenya bombing, and strategies women can apply to be heard in patriarchal environments. I briefly tried consulting with senior executives at other federal agencies and found them uninterested in practicing leadership. It is so much more fun to make policy as individual contributors. A group of political appointees and career executives in one case agreed with my findings that they were terrific individual achievers and lousy team players. I invited a discussion of next steps, and they hosted a farewell lunch for me.

By word of mouth, my speaking and training gigs increased in enough numbers to fund garden projects, home improvements, and eventually overseas trips. Gerry, my father, died at ninety, and Dufie decided she did not want to live without him, leaving us a year later. Richard and I settled into an inner Northern Virginia suburb with an alphabet soup of ethnicities and matching restaurants. Our two Kenyan cats adjusted, and I found life as an American woman, Ambassador (Ret.), to be okay.

I had to deal with the symptoms of post-traumatic stress disorder before life became better than okay. I had learned to stuff it all into a drawer that stayed shut—unless it popped open. When it did, I found emotional rubble still fresh from the bombing.

Anger was paramount, revived when I learned I was barred from consideration for a job in the State Department during Secretary Hillary Clinton's tenure because "Pru had health issues." Now that was closure. I was "obsessed" before the bombing when I would not stop sounding out about vulnerabilities of our chancery; I was "headed over the edge" when I demanded attention after al-Qaeda blew up our work community and thousands of Kenyan neighbors; and now, years later, I had "health issues."

Another bomb survivor had recommended EMDR—eye movement desensitization and reprocessing—which uses rhythmic eye movements or applied sensations to dampen the power of emotionally charged memories of past traumatic events. Who knows how it works, but it did for me. Not perfectly, but I was looking for relief, not perfection. I took up knitting and earned praise for being "prolific and persevering." Years later, I am still pursuing "talented" and "creative." Eventually I decided to research and write about the August 7 bombing.

Countless authors had penned material about September 11, 2001, with reports, books, articles, self-congratulating memoirs, and the 9/11 Commission Report. I wanted to understand the people, the decisions, and the policies related to August 7, 1998. What had prevented the United States from protecting vulnerable diplomatic facilities in East Africa from a terrorist group hiding out in Afghanistan?

When Osama bin Laden attacked us, he was stateless and significantly short of resources. The Saudi government had revoked his citizenship and frozen his assets two years earlier, and the government of Sudan, which had hosted him for years, had asked him to leave in 1996. Bin Laden went to Afghanistan to live under the protection of the Taliban-Islamist warriors trained in Pakistan, who now controlled several regions with ruthless repression and misogyny. He was under the surveillance of the CIA, the FBI, the NSA, and the National Security Council. How did he manage to blow up two American embassies in distant countries given that level of scrutiny? What had kept the U.S. government from listening to the security concerns of its ambassador in Kenya?

It was fascinating and unpleasant to spend a series of winters sequestered with the faces of scowling jihadists and smug American political figures staring at me from book jackets. I knitted copiously, and I wrote copiously. Who needs another book about al-Qaeda? Who wants to hear about betrayal or read about policies gone awry? And why in the world did I want to spend time in the museum of past hurts? Richard said I needed to write the story, and family and friends agreed. I persevered with my knitting, and I persevered with the writing, meanwhile producing lots of sweaters and promoting leadership among federal executives.

Eventually, like my sweater projects, the story of the August 7 bombing in Nairobi came together. Ironically, it begins the same year I decided to join the Foreign Service.

1979: Washington DC

The fall of the shah of Iran was a strategic surprise. President Jimmy Carter had been in office two years when our ally was chased from his country in a revolution that replaced him with a radical theocracy. The event inspired attention throughout the Muslim world and astonishment in Washington DC. It was not supposed to happen. The shah was our guy, and the militant Ayatollah Khomeini was barely known to us. Under the ayatollah's watch, sixty-six U.S. government representatives were taken hostage at our embassy in Tehran by Shia Muslim students. A few weeks later, fifty American representatives in our embassy in Islamabad, Pakistan, were almost burned to death in an assault carried out by Sunni Islamists. These things were not supposed to happen, either. At year's end, the Soviet Union invaded Afghanistan. This is where the story of August 7, 1998, begins.

Once upon a time we thought the shah of Iran would never fall. We nurtured policies to support him because he was vital to our Middle East interests—oil, Israel, and the Communist threat—and we had no Plan B should something happen. We had initiated a coup d'état in 1953 to put the shah at the head of a geostrategically important government and then spent decades providing billions of dollars of economic and military assistance in return for platforms for the CIA to keep tabs on Russia, for cheap oil, and for a moderate stance toward Israel. The deal worked for years. The shah implemented draconian policies to force a secular culture on a conservative Shia Muslim community, invested in guns not butter, enabled government corruption, and kept everyone under control with a violent and ruthless intelligence service. As we spied on the USSR, we played deaf, dumb, and blind to realities in Iran.

I knew at the tender age of eighteen that the shah was feared and despised. In Iran's countryside it was equally clear that people did not embrace the westernized dress and customs of elites in Tehran. I felt a tension in this Muslim country I had not found in Pakistan, and I was hardly an embassy political reporting officer. The tensions mounted over the years, but Washington policy makers would hear or see none of it. The willful ignorance of facts that belie policy—a tendency of administrations across party lines—would contribute to our fate years later.

After a particularly bloody protest on "Black Friday" in 1979, when the shah's forces gunned down hundreds of demonstrators, the U.S. embassy issued a public statement: "The monarchy is a deeply important institution in Iran, and the Shah is, in our view, the individual most suited to lead the Iranian people to a more democratic system."[1] Meanwhile, the Washington intelligence community was concluding in its National Intelligence Estimate, "Iran after the Shah," that "the government of Iran has the ability to use as much force as it needs to control violence, and the chances that the recently widespread urban violence will grow out of control is [sic] relatively small."[2]

Not everyone at the embassy agreed with that conclusion. Ann Swift, chief of the political section, had this to say:

> The people who had been stationed at the embassy through the earlier period thought things were getting better. To somebody like me coming in August, this was the craziest, most lawless situation I'd ever been in. There were mounting demonstrations against the embassy. I mean, you had demonstrations all the time, huge demonstrations. This place was crazy and extremely, extremely dangerous. And for the older officers to minimize what was going on was insane and that's what they were doing. And they were doing it on orders from Washington.

I was told I was stupid, I knew nothing of what I was talking about, I knew nothing about Iran. I had no experience in Iran and shut up small child, and forget it. I still get angry. This was two weeks before we were taken.[3]

Ann Swift spent 444 days in captivity.

When the Khomeini government refused to release the majority of the Americans taken hostage by student demonstrators, Washington policy makers were outraged and powerless. Rescue efforts failed, and President Carter lost his bid for a second term as president.

Like U.S. presidents before and since, Carter came into office with a domestic agenda—innovative approaches to health care, urban problems, welfare, and energy dependence. In foreign affairs he was fighting a cold war, and he selected a cold warrior, Zbigniew Brzezinski, as his national security advisor. Carter claimed that only an outsider could fix Washington, and he had four short years to make good on his promises.

He tackled his agendas at breakneck speed. The administration created the Department of Energy and the Department of Education, established a national energy policy, took measures to improve the environment, and began the process responsible for deregulating the airline, trucking, rail, communications, and finance industries. In foreign affairs Carter and Brzezinski introduced human rights into policy considerations, negotiated the Camp David Accords between Israel and Egypt, returned the Panama Canal to Panama, and initiated another round of Strategic Arms Limitation Talks (SALT II) with the Soviets.

Then came the fall of the shah and the new Islamic Republic of Iran. That was not the only theocracy to emerge in 1979. In Sudan the military president invited an Islamist scholar, Hassan al-Turabi, to help his government create a pure Islamic state. In Pakistan Gen. Muhammad Zia-ul-Haq, having hanged his civilian predecessor, announced that he would bring a "genuine Islamic order" to his country. As a group of radical Muslim zealots attacked the U.S. embassy in Islamabad, he waited five hours to make good on his international obligation to safeguard foreign diplomats. By the time his security forces arrived, two people lay dead from the initial assault and others suffered injuries and trauma. That night President Carter publicly thanked Zia for saving Americans. Little over a month later, the U.S. government embarked on a strategic partnership with Pakistan.

On Christmas Eve 1979, the Russians invaded Pakistan's neighbor, Afghanistan, to prop up their allies in the Communist government against persistent insurgents. When Brzezinski learned about it, he had what he called "an excellent idea."[4] Step up covert assistance to Afghan rebels, the warlords who were rebranding themselves mujahedin, or "holy warriors," to fight the infidel Russians. Use Zia's intelligence service, ISI, to disseminate U.S. assistance and give Pakistan permission to develop nuclear capability. "[We] must both reassure Pakistan and encourage it to help the rebels. This will require a review of our policy toward Pakistan, more guarantees to it, more arms aid, and alas, a decision that our security problem toward Pakistan cannot be dictated by our nonproliferation policy."[5] It did not matter that the professionals in the field left to fry in a burning embassy considered Zia untrustworthy. Washington and Brzezinski knew better.

Years later Brzezinski was still congratulating himself: "That secret operation was an excellent idea. It had the effect of drawing the Russians into the Afghan trap, and you want me to regret it? The day that the Soviets officially crossed the border, I wrote to President Carter. We now have the opportunity of giving to the USSR its Vietnam War. Indeed, for almost ten years, Moscow had to carry on a war unsupportable by the government, a conflict that brought about the demoralization and finally the breakup of the Soviet empire."[6] Over the next decade, billions of American dollars went to the Pakistani ISI, matched dollar for dollar by Saudi Arabia. The Pakistani intelligence service members, in turn, funneled the funds to militias of choice that practiced a radical brand of fundamentalist Islam.

The call for "jihad," a holy struggle against the Soviets, echoed throughout the Muslim world. Firebrands like world-renowned Abdullah Azzam and other scholars inspired thousands of men to heed the call. They poured into the border town of Peshawar,

Pakistan, to sign up. Among them was a wealthy Saudi construction engineer by the name of Osama bin Laden, an Egyptian physician, Dr. Ayman al-Zawahiri, and an Egyptian cleric, Sheikh Omar Abdel-Rahman. Their recruits would blow up the U.S. embassies in Kenya and Tanzania.

I began the process to join the Foreign Service in 1979 with no inkling of the path that was unfolding. It never occurred to me that I might face the violence of a genocide or a terrorist attack any more than it occurred to me to aim for the rank of ambassador. I had known the culture and the pecking order of the department from childhood. Management people maintained the platform, services, and cocoon within which U.S. government agencies operated. Consular people adjudicated visas and provided services to Americans. Political and economic policy people ran the place. I was going into management.

1989: Washington DC

Ronald Reagan won the U.S. presidency on a campaign of "Morning in America." Iran released the hostages after Jimmy Carter left office. Reagan announced that America's biggest problem was its huge government. He deregulated industries, closed out social programs, and ran up the national debt. He did not change course in international affairs, however. The Cold War against the Soviet Union, aka "Evil Empire," continued. The Reagan administration adopted the policy of its predecessor to support Afghan warlords and the mujahedin they led. Pakistan's ISI continued to serve as the funnel for money and weapons; the CIA continued to serve as the lead agency.

The Central Intelligence Agency had been around since the end of World War II, born of the same legislation as the National Security Council. Harry Truman had negotiated the act to bring together the three branches of the military, now under civilian leadership, with the State Department in order to defeat the worldwide threat of communism. Each of the military services came to the table with its own intelligence units. State had but a small, respected division of analysts; it was at a disadvantage from the first. The CIA was created to coordinate intelligence from outside U.S. borders, while the FBI clung jealously to its jurisdiction within the borders. It did not take long for presidents and their national security advisors to recognize and use CIA's operational capabilities. Unlike other departments accountable to Congress and the American people as well as to the president, the CIA and the NSC had only the president as a client. NSC members needed no Senate confirmation, remained unimpeded by regulation, and, thanks to the CIA, had the means to conduct secret operations anywhere outside of U.S. borders. Its senior advisors could serve as policy counselors, coordinators, micromanagers, or operators. Reagan ran through six national security advisors in eight years and ended up confronting the scandal called Iran-Contra. He did not, however, change his CIA director. William Casey spent six activist years in office and embraced the concept of bringing down the Russians through a proxy war.

According to Coll, "At the CIA station in Islamabad, the new era arrived in the form of visiting delegations from Washington: Pentagon officials carrying satellite maps; special forces commandos offering a course in advanced explosives; and suitcase-carrying congressional visitors who wanted Disney-quality tours of mujahedin camps and plenty of time to buy hand-woven carpets."[7] The men receiving this military largesse adhered to a fundamentalist strain of Islam, to which Washington policy makers showed ignorance and indifference. They did not appear to understand Islam as a religion, either. As a religious historian explained,

> In Islam, Muslims have looked for God in history. Their sacred scripture, the Quran, gave them a historical mission. Their chief duty was to create a just community in which all members, even the most weak and vulnerable, were treated with absolute respect. . . . The political well-being of the Muslim community was a matter of supreme importance. Like any religious ideal, it was almost impossibly difficult to implement in the flawed and tragic conditions of history, but after each failure Muslims had to get up and begin again.[8]

Islam integrated religion into the community's daily life, and like all religions, it bred moderates and extremists. The latter rallied around fundamentalist political thinking that produced Wahhabism in Saudi Arabia, the Muslim Brotherhood in Egypt, and the Ayatollah Khomeini in Iran. Their interpretation of the Koran was severe. Their resentment of western ways of thinking and governing dated back to the Crusaders. It was fueled by modern history: political borders redrawn at the whim of colonial powers at the end of World War I; the recognition of the state of Israel in 1948 and humiliating losses of wars and territory to Israel during the 1960s; and westernized social norms. Ignoring their worldview, the United States used these groups during the Cold War as foils against nationalist leaders like President Gamal Abdel Nasser of Egypt and Prime Minister Mohammad Mosaddegh of Iran when they defied American interests.[9] Now Director Casey and his case officers were pushing billions of dollars in kind and in weapons to them through ISI. They brought rabid Islamists to the United States to recruit holy warriors, and they even obtained a legal exemption from reporting on officers, agents, or assets involved in drug smuggling.[10]

Like most Americans, I was oblivious to our proxy war activities. In the "administrative cone," as my career track was called, I ran my operations in Dakar and Bombay largely detached from the policy issues that my "substantive" colleagues enjoyed. While the people in political and economic "cones" held most of the top jobs, they had little experience or interest in management. "Training is for dogs," growled a political officer to me when I returned to Washington as director of the Executive Development Division of the Foreign Service Institute, the department's "schoolhouse." Training political and economic reporting officers in management "can't be done," said some of my colleagues, never mind that Congress has mandated that it would be done. Most of them never had to manage until they reached senior positions, and then they delegated. For purely pragmatic reasons we changed the focus to leadership, and I started looking at my work world through a new prism.

We interviewed respected senior career colleagues as we designed the seminar. While they told us that teamwork was important, what we actually saw senior people do was negotiate

with other Washington peers about decisions, policy pronounce-
ments, and legislative coups in dawn-through-dusk meetings
together. That, in turn, generated more meetings and lots of paperwork for their staffs. Ironically, the department's influence within
the Washington national security community had already diminished, along with its resources.[11] The cost of getting one's boss
into the right meeting with the right talking points did not yield
the benefits of long-term funding or respect from the interagency.

I was taken aback by the disdain for strategic thinking, long-
term goals, and short-term measurements. Diplomacy cannot be
measured, officials would sniff; it is too dependent on external fac-
tors. As to resources, that was the job of the budget people, just
like taking care of people was an administrative task.

I had a mandate to confront that attitude, great bosses who
gave us resources and attention, and an innovative team. Together
we created and delivered state-of-the-art leadership training. It
was a tremendous success. "I can't believe you are an admin officer," said an economic colleague who was complimenting me on
the outcome. "I'd hire you any day!" By the time I had helped
to deliver almost a dozen offerings of the Foreign Affairs Leadership Seminar, I had concluded that State was a second-rate
organization filled with first-rate people, and I wrote about it in
an article I entitled "Leadership at State: The Neglected Dimension." Richard and I returned to Senegal five years after we had
left. This time I was deputy chief of mission for Ambassador
George Moose. I would have the chance to practice what we had
been preaching and see if it worked in reality.

1989: Afghanistan

Osama bin Laden trained, recruited, and waged war with radical
Egyptian friends like Dr. Ayman al-Zawahiri and the blind scholar,
Omar Abdel-Rahman. The three shared a vision of a pure Islamic
state, starting with a victorious holy war in Afghanistan. Their
policy was to kill Russian infidels, and their leadership expertise
in business, recruitment, training, and battle plans would make
it happen. From a wealthy construction family with close ties to
the Saudi royal entourage, bin Laden built roads, set up training

camps, and even experienced a battle. Tall, quiet-spoken, and polite, he was popular for living a humble life and giving away a lot of money. Al-Zawahiri, a bespectacled man of ordinary features who cultivated a mark in the middle of his forehead to show how fervently he prayed, was a surgeon from an Egyptian family of doctors and scholars. An active member in the Muslim Brotherhood opposition movement, al-Zawahiri was imprisoned and tortured by the Egyptian government after President Anwar Sadat was assassinated. After his release, he headed the militant Islamic Jihad Movement. Abdel-Rahman was a renowned cleric who ran his own radical group opposed to Egypt's secular government, al-Gama'a al-Islamiyya.

Each of the three men brought singular contributions to their effort to kill infidels. Bin Laden had business skills and a significant bank account. He created a worldwide infrastructure and financed recruiting centers that Abdel-Rahman and al-Zawahiri used as cells and bully pulpits to organize radical Muslim men who also wanted jihad. Washington policy enthusiasts likened them to the international brigade of volunteers who flocked to Spain to fight Franco in the 1930s. The CIA chief then in Islamabad commented that Osama bin Laden "actually did a few good things. He put a lot of money in a lot of right places in Afghanistan."[12] Abdel-Rahman contributed a huge following and preaching skills—he was sent to Brooklyn, New York, where he became known as the Blind Sheikh at the al-Farooq Mosque. Al-Zawahiri brought the experience of militant activities, torture in Egyptian prisons, and enthusiasm for violent action. By the time the Soviets departed Afghanistan in 1989, bin Laden and his associates had established recruiting offices in thirty cities in the United States and more around the world, trained thousands of fervent radicals, and defeated a superpower.

Bin Laden proudly boasted: "The Soviet Union entered Afghanistan in the last week of 1979 and, with Allah's help, their flag was folded a few years later and thrown on the rubbish heap, and there was nothing left to call the Soviet Union. That victory cleared from Muslim minds the myth of the superpowers."[13] He was now ready to form a base for more holy war.

The purpose of al-Qaeda was "to establish the truth, get rid of evil, and establish an Islamic nation." Recruits were required to have references, good manners, and a willingness to obey instructions. In return for a loyalty pledge to bin Laden, they would receive a salary commensurate with polygamous family needs, health benefits, yearly vacations, and an annual round-trip ticket home, as well as a buy-out option.[14] Bin Laden put himself at the top of the organization, established a clear chain of command heavily influenced by Egyptians, and looked for another jihad. Ayman al-Zawahiri and Sheikh Abdel-Rahman became affiliates, sharing al-Qaeda's mission and passion for jihad while remaining heads of their own groups. The three represented the policy makers. To make war, they needed implementers. Al-Zawahiri provided the one who played a prominent role in blowing us up in 1998. His name was Ali Mohamed.

Mohamed was mustered out as a major from the Egyptian army after members of his unit assassinated Anwar Sadat. In 1985 in Hamburg, Germany, the CIA hired him as an informant and then fired him for disclosing his role to one of his targets. Nonetheless, he received a "special" visa to the United States, and on his flight to California, he sat next to an American woman whom he married a few weeks later. He was buff, well-educated, and multilingual. The couple settled in Santa Clara, California, where Mohamed promptly established a clandestine cell for al-Zawahiri that would serve as a regional communications hub for al-Qaeda. Ali Mohamed also became a U.S. citizen.

He enlisted in the U.S. Army as a private in 1986, and the army assigned him to a two-year stint at the JFK Special Warfare Center in Fort Bragg, North Carolina. He was promoted to supply sergeant, but he was not just any supply sergeant. He lectured about Islam to Special Forces audiences headed for the Middle East, with little effort to hide his fundamentalist Islamist views.[15]

On weekends Ali Mohamed left base to train al-Qaeda recruits headed for Afghanistan (even after the war had ended) as they came through one of the branch offices funded by bin Laden, the al-Kifah Refugee Center in Brooklyn. In 1988 Mohamed told his military superiors of his plans to take annual leave to kill some

Russians in Afghanistan. Yes, Mohamed told his ranking officer, he knew it was against regulations, but he was going anyway. He met up with al-Zawahiri and bin Laden, trained new jihadists calling themselves "Arab-Afghans," and may even have enjoyed a battle. He returned to the U.S. Army with ne'er a negative consequence and got an honorable discharge in 1989. That was the year that his mentor, al-Zawahiri, traveled to the United States on a stolen passport raising money for more holy wars. Abdel-Rahman would come a year later to settle into the al-Kifah Refugee Center in Brooklyn, never mind that he was on a "terrorist watch list."[16] In 1989 bin Laden created al-Qaeda, and the last of the Soviet troops departed Afghanistan, a country still at war with itself. It was the year the Berlin Wall crumbled, and it was the year the Cold War ended. It was the year in which a new war machine started.

1. Near the rear wall of the U.S. embassy. Nairobi citizens rush to the rubble of the Ufundi House office building to search for survivors on August 7, 1998. AUTHOR'S COLLECTION.

2. Colleague Riz Khaliq and I pass a marine guard in front of the U.S. embassy after escaping the Cooperative Bank Building together on August 7, 1998. AUTHOR'S COLLECTION.

3. The author's parents, Dufie and Gerry Bushnell, enjoy Nice, France, in 1950. AUTHOR'S COLLECTION.

4. (*opposite top*) Susan and Prudence on ship to Germany, 1950. AUTHOR'S COLLECTION.

5. (*opposite bottom*) Susan and Prudence dressed for a day in school in Vaucresson, France, 1956. AUTHOR'S COLLECTION.

6. (*opposite top*) Susan and Prudence on
Easter Sunday in Vaucresson, 1960.
AUTHOR'S COLLECTION.

7. (*opposite bottom*) Family photo on Christmas
Day in Karachi, Pakistan, 1960.
Clockwise: Gerry, Susan, Prudence, Peter, and
Jonathan Bushnell. AUTHOR'S COLLECTION.

8. (*above*) Chargé d'affaires in Dakar, Senegal,
cutting the cake at the Marine Corps Ball in
November 1990. AUTHOR'S COLLECTION.

9. Duncan Musyoko, ambassador's driver, and the burgundy Cadillac, 1997.
AUTHOR'S COLLECTION.

10. Farewell to Americans killed in the bombing. Standing next to Foreign Minister Boyana Godana, August 10, 1998. AUTHOR'S COLLECTION.

11. Walking away after laying a wreath at the bomb site after the Israeli Defense Forces completed their search and rescue mission, August 15, 1998. This photograph won the 1999 Pulitzer Prize for Photojournalism.

PERMISSION GRANTED BY PHOTOGRAPHER JOHN MCCONNICO.

12. Secretary Albright's visit to downtown Nairobi, August 18, 1998.
AUTHOR'S COLLECTION.

13. Holding the inscribed Ka-Bar knife presented by a gunnery sergeant at the Marine Corps Ball, November 1998. AUTHOR'S COLLECTION.

14. Greeting U.S. Secretary of Commerce William Daley with Kenyan Minister of Commerce Joseph Kamotho in December 1998.
AUTHOR'S COLLECTION.

15. Ambassador Extraordinary and Plenipotentiary in her garden, August 1997. AUTHOR'S COLLECTION.

16. Memorial park. The names of those who died in the Nairobi bombing on August 7, 1998, are inscribed on the wall surrounded by bricks.

17. Colleagues and families of those who died on August 7, 1998, line up to view memorial fountain at Remembrance and Recognition Ceremony, January 1999.

18. With Assistant Secretary for African Affairs Susan Rice and George Mimba, president of the Foreign Service Nationals Association, at Remembrance and Recognition Ceremony, January 1999.
AUTHOR'S COLLECTION.

19. Farewell gift of a wooden giraffe presented at the Nairobi embassy surprise farewell party, May 1999.
AUTHOR'S COLLECTION.

20. Women's Community Banking Group in Tecpan, Guatemala, spring 2000.

21. Richard Buckley, aka Don Ricardo, with women's group in Guatemala, spring 2000.

22. Reverend Jesse Jackson's visit to the Rift valley to call for peace, January 1998. AUTHOR'S COLLECTION.

23. Dressed up by the women of Lamu, Kenya, in June 1998. AUTHOR'S COLLECTION.

24. (*opposite top*) Dressed up by women of eastern
Kenya in June 1998. AUTHOR'S COLLECTION.

25. (*opposite bottom*) Dressed up by Masai women in
May 1998. AUTHOR'S COLLECTION.

26. (*above*) On a field trip with U.S. and Kenyan
militaries, 1998. Fatigues and boots courtesy of a
Marine Corps field general. AUTHOR'S COLLECTION.

27. Dressed for the Marine Corps Ball
with Top Spouse, Richard Buckley,
November 1997. AUTHOR'S COLLECTION.

28. President Daniel arap Moi attends
the July 4, 1998, celebration.

29. Arlington Cemetery marker dedicated to the
memory of those who died on August 7, 1998.

8

THE BLOWBACK

1990: Washington DC, New York City

The United States was at peace with the Soviet Union for the first time in fifty years, and Ronald Reagan's vice president had been elected president. George H. W. Bush inherited a world in transition. Domestically he struggled with an economic recession, increased unemployment, and a significant budget deficit. Internationally he faced the breakup of the Soviet Union and the emergence of what he called "a new world order." When Iraq invaded Kuwait in the summer, Bush faced a new world order crisis and called up the troops for Operation Desert Storm. Unlike many of his predecessors, Bush had both foreign policy experience and interest, having served as ambassador to China and director of the CIA. Although the Soviets were out of Afghanistan, the president continued to approve the policy to back our favored Pakistan-vetted local militias in what was now a civil war. The Soviets funded their favored militias as well. Each side hoped "his" guys would win. Meanwhile, wannabe jihadists kept coming into the area even though the infidels had left. A reporting officer in the U.S. embassy noticed. These were "well-financed Arab fanatics, extolling a virulent anti-American line, in contrast to the embassy perception of the groups that have been supported by the United States during the conflict with the Soviet Military forces."[1]

In the United States, some of these recruits had come to the attention of New York City's Joint Terrorism Task Force (JTTF). Made up of New York City police and members of the local FBI office, the JTTF learned that members of the al-Kifah Refugee Center and al-Farooq Mosque were negotiating for illegal arms. Someone later photographed men from al-Kifah receiving arms training at a shooting range near New York City. What were they training for? Was the Afghan war over or not? It was an open secret that the "refugee center" had links to the CIA, so the JTTF figured the CIA would know.[2] What was certain, for anyone who looked closely enough, was that al-Kifah was a busy place.

> One week on Atlantic Avenue, it might be a CIA-trained Afghan rebel travelling on a CIA-issued visa; the next, it might be a clean-cut Arabic-speaking Green Beret, who would lecture about the importance of being part of the mujahedin, or "warriors of God." The more popular lectures were held upstairs in the roomier Al-Farooq Mosque; such was the case in 1990 when Sheikh Abdel-Rahman, travelling on a CIA-supported visa, came to town. The blind Egyptian cleric, with his ferocious rhetoric and impassioned preaching, filled angry, discontented Arab immigrants with a fervor for jihad—holy war. This was exactly what the CIA wanted: to stir up support for the Muslim rebels and topple the Soviet-backed government in Afghanistan.[3]

In November 1990 the head of the Jewish Defense League, Rabbi Meir Kahane, was shot and killed after giving a speech in a New York City hotel. Police caught the gunman, an al-Kifah Center member, minutes later. In his apartment the JTTF found two associates, whom they took in for questioning, and dozens of boxes of materials: bomb-making manuals, maps of New York City landmarks, and top-secret training materials from the John F. Kennedy Special Warfare Center at Fort Bragg.

The police and the district attorney decided to make a "lone gunman" case.[4] Police were told to release all but the gunman. An officer later noted: "The fact is that in 1990, myself and my detectives, we had in our office in handcuffs the people who blew up the World Trade Center in '93. We were told to release them."[5] The FBI took the boxes they had found and left them in an office to collect dust for the next couple of years. The accused was tried and acquitted of all but lesser firearms offenses.

In Tucson, Arizona, another bin Laden recruit, Wadih el-Hage, also attracted attention in 1990 when he became a person of interest to law enforcement authorities. El-Hage was born a Christian in Lebanon and converted to Islam as a teen. He attended college in the United States, married an American woman, and became a citizen. El-Hage was associated with the Islamic Center of Tucson, al-Qaeda's first recruiting center in the United States. When the imam of a rival and progressive mosque was assassinated in 1990, leads brought police to el-Hage's door. He had hosted the primary murder suspect, who subsequently disappeared, and he also admitted he was glad the victim was killed. But there was no evidence to arrest him.[6] Wadih El-Hage would play a central role in the 1998 bombings.

With an honorable discharge in hand, Ali Mohamed, the jihadist trainer, applied for a translator's job in two FBI offices, and although neither hired him, the San Francisco office did take him on as an informant in a case involving local document forging. Mohamed did not include in his sales pitch the fact that he was escorting his boss, Ayman al-Zawahiri from the Egyptian Islamic Jihad (EIJ), on a fund-raising trip. Mohamed never had to take a polygraph test. "One of the most unbelievable aspects of the Ali Mohamed story," said an agent later, "is that the Bureau could be dealing with this guy and they didn't polygraph him. . . . The first thing you do with any kind of asset or informant is you polygraph him and if the relationship continues, you make him submit to continued polygraphs down the line."[7] FBI field offices served local priorities, not national ones, with archaic technology that made it difficult to communicate or share information.[8] Ali Mohamed operated below the radar for years.

I was in Senegal, a majority Muslim country practicing a moderate brand of Islam utterly different from the one for which Ali Mohamed planned killings. Like FBI field offices, U.S. embassies do their work independent of one another. Unlike the FBI, embassies focus on national issues to implement policies established by headquarters. In our case, Washington's policy toward sub-Saharan Africa could be summarized as "peace, prosperity, and democracy." Our job in Senegal was to successfully manage shared interests ranging from aviation safety to international peacekeeping. My job as deputy to Ambassador George Moose and later to Katherine Shirley was to manage the State Department component of the embassy and harmonize the agendas of other government agencies represented on the country team.

Chiefs of mission are responsible for the safety and overall performance of all government employees except those under a military command. But, I quickly learned, they have no control over the budgets, agendas, rewards, promotions, or assignments of anyone outside of the State Department. You either used the leadership necessary to bring people to the same policy page, or you ceded the power of the office. The mechanism I found to help my bosses exercise leadership was the mandatory "mission program planning" process. Boring and a waste of time for some, I found it key to finding common policy ground with other agencies. Smile on my face, magic marker in hand, flip chart by my side, I led sessions to translate Washington's myriad injunctions into tangible results through programs like economic and military assistance, through trade delegations and cultural exchanges, and through achievements in shared political objectives. I also learned how effective ambassadors influenced Washington. They exercised leadership.

1991: Washington DC, Khartoum, Dakar

In his mid-January State of the Union address, President George H. W. Bush proposed sending troops into Kuwait to force Iraqi president Saddam Hussein's invading military to leave. He also said he would reduce spending and taxes to fix the economy. His appointees across government went about diminishing missions, resources, and morale among public servants. Secretary of State James Baker offered to open new embassies in the former Soviet republics without asking for supplemental funds, and the Congress took him up on it; resources at the department would shrink by a third. Job vacancies created by a hiring freeze became positions to eliminate, while security regulations were waived to fit the budgets. The CIA was no better off. Its focus evaporated with the fall of the Soviet Union; leadership floundered as people left. A scandal erupted over the agency's relationship with BCCI, a bank accused of money laundering and other nefarious activities. Even defense spending plunged as the military repositioned itself for a new world. The Soviet threat was gone. No one cared about the civil war still churning in Afghanistan with the help of U.S., Saudi, Pakistani, and Russian support.

Osama bin Laden had left Afghanistan, returning to Saudi Arabia to stir up enthusiasm for a jihad in neighboring Yemen. When Iraq invaded Kuwait in the summer of 1990, he offered the Saudi royal family al-Qaeda's military talents for protection as defense against the Iraqis. Instead, the Saudis turned to the United States, offering to host our military bases as we pushed Iraqis back into their borders. Bin Laden and others were outraged that the keeper of the two holy mosques of Islam would permit armed infidels on its soil. He left the country in a snit, and with Ali Mohamed's help, he moved his wives, children, and operations first to Pakistan and then to Khartoum, Sudan. He was welcomed by President Omar al-Bashir, who had come to power in 1989 via military coup and who cultivated a vision of a pure Islamist society in Sudan. Under the influence of his powerful Islamist scholar-in-residence, Hassan al-Turabi, he saw his country at the center of ever-extending waves of holy war throughout the world. Together, al-Bashir and al-Turabi put up the welcome sign for jihadists of all stripes, bin Laden and al-Qaeda included.[9]

"Sudan in the early 1990s was an anything-goes cesspool of a place," wrote CIA contractor Billy Waugh, "free-for-all for terrorists and rogues from throughout the Middle East. I could go on a long run from my residence in the al-Riyadh section and run past the homes or support sites of bin Laden, Abu Nidal, various members of Hezbollah, the Egyptian Gama'at al Islamiyya, the Algerian Islamic Jihad, HAMAS, the Palestinian Islamic Jihad, and a bunch of badass Iranians loyal to the Ayatollah Khomeini's 'Death to America' craziness."[10]

Waugh was asked to watch bin Laden's activities and photograph him.

My first task was to find an observation post close enough to his residence to keep an eye on his movements. The CIA didn't know much about him, but it wanted me to be in a position to know more. They knew about the personal bank account, but they wanted to know more of his associations, his habits, and whether he was training some of these al-Qaeda folks to do harm to our interests. The chief of station gave me the authorization to spend whatever money necessary to establish an observation post that would enable me to watch and photograph UBL. It was clear this tall, languid man with the curious background was working his way onto our radar range.[11]

Bin Laden bought a house and a guesthouse; he farmed, bred thoroughbred horses, and started developing the country's crumbling infrastructure with his construction company. He also set up guerilla training camps, organized jihadist networks around the world, and ran an international finance system to help support them. He had gung-ho lieutenants like Ali Mohamed, and he was about to transfer Wadih el-Hage and his family from Arizona to Khartoum to serve as his personal secretary.

El-Hage was once again in hot water in the United States, this time in connection with the murder of the heretofore head of the al-Kifah Refugee Center in Brooklyn. The incumbent had argued over money with the Blind Sheikh and ended up shot, stabbed, and bludgeoned in his own home. It so happened that el-Hage knew the victim and arrived in New York on the day he was murdered. The FBI found out about el-Hage's connection to the murder of a liberal imam in Arizona and discovered that he had visited Rabbi Kahane's assailant in prison. Bad company, but insufficient evidence to charge el-Hage. He was free to leave the country, and he did.[12]

Ali Mohamed was racking up his own frequent flyer miles as he helped move bin Laden and his entourage of two thousand from Afghanistan to Sudan. Mohamed also set up three new al-Qaeda training camps so he could teach recruits to create cells, make bombs, wage urban warfare, and kidnap people.[13]

In Dakar, Senegal, we went on terrorism alert, along with every other embassy in the world, when U.S. troops hit the ground in Kuwait. A contingent of Senegalese troops joined the U.S.-led coalition that chased Saddam Hussein's troops out of Kuwait in three short months. The French-language equivalent of "chemical warhead," "rules of engagement," and sundry military armaments grew my vocabulary. Conversations with the government were broadening from agricultural reforms and economic structural adjustment to continuing ethnic tensions in Mauritania to the north, conflicts in Mali to the east, and increasing chaos from clashes in Liberia to the south. As we pressed the Senegalese to use their effective military for peacekeeping in Liberia, I grew more conversant in issues of refugees and conflict. I was gaining expertise in new world order.

1992: Washington DC, Mogadishu

Presidents George Bush and Boris Yeltsin formally declared an end to the Cold War. A vicious conflict began in the Balkans as former parts of Yugoslavia declared independence and turned on one another. In the newly independent, multiethnic republic of Bosnia and Herzegovina, Serbian citizens marshaled forces against their Bosnian Muslim and Catholic Croat compatriots. The new world order was not pretty.

In Sudan Osama bin Laden formally declared war against the United States through a religious ruling, *fatwa*, condemning us for choosing to keep our base in Saudi Arabia even after Iraqi troops no longer threatened Kuwait.[14] Ali Mohamed continued to serve as his go-to guy for various sorts of training, from countersurveillance to assassination. On one trip from Afghanistan, Italian airport authorities asked him about the false compartments in his luggage, but he convinced them he was fighting terrorists, and they let him go.[15] Many of Ali Mohamed's trainees were headed for Bosnia to fight alongside Muslim citizens battling Serbs. A post-Afghanistan generation of mujahedin had a new jihad, fully funded by Saudi Arabia and once again assisted by the United States.[16]

President Bush could not keep his promise of no new taxes, and the American people voted him out of office in favor of a Washington outsider, Bill Clinton. In his last months in office, Bush committed U.S. troops to Somalia as a humanitarian gesture to help the United Nations peacekeepers distribute food amid a vicious inter-clan war. We had, after all, won a desert war in the Middle East and a cold war with the former Soviet Union. In neighboring Kenya, the U.S. ambassador did his job by warning Washington that "Somalis, as the Italians and the British learned to their discomfiture, are natural-born guerrillas. They will mine the roads. They will lay ambushes. They will launch hit-and-run attacks."[17] Washington did not listen.

On a dark December night, in the blaze of the media's bright lights, American military units splashed onto a beach outside of Mogadishu, the Somali capital. Days later, two hotels in Yemen that had served as barracks blew up. The soldiers had already left, but two tourists were killed. Osama bin Laden had just launched his first direct attack on the United States. What Americans considered humanitarian assistance, bin Laden and al-Qaeda saw as yet another power move and acted immediately. When the U.S. military relocated its barracks, bin Laden preened. As Michael Scheuer reported, "The United States wanted to set up a military base for U.S. soldiers in Yemen, so that it could send fresh troops to Somalia. The Arab mujahedin related to the Afghan jihad carried out two bomb explosions in Yemen to warn the United States, causing damage to some Americans staying in those hotels. The United States received our warning and gave up the idea of setting up its military bases in Yemen. This was the first al-Qaeda victory scored against the Crusaders."[18] Bin Laden was keeping score of victories in a war which the U.S. national security community was unaware existed.

In Senegal, Richard and I entered what would amount to our fifth year in Dakar. I was familiar and comfortable despite the difference of my skin color, religion, language, culture, and in many cases gender. Interactions with Senegalese were easy, especially with courtesies observed. Few talked about the fact that 750,000 people from the Senegambia area were kidnapped and shipped to the Americas for more than three centuries.[19] We laughed at the same kinds of jokes, and we found ourselves on the same side of the policy agendas. When our public diplomacy colleagues introduced the queen of Zydeco from Cajun country to a Senegalese public, we witnessed a love fest.

Senegal was the third majority-Muslim country I had lived in and by far the most open. Their interpretation prescribed no veils, no religious police, and no intolerance. Dakar moved to the rhythm of the Muslim lunar calendar with western and African style and sophistication. Beautiful men and women in French-cut suits and long, gorgeously embroidered *boubous* integrated us into conversations and celebrations of faith I had not encountered in Pakistan or Iran.

I was comfortable enough to ask questions about what it was like to live in a polygamous family. As a teen I was curious, and as a feminist I was repelled, but what did I actually know? African cultures, I learned, had practiced polygamy long before Islam. Subsistence agriculture needed many hands, and the vast, semi-arid landscape needed more people to cultivate it. Islam actually limited the number of wives to four, all to be treated equally. In contemporary, expensive Dakar, one or two wives were the norm. Senegal's secular laws entitled a woman to know her spouse's intentions before she legally married him. Senegalese professional women in our conversations generally opposed polygamy, but if pressured into a plural marriage, they advocated the status of second wife. First wives have to struggle as their husbands start careers, finish graduate school, find jobs, and build reputations, only to face the humiliation of learning in middle age that he has taken a second, usually younger wife. At that point in the conversation, we American women would be nodding in understanding. Yup, it happened in the United States, too, only serially. Far easier, our Senegalese female friends would continue, was to come second, seizing the advantage of a husband's absence for business trips or simply enjoy a few days of a life of one's own.

From the men I got different perspectives. Rural men lounging under neem trees said polygamy was the natural order of things, and the women liked it because they had someone to share the work. Said wives were usually toiling in the fields, baby strapped on back, while these conversations took place. Urban men gave more nuanced commentaries and less enthusiasm for the practice. Many talked about the pressure when they were children to successfully compete with multiple stepbrothers for their father's approval. Their mother's status often depended on their performance in school and in the paternal eye. While the extended family created an effective safety net for those who needed it, it was also a burden for employed family members who provided it. As to supporting more than one wife and family, that was both costly and stressful. Our conversations about religious differences came naturally and without tension. Cherishing the tenets of the holy Koran did not translate into intolerance. I was a smarter person by the time Richard and I left Senegal.

9

THE PLOTS

Bill Clinton was elected president on a platform of domestic reforms, budget reductions, and new policies regarding gay people in the military. Foreign affairs held little interest for him. Tony Lake, his national security advisor and a former Foreign Service officer, would take care of things. The federal budget cuts continued. It was "the economy, stupid," and Clinton vowed to improve it.

Soon after his inauguration, two terrorist attacks occurred on U.S. soil. The first took place only a few miles from the White House five days after Clinton took the oath of office. A lone gunman stood at the entrance of CIA headquarters and shot incoming employees. He killed two and wounded three more before making a getaway to Pakistan. A few weeks later, a truck bomb exploded in the underground parking lot of the North Tower of the World Trade Center in New York City. Six people died, and a thousand were injured. The mastermind, Ramzi Yousef, got away.

It took only a few days after the bombing for authorities to focus on the al-Kifah Refugee Center and its companion, al-Farooq Mosque. The FBI once again rounded up the men who had been taken into custody and released in the Rabbi Kahane murder case and dusted off the boxes from the assailant's apartment that had been stored in someone's office. In them they found classified Special Operations training manuals, secret documents, bomb-making instructions, and maps of New York City and landmarks, along with lots of documents written in Arabic and videotapes of Ali Mohamed's lectures on Islam.[1]

Abdel-Rahman, the Blind Sheikh, imam of the al-Farooq Mosque, was hauled into custody. He was already under suspicion after Egyptian authorities told the FBI that his gang, al-Gama'a al-Islamiyya, was behind the attack on western tourists in November 1992. The Egyptians also shared information on a plot to kill Egyptian president Hosni Mubarak during a planned visit to New York. The Mubarak trip was canceled. Then the FBI learned through its informant in the Blind Sheikh's entourage that Abdel-Rahman had plans to blow up the Lincoln and Holland Tunnels, the United Nations headquarters, and the New York FBI offices. In late June the FBI had enough evidence to arrest the Blind Sheikh and did so after a public standoff with his supporters. The conspiracy was like none they had seen. Never mind how hard conspiracies are to prove—this one was worth it. They called it the Landmarks case.

Bin Laden's name kept coming up. Over the summer, the CIA noted he was paying for members of the Blind Sheikh's al-Gama'a al-Islamiyya to train in Sudan, and the State Department reported other links between bin Laden and the Blind Sheikh. By summer's end, the United States had officially designated Sudan to be a "state sponsor of terrorism," subject to a variety of sanctions, and put bin Laden on its TIPOFF watch list to prevent him from entering the United States.[2]

By the fall, the New York office of the FBI wanted to speak with Ali Mohamed. He had already been stopped by Canadian authorities in June for helping a man with false passports into the country, but the FBI's San Francisco office had vouched for him. Now the New York office wanted to see him in connection with stolen documents from Ft. Bragg found in the apartment of the perpetrators of the World Trade Center bombing. Mohamed readily admitted his relationship to Osama bin Laden and al-Qaeda, which, he said, was interested in overthrowing the Saudi government. Yes, Mohamed informed them, he had provided military and intelligence training to them in Afghanistan and Sudan, but, no, he was not a criminal. The FBI let him go but began monitoring his phone calls.[3]

By now the White House wanted its own team to monitor terrorism-related events. In Washington, if an issue becomes really important, the White House steps in to "coordinate." The World Trade Center bombing was important. The NSC staff person assigned to deal with terrorist attacks was Richard Clarke, then head of International Programs, a portfolio vague enough to include almost anything. Clarke thrived in both Democratic and Republican administrations. He had a reputation for getting things done and did so with a strategic focus and an autocratic hand, as I learned getting to know him from my vantage as one of State's deputy assistant secretaries for African affairs.

"The notion that terrorism might occur in the United States was completely new to us then," Clarke recalled. He asked his contacts in the FBI and the CIA about al-Kifah and its followers. "The FBI and CIA should have been able to answer my question, 'Who are these guys?' But they still could not." As to any link to al-Qaeda, Clarke wrote: "Usama bin Laden had formed al-Qaeda three years earlier. Not only had no one in the CIA or FBI ever heard of it, apparently, they had never heard of bin Laden either. His name never came up in our meetings in 1993 as a suspect in the World Trade Center attack."[4] Instead, the FBI told the White House the bombing had been planned by one man, Ramzi Yousef.

On October 3, seven months after the World Trade Center bombing, eighteen American soldiers died in the battle of Mogadishu, the capital of Somalia. The intention to help food distribution had morphed into an effort to do away with warlord Farah Aideed, whose men were getting in the way. In the United States, people watched helplessly as television networks showed the body of an American soldier dragged through the streets of Mogadishu after a Black Hawk helicopter had been shot down. Dick Clarke wondered who was behind the shooting. "I repeatedly pressed CIA to track down rumors in the foreign press about terrorists who might have trained Aideed's militia. They discounted them."[5] In fact, the killers had been trained by Ali Mohamed, together with the al-Qaeda cohorts who participated in the battle.[6]

Osama bin Laden interpreted the U.S. reaction in Somalia as another victory and a sign of weakness. Quotes Michael Scheuer,

"The youth [al-Qaeda fighters in Somalia] were surprised at the low morale of the American soldiers and realized more than before that the American soldier was a paper tiger and [would] after a few blows run in defeat. And America forgot all the hoopla and media propaganda . . . about being the world leader and the leader of the New World Order, and after a few blows they forgot this title and left, dragging their corpses and their shameful defeat."[7]

Bin Laden then planned attacks against other U.S. targets. He tasked Ali Mohamed with setting up al-Qaeda fronts on the East African coast, including a fishing business, two charities, and a gemstone enterprise in Kenya. Then he gave Mohamed another assignment: "In late 1993, I was asked by bin Laden to conduct surveillance of American, British, French, and Israeli targets in Nairobi. Among the targets I did surveillance for was the American Embassy. . . . These targets were selected to retaliate against the United States for its involvement in Somalia. . . . I later went to Khartoum, where my surveillance files and photographs were reviewed by Osama bin Laden. . . . Bin Laden looked at the picture of the American Embassy and pointed to where a truck could go as a suicide bomber."[8]

The death of eighteen soldiers in Somalia gave bin Laden the confidence to start targeting Nairobi as a place to kill more Americans. In Washington the national security community was clueless. Dick Clarke noted that in 1993 the administration did not know that bin Laden or al-Qaeda existed.[9] CIA director George Tenet remembered differently. "As early as 1993, [the CIA] had declared bin Laden to be a significant financier backer of Islamic terrorist movements. We knew he was funding paramilitary training of Arab religious militants in such far-flung places as Bosnia, Egypt, Kashmir, Jordan, Tunisia, Algeria, and Yemen."[10] Billy Waugh, the CIA contractor in Khartoum, corroborated this: "In the early 1990s, though, it was impossible to read his intentions. He was an enemy, definitely, but he was not considered an imminent threat."[11] What was considered an imminent threat to the Clinton administration's domestic image that year was the Somalia debacle. The U.S. intervention had, in fact, ended the famine, but the White House saw it as one more budget-cutting reason to avoid peacekeeping operations in general and peacekeeping in Africa specifically.

The effects of that policy directed how I spent many a day for the next few years. Richard and I were back in Washington, and I was again working for George Moose, this time as one of three deputy assistant secretaries (DAS) and seven office directors, most of them former ambassadors, with forty-six sub-Saharan countries in our policy portfolio. Among top priorities were Somalia's humanitarian assistance; South Africa's transition to democracy; Angola and Burundi, both on the verge of major ethnic conflicts; peace efforts to stop Rwanda's war between Tutsis and Hutus; regional efforts to stop expanding chaos in Liberia; a civil war in Congo; terrorism from Sudan; and the rest of sub-Saharan Africa.

I was charged with "transnational issues," meaning everything that crossed borders, including women, democracy, HIV/AIDS, peacekeeping, conflict resolution, humanitarian assistance, refugees, and the bureau's management functions. When George Moose and my DAS colleagues divided other responsibilities, including the shared tasks of tending the bureaucratic machinery, I got oversight of Rwanda, Burundi, and Liberia.

Now that the Cold War was over, Americans wanted a peace dividend and a balanced budget, and the only way to make that happen was to shift the priorities. Africa was the loser. USAID began closing up shop all over the sub-Saharan continent to open new ones in the former Soviet republics. The CIA downsized in sub-Sahara as well. We were still promoting democracy, prosperity, and peace but with less money. When I was admonished by a very senior colleague that the Africa Bureau was not "forward-leaning" enough, I was astonished, in part because he could not define what that meant. I was in fact backward-leaning, clutching programs and peacekeeping operations to my bosom in countless interagency meetings focused on directing funds out of Africa. As our crises expanded and South Africa moved toward democratic elections, the bureau was thankfully left to fend for itself. We had a good boss, a decentralized decision-making structure, and experienced staff at many levels. Most important, AF had the reputation for taking care of its people. If Africa were at the bottom of the Clinton regional priority list, we would make the best of it.

As the United States divested from the sub-Sahara, al-Qaeda expanded there.

1994: Washington DC

President Clinton proposed health care reform and a negotiated nuclear weapons deal with the Russians. News of a longtime Soviet spy in the CIA rocked the national security world, while the attack on figure skater Nancy Kerrigan rocked the sports world. In November the Republicans rocked everyone's world by taking control of both the House and the Senate.

Dick Clarke was also busy. He organized a top-secret Counterterrorism Security Group (CSG) to bring military, diplomatic, intelligence, and law enforcement assets under his direction. He also wrote a presidential directive to "deter, defeat, and respond to" potential terrorist attacks. The counterterrorism portfolio traditionally belonged to the State Department, but that was easily fixed. "Early in Clinton's first term," a colleague observed, "Clarke, characteristically, threw a bureaucratic elbow at the State Department by announcing that he would not attend their meetings; from now on, they would be attending his."[12]

Only the most senior people in the Departments of Defense, State, and Justice—along with the CIA and the FBI—could attend the meetings, and they were not allowed to pass on information. Not that anyone but the CIA and FBI had a particular interest in counterterrorism. The Defense Department concerned itself with "preventive defense" now that the Cold War was over. The State Department had a sole counterterrorism coordinator with almost no resources or staff, and neither Secretaries Warren Christopher nor Madeleine Albright showed interest. Justice Department was equally unconcerned and under-resourced, so that left the FBI and the CIA to address the threats. They both had other distractions.

FBI director Louis Freeh complained in his memoir, "As director, I sometimes thought I was running a huge crisis-intervention unit, except that each new crisis seemed to add permanent responsibilities to the Bureau's purview without necessarily expanding the resources to take them."[13] The CIA was still suffering from a lack of mission, the legacy of the Iran-Contra scandal, a brain drain from rank-and-file departures, and the discovery of a Soviet mole, Aldrich Ames, uncovered by none other than the FBI. Neither CIA director James Woolsey nor Freeh had a relationship with President Clinton, and the turf issues between the agencies meant their relationship was none too cooperative, either.

The two organizations nurtured enmities going back to J. Edgar Hoover; they loved secrets, and they hated to share information. The CIA relied on "protection of sources and methods," and the FBI invoked "chain of evidence" and "grand jury secrecy." To force the FBI to share information with the White House, Clarke came armed with a permission slip signed by both National Security Advisor Tony Lake and Attorney General Janet Reno. "Usually, the FBI acted like Lake-Reno was a resort in Nevada," he later wrote.[14]

As the Counterterrorism Security Group suited up to confront Osama bin Laden, it was distracted by resource cuts and weakened by historic animosities, big egos, and turf battles. Osama bin Laden, meanwhile, thrived. As Peter Bergen remembered later, "During this time the youth from all Arabic countries began to come to Sudan—Libyans, Saudis, Emiratis. They gave [bin Laden] the title of 'Sheikh Osama.' Quickly he became very popular. They like him and they listen to him and especially [as] he has money. He can solve their problems."[15]

Abdel-Rahman was in an American jail, but his Egyptian confederate, Ayman al-Zawahiri, and the ever-helpful Ali Mohamed were on the move. They established a public relations office in London, expanded jihad training in Malaysia, and sent assets to Kenya. Al-Zawahiri connected with jihadists in Yemen and created an al-Qaeda base in the Balkans that included "humanitarian" organizations in Bosnia-Herzegovina and Kosovo to direct arms and money to Bosnian Muslims.

Bin Laden also expanded his base, sending Wadih el-Hage to Nairobi to direct the cell Ali Mohamed had set up and to oversee the fronts Mohamed and others had created. Bin Laden sent a veteran of Somalia, Mohammed Saddiq Odeh, to the Kenyan coast where he was assigned a fishing business to smuggle people, arms, forged documents, and fish. He married a local woman, settled in, and later helped make the bomb for the truck that blew us up.

Mohamed, meanwhile, continued to travel between his California home and Khartoum, sometimes for the meetings that the Government of Sudan hosted for international Islamist terrorist groups. During one of them, he introduced bin Laden to the head of Hezbollah, Iran's go-to terrorist organization. Mohamed later said: "I was aware of certain contacts between al Qaeda and al Jihad organization, on one side, and Iran and Hezbollah on the other side. I arranged security for a meeting in the Sudan between [Imad] Mugniyeh, Hezbollah's chief, and bin Laden. [Mugniyeh had masterminded the 1983 attack on the U.S. Marine Corps barracks in Beirut that killed 241 U.S. soldiers and led to the withdrawal of U.S. troops.] Hezbollah provided explosives training for al Qaeda." Mohamed also pointed out that the objective was to force western countries out of the Middle East using tactics like the Marine Corps barracks bombing.[16]

For a while it looked as though Ali Mohamed's days were numbered. The Landmarks trial—the conspiracy case against the Blind Sheikh and associates—included none other than Rabbi Kahane's assailant. Once considered a lone gunman, he was now a co-defendant. His lawyers argued that his activities at al-Kifah were part of a U.S.-sponsored covert operation to train and arm people for the Afghan war. The *Boston Herald* publicized an internal CIA report concluding that the agency was "partially culpable" for the 1993 World Trade Center bombing because it helped train and support some of the bombers.

> It was determined that a significant amount of blowback appeared to have occurred. A U.S. intelligence source claims the CIA gave at least $1 billion to forces in Afghanistan connected to Gulbuddin Hekmatyar. More than a half-dozen of the WTC bombers belonged to this faction, and some of the CIA money paid for their training. The source says, "By giving these people the funding that we did, a situation was created in which it could be safely argued that we bombed the World Trade Center." Those connected to the bombing who went to

Afghanistan include Sheikh Omar Abdul-Rahman, aka the Blind Sheikh, and others."[17]

At the trial, lawyers for the defense provided evidence of the documents Ali Mohamed stole from Ft. Bragg and the training he provided al-Kifah. The defense wanted to call Mohamed as a witness but could not locate him. The FBI could. They were monitoring his telephone and discovered Mohamed at Wadih el-Hage's house in Nairobi. They told him they wanted to talk. Mohamed later testified, "I flew back to the United States, spoke to the FBI, but didn't disclose everything that I knew." The FBI already knew that he worked for bin Laden and that bin Laden had been paying for the Blind Sheikh's living expenses.[18] They knew Mohamed often talked with Wadih el-Hage because they were tapping his phone in California and el-Hage's phone in Nairobi. They may have known a lot more, but they let him go nevertheless. Ali Mohamed was never called to testify by the federal prosecutor in the Landmarks trial, and the defense attorneys never found him. His name was on the list of unindicted co-conspirators, along with bin Laden's, but that was it.[19]

Luck initially held as well for bin Laden, still in Khartoum. Assassins had tried to kill him and his son in a shootout after morning prayers early in 1994 but were unsuccessful. Bin Laden sent for Ali Mohamed to train a new crew of bodyguards, all of them Egyptian. Then family problems began for bin Laden. He later recounted, "They sent me my mother, my uncle, and my brothers in almost nine visits to Khartoum asking me to stop and return to Arabia to apologize to [Saudi] King Fahd. . . . I refused to go back."[20] Saudi Arabia revoked his citizenship and froze his assets, and without his allowance, bin Laden began to lose money. One of his wives divorced him, taking three children with her. His work life may have been fine, but his personal life was not.

Islamist terrorist attacks around the world stepped up: Hezbollah blew up a Jewish cultural center in Buenos Aires; the Armed Islamic Group, an Algerian organization, hijacked an Air France jet; the Blind Sheikh's followers attacked tourists in Egypt a dozen times over the year; and suicide bombers opposed to the Arab-

Israeli peace process stepped up the scale and frequency of their attacks in Israel, the West Bank, and Gaza. By the end of 1994, the State Department had enough evidence to note in its annual report, *Patterns of Global Terrorism*, that "transnational terrorists with access to modern communications and substantial funding who had trained in militant camps in Afghanistan were now on the scene." The CIA also published a National Intelligence Estimate about extremists angry at the United States in possession of weapons, money, assorted benefactors, and international networks.[21] Nonetheless, Dick Clarke and the Counterterrorism Security Group at the NSC remained in the dark. Clarke wrote, "Although bin Laden's name surfaced with increasing frequency in raw intelligence in 1993 and 1994, CIA analyses continued to refer to him as a radicalized rich kid, who was playing at terrorism by sending checks to terrorist groups."[22]

While parts of the national security community were learning about Islamists, I was learning about the policy-making process of the national security community. It was rough, tough, and nasty. War metaphors peppered our vocabulary. We would "gird our loins" going into meetings and return either "winning the battle" or "ready to fight another day." "Allies" were fine; "collaborators" were unheard of. The "enemy" was often another agency, and "spies" were the people who attended meetings not to contribute but to report back to persons unknown. State Department people considered the CIA full of "cowboys," and we were "weenies" to them. The one thing that the civilian side could agree upon was that the Defense Department was "eating our lunch."

The terrorists I encountered in the course of my work on the African continent were ethnic ideologues, not religious ones. Warlords in Liberia talked to me about cannibalism—the other guy did it—and one in particular, Charles Taylor, kicked me out of his office when I told him to stop calling me "my dear." Genocide perpetrators in Rwanda tried to tell me their "civil uprisings" were "spontaneous." Militaries and militias in Burundi spoke of "kill or be killed." A variety of thugs in and out of uniform in other places reminded me that my place as a woman was secondary and ordained by God. Almost all of them were put out by a woman, a white one at that, looking straight into their faces and telling them to stop the killing. I did so with pleasure on behalf of the U.S. government and women everywhere.

On trips to the region, I saw creative strategies to address conflict unheard of in Washington. In Burundi, the UN's senior representative called for meetings between combatants at odd and various times of day or night because "when they are talking with me they are not killing each other." The U.S. embassy used local radio to discourage violence. I visited with a colleague at a particularly tense time and followed the country team's advice to counsel peace on the local radio. That night ended without a killing. The next morning, a woman approached me on the street. "Was that you on the radio? Thank you. We passed a night in peace." A few months later we supported a "peace radio station" to bring the communities together.

In Liberia an older woman described to me how she and her friends brought desperately needed food into Monrovia past hostile militia blockades. On the way out of town, they packed their suitcases with dirty underwear ready for the inevitable baggage checks and thefts. As the boy soldiers rifled through their suitcases, dropping the clothes in disgust, the women were taking them to task. "Don't point that gun at me!" "Why aren't you in school?" "Where's your mother?" "What is your family's name?" They returned with the same bags filled with food, to be hastily waved through each checkpoint. A decade later the women of Liberia themselves brought peace to the country through a strategy of nonviolence described in the film *Pray the Devil Back to Hell*. I used the film in leadership seminars for college students to show what the practice of leadership looks like. The women of Liberia also elected the first female president in sub-Saharan Africa, Ellen Johnson-Sirleaf.

In Washington, by contrast, conflict resolution strategies invariably turned to military means. In our case we were greeted with significant pushback from our Defense Department colleagues explaining why something could/should/would not work in Africa. Creative strategies were never considered. My phone calls to the perpetrators were ridiculed. Meanwhile, the Counterterrorism

Security Group at the White House had missed the fact that we were engaged in an entirely new type of conflict and that al-Qaeda had the upper hand.

1995: Washington DC

The Republican majority in Congress promised smaller government, lower taxes, and pro-business policies. It lost no time cutting federal funds and snarling over the next year's budgets. In November the government closed for five days, and again for twenty-one days in late December and early January. The continuing O. J. Simpson trial, Christopher Reeve/Superman's paralysis after falling off a horse, the Million Man March, and the Unabomber's manifesto kept the media and public engaged.

For the small Washington counterterrorism group, the year began on a good note with the discovery of Ramzi Yousef in Manila. The architect of the 1993 World Trade Center bombing was making a bomb in his apartment when he started a fire. The police investigated and took into custody his associates and his laptop computer. On it was this: "All people who support the U.S. government are our targets in our future plans and that is because all those people are responsible for their government's actions and they support the U.S. foreign policy and are satisfied with it. We will hit all U.S. nuclear targets. If the U.S. government keeps supporting Israel, then we will continue to carry out operations inside and outside the United States to include—"[23] The document came to a halt in midsentence.

Investigators also found plans to detonate bombs on eleven U.S. flights and indications that Yousef had already caused one explosion that killed a man on Philippines Airline Flight 434 in late 1994. As they dug deeper, they uncovered evidence that Yousef and his uncle, Khalid Sheikh Mohammed (KSM), planned to assassinate the pope and ram a dozen hijacked aircraft into key American landmarks, including the CIA. The files included names and photos of associates and trails of money transfers.

The plot was named "Bojinka," and copies of the computer files were handed over to the CIA. The CIA, in turn, gave other copies to the FBI, which found multiple program deletions. The FBI accused the CIA of destroying evidence.[24] Meanwhile, Ramzi Yousef and KSM had fled the Philippines. Their associates were released.

In February Yousef was betrayed to U.S. authorities for reward money and picked up at a building owned by bin Laden in Islamabad, Pakistan. On the way to the United States, Yousef talked about the 1993 World Trade Center bombing, about his colleagues, and about bin Laden. The FBI listened. When they tracked the money, the phone calls, and the plane tickets that supported Yousef's bombing exploits, they found Osama bin Laden at the other end.

In March members of a religious cult unleashed sarin gas in the Tokyo subway system, killing thirteen and injuring many more. Dick Clarke made sure the new presidential decision directive on terrorism he was drafting addressed the possibility of finding chemical, biological, or nuclear materials in terrorist hands.

On April 19 a truck bomb ripped apart the Murrah Federal Building in Oklahoma City. One hundred sixty-eight people lost their lives; hundreds more were injured. Was this the act of Middle East terrorists? People buzzed about it, but in short order two Americans were charged, Timothy McVeigh and Terry Nichols. It just so happened that Nichols had visited Cebu, a small island in the Philippines where his wife lived, at the same time Ramzi Yousef was there. Clarke wondered about the connection. "Could the al-Qaeda explosives expert have been introduced to the angry American who proclaimed his hatred for the U.S. Government? . . . We do know that Nichols's bombs did not work before his Philippine stay and were deadly when he returned."[25]

Terrorist attacks continued. In June assassins associated with both the Blind Sheikh and Ayman al-Zawahiri barely missed killing Egyptian president Hosni Mubarak during a visit to Addis Ababa, Ethiopia. Sudan's help was clear.[26] Egypt, Ethiopia, and the United States persuaded the UN Security Council to impose sanctions on Sudan. Perhaps to show he had gotten the message, Sudanese president Omar al-Bashir asked Ramzi Yousef's uncle, KSM, living in Khartoum, to leave the country and then tipped the U.S. authorities that he had gone to Qatar.[27] The CIA planned the operation to pick him up, but, according to one account, "When the FBI was briefed, the [overseas FBI office] based in Rome moved in and tried to take over the operation without concern for CIA equities on the ground or Qatari political tendencies."[28] KSM got away.

In the fall, the Algerian Armed Islamic Group attacked the Paris Metro, and in November radicals bombed the Saudi National Guard headquarters in Riyadh, killing five American soldiers and two Indian soldiers. Before the FBI could speak to the perpetrators, Saudi authorities had rounded them up. They confessed their guilt on national television and lost their heads, literally, within days. At least one of them noted Osama bin Laden's influence. Six days later, Ayman al-Zawahiri's group drove two cars filled with explosives through the gates of the Egyptian embassy in Islamabad, killing sixteen people.

Dick Clarke responded systematically. He wrote an executive order making it a felony to give money to terrorist organizations or fronts; he penned a presidential order directing more integrated efforts to counter money laundering. He requested more funding and new legislation and, although it took a year, got both.[29] He also responded tactically. After the failed attempt to assassinate President Mubarak in Ethiopia, Clarke asked the Defense Department to propose a plan to retaliate against Sudan. Clarke described this exchange in the office of the national security advisor, Tony Lake.

> While the Joint Staff dutifully briefed on the plan, they recommended strongly against it. "I can see why," Lake replied after seeing the details. "This isn't stealth. There is nothing quiet or covert about this. It's going to war with Sudan."
>
> The military briefing leader nodded. "That's what we do, sir. If you want covert, there's the CIA."[30]

In June President Clinton signed off on a CIA proposal to abduct Ayman al-Zawahiri's Islamic Jihad militants from their various hiding places and send them to Egypt for interrogation and likely torture. "It was begun in desperation," wrote Michael Scheuer, one of the authors. "We were turning into voyeurs. We knew where these people were, but we couldn't capture them because we had nowhere to take them, due to legal and diplomatic complications. . . . We had to come up with a third party."[31]

In December U.S. authorities arrested Osama bin Laden's brother-in-law, Mohammed Jamal Khalifa, for funding exactly the kind of terrorist group the administration had in mind when it issued its executive order. His name was in Ramzi Yousef's computer, and when he was arrested, his luggage contained explosives, weapons, and books advocating assassination. He was released to the government of Jordan, however, after Secretary of State Warren Christopher and Attorney General Janet Reno approved his deportation per Jordan's request. Once in Jordan, Khalifa was released. He found his way back to Saudi Arabia as a hero and went on to create another al-Qaeda cell. A CIA analyst later reported, "I remember people at the CIA who were ripshit at the time. Not even speaking in retrospect, but contemporaneous with what the intelligence community knew about bin Laden, Khalifa's deportation was unreal."[32] Ali Mohamed also avoided authorities, although the FBI continued to tap his phone.

By the end of 1995, it was clear from worldwide terrorist activities that the counterterrorism community needed to get its act together. The CIA detailed a small staff of analysts from the Counterterrorism Center to a virtual station named Alec Station, dedicated exclusively to tracking bin Laden and al-Qaeda. "If you were an up-and-coming CIA officer," commented a former case officer, "you didn't want to get sent down there to sit around with those FBI guys."[33] The FBI, in turn, formed what it called the I-49 Squad. Staffed with people who had worked with the New York JTTF, it was charged with overseeing Middle East terrorist cases in general and developing evidence for a secret grand jury investigation against bin Laden specifically. To ensure cooperation between the two units, FBI agents from the I-49 Squad were sent to Alec Station.

Alas, the three organizations with capabilities to intercept information—the FBI, the CIA, and the NSA—each had their own wall of secrecy, and no agency would fully share data with the others. The FBI could not even share with colleagues in the Justice Department because of "the wall." Aptly named, the new regulation prevented FBI agents who had access to intelligence about terrorist cells from passing on the information to the lawyers prosecuting cases against them—unless someone at headquarters approved. It was a bureaucratic power move, and complaints began immediately. At the tenth public hearing of the 9/11 Commission on April 23, 2004, Attorney General John Ashcroft said that "the single greatest structural cause for September 11 was the wall that segregated criminal investigators and intelligence agents." It was the reason that U.S. Attorney Mary Jo White and her assistant, Patrick Fitzgerald, apologetically explained to Richard and me in 2001 why they had not shared information about al-Qaeda's activities in Nairobi before we were attacked. At the time, we had no idea what they were talking about.

In the State Department, the wall against which I was banging my head was called resources. I was part of an ad hoc group of career people serving as a sounding board to State's chief financial officer. We were way beyond the charade of "doing more with less" and deep into conversations about fixing the plumbing in the department vs. hiring more Foreign Service members to meet ongoing need. We could not do both. Not once did we consider how to challenge the senior "leaders" to secure more funding. It was understood they would not do anything. That was just the way it was.

10

THE PLANS

1996: Washington DC

This was an election year. But in case Americans were not interested in politics, they could watch the Summer Olympics, read about the Whitewater investigations into President Clinton's prior investments, or watch the start of the riveting O. J. Simpson murder trial on television. There was plenty to keep them busy.

In Washington Richard Clarke put policies, resources, and people in place to confront the growing menace of terrorism. Clinton had signed a "finding" declaring Osama bin Laden a danger to national security, so the paperwork was in order, and he officially sanctioned FBI-CIA cooperation. Coordinating the effort was Clarke's staff and the super-secret Counterterrorism Security Group (CSG).

In Khartoum, bin Laden was thinking about moving. Someone had tried once again to kill him. The Saudi government had frozen his assets. The Sudanese government had fleeced him by paying their bills for the construction projects he financed with properties like a tannery factory rather than in cash. Further, President Omar el-Bashir's mood was shifting. What with a never-ending civil war, two irritated and militarized neighbors, Egypt and Ethiopia, and the economic bite of UN economic sanctions, bin Laden's appeal had waned. As moderates pushed radicals aside in his government, el-Bashir was showing signs he wanted to get back into Washington's good graces—or at least get out of the doghouse—especially after we closed the U.S. embassy in Khartoum. That was done over the objections of Ambassador Timothy Carney, but with the insistence of the CIA. The asset who reported that embassy personnel were in jeopardy was later proved a liar, but at the time it was imprudent to take chances, especially as an alleged threat was also made against Tony Lake, Clinton's national security advisor. Finally Sudan's foreign minister resorted to sending Tony Lake a message when they were both attending the same conference in Algiers: "I am not trying to kill you," it read. Lake responded, "I am not trying to kill you either."[1]

As the embassy pulled out of Khartoum, Carney made clear to Sudan's government that if it wanted to impress Washington, it had to close down the likes of Hamas, Hezbollah, and al-Qaeda in Sudan and deport Ayman al-Zawahiri and Osama bin Laden. Speaking for the government, the defense minister said fine. Sudan was also ready to arrest bin Laden and hand him over. (They had provided the French with a similar service when they rendered Carlos the Jackal a few years earlier.)[2]

If the U.S. government had an opportunity, the NSC had an attitude. Christian evangelicals, influential congressional staffers, nongovernmental organizations, and members of the Congressional Black Caucus had maintained pressure for a strong anti-Khartoum policy for years. The reports about threats to Americans only hardened positions. Richard Clarke and Susan Rice, his NSC Africa director colleague, would not be persuaded to interact with the Sudan government.

"There were lots of reasons to be unhappy with Sudan," Ambassador David Shinn, director of East African Affairs at State, later told the 9/11 Commission. "I did not dispute that the Sudan was subject to severe criticism on many counts. But I saw no point in turning Sudan into an obsession that was not going to achieve any positive results.[3] Dick Clarke denied that an offer from Sudan had even been made. He wrote, "The only slivers of truth in this fable are that (a) the Sudanese government was denying its support for terrorism in the wake of the UN sanctions, and (b) the CSG had initiated informal inquiries with several nations about incarcerating bin Laden or putting him on trial. There were no takers."[4]

According to other reports, the Clinton administration struggled to find a way to accept Sudan's offer of rendition, either to the United States, Egypt, or Saudi Arabia, but ultimately they gave up. The Saudis did not want bin Laden fomenting trouble, and so they resorted to paying him—and other Islamist extremists—large sums of money to stay quiet as they decided the delicate royal succession of the day. Egypt did not want him either. The United States was out: the FBI, according to Tony Lake's successor, Sandy Berger, did not believe the United States had enough evidence to indict bin Laden at that time and therefore opposed bringing him to the United States. Michael Scheuer, head of the CIA's special bin Laden unit, later explained, "The thinking was that he was in Afghanistan, and he was dangerous, but because he was there, we had a better chance to kill him. But at the end of the day, we settled for the worst possibility—he was there and we didn't do anything."[5]

In May Ali Mohamed helped to move bin Laden, his wives and children, and chosen operatives to Taliban-controlled Afghanistan. Discussions about catching bin Laden in Sudan were now moot. On to other options. The FBI's Squad 1-49 began the legal case against bin Laden under the direction of Assistant U.S. District Attorney Patrick Fitzgerald. A member of his team was seconded to work with the CIA's Alec Station, headed by Michael Scheuer, to collect intelligence. Others at Alec Station were to coordinate with Agent John O'Neill at the FBI's New York Office. Clearly 1-49 had found a way around "the wall" that prohibited intelligence gatherers from sharing with prosecuting attorneys.[6]

The CIA and NSA began intercepting communications in Nairobi to better understand what Wadih el-Hage and others were doing. They listened to bin Laden in Afghanistan and Ali Mohamed in California.[7] Better than any intercept, however, was an informant. In June Jamal al-Fadl, whom the FBI would call "Junior," walked into a U.S. embassy in East Africa and said he wanted protection from al-Qaeda. He had stolen money from bin Laden's coffers and feared the repercussions. During subsequent months of debriefings, Junior described al-Qaeda's background, structure, mission, objectives, and financial infrastructure. He explained al-Qaeda's networks and its collaborations with other terrorist groups, including those at the al-Kifah Refugee Center. He gave details about al-Qaeda activities against U.S. soldiers in Somalia and more recent activities in Bosnia. He divulged plans to attack inside the United States or overseas U.S. embassies. He described his own involvement in bin Laden's efforts to acquire weapons of mass destruction.[8] In mid-June an attack in Khobar, Saudi Arabia, gave his interrogators even more questions to ask. A truck bomb had exploded next to one of the Khobar Towers, buildings that housed U.S. Air Force personnel. Nineteen U.S. servicemen were killed, and 498 of many nationalities were wounded. Al-Qaeda was the chief suspect.

While the combined efforts of the FBI and CIA made perfect sense on paper, leading players in these communities proved incapable of overcoming personal animosity and agency prejudices. As al-Qaeda planned war, American protagonists fussed and feuded. FBI agent O'Neill could not abide the CIA's Michael Scheuer, the head of Alec Station, and they refused to cooperate with one another. Scheuer could not stand Dick Clarke either: "Mr. Clarke was an interferer of the first level, in terms of talking about things that he knew nothing about and killing them. . . . Mr. Clarke was an empire builder. He built the community, and it was his little toy. He was always playing the FBI off against us or us against the NSA." For his part Dick Clarke said this about Scheuer: "Throwing tantrums and everything doesn't help. . . . Fine that you came to the same conclusion that we all came to, fine that you're all worked up about it, and you're having difficulty getting your agency, the rest of your agency, to fall in line, but not fine that you're so dysfunctional within your agency that you're making it harder to get something done."[9] Nor did Clarke like FBI director Louis Freeh. This is what he had to say about Freeh's race to Saudi Arabia after the highly publicized Khobar Towers bombing:

> Freeh should have been spending his time fixing the mess that the FBI had become, an organization of fifty-six princedoms (the fifty-six very independent field offices) without any modern information technology to support them. He might have spent some time hunting for terrorists in the United States, where

THE PLANS

al-Qaeda and its affiliates had put down roots, where many terrorist organizations were illegally raising money. Instead, he reportedly chose to be chief investigator in high-profile cases like Khobar, the Atlanta Olympics bombing, and the possible Chinese espionage at our nuclear labs. His back channels to the Republicans in the Congress and to supporters in the media made it impossible for the President to dismiss him without running the risk of making him a martyr of the Republican Right and his firing a cause célèbre.[10]

Meanwhile, the NSA would not share the information from their taps of bin Laden's phone with the 1-49 squad. Nor would it share with the CIA. When it finally did release documents to 1-49 after it threatened to build its antennas in Afghanistan, this proved a onetime deal.[11]

Bin Laden was now settled in the Hindu Kush Mountains under the protection of the Taliban, another set of Islamist jihadists nurtured by Saudi Arabia and Pakistan. With the theatrical backdrop of his Tora Bora cave, he gave press interviews and issued *fatwas,* religious edicts: kill American troops to get them out of the Arabian Peninsula. This was the consensus of Islamist terrorist groups from Egypt, Algeria, Iran, the Palestinian Liberation Organization, Lebanon, Great Britain, the Balkans, the Persian Gulf, Pakistan, Afghanistan, and Sudan. They had overcome rivalries and animus to confer together and agree "to use force to confront all foreign forces stationed in Islamic land."[12] Bin Laden appeared only too happy to deliver the message.

In July, during the Summer Olympics in Atlanta, a bomb exploded at the Centennial Olympic Park, killing one person. Barely a month later, TWA Flight 800 exploded into a ball of fiery debris over the Atlantic just off New York City. All 240 people aboard were killed. Witnesses swore they had seen evidence of a missile attack from the ground. Washington's attention turned. The perpetrator of the Atlanta bombing turned out to be an American, Eric Rudolph. The cause of the plane crash turned out to be mechanical. It took time and attention away from al-Qaeda to reach those conclusions.

As this was going on, I was spending the summer becoming an ambassador, "extraordinary and plenipotentiary." I filled out lots of forms concerning our assets; how much money our relatives, dead or alive, had contributed to a political party; whether Richard had ever been arrested; and whether I had ever done anything that, if it became public, would embarrass President Clinton. Once the Senate confirmed me as ambassador designate, I raced around town learning all I could about the interests of the seventeen agencies represented in the embassy. The Defense Department admired the Kenyan military and saw its geostrategic advantages. Commerce saw possibilities marred by corruption. Other agencies predicted that nothing good could happen in the areas of democracy, human rights, poverty reduction, health, or environment as long as Daniel arap Moi remained president. In brief, Kenya at the time was too corrupt for business and development interests, too autocratic for political hopes, and too far away for all but a smattering of American tourists and well-meaning missionaries to care about. That said, Kenya was also a regional economic power, an island of relative peace, a positive player in regional affairs, and an important hub for international organizations and regional transportation.

Colleagues in Diplomatic Security told me Nairobi was a major threat post for crime and a lesser threat for terrorism. I already knew about some of its nefarious residents, including Somali warlords who came to be hosted by the international community to talk peace in five-star hotels. The CIA advised me that a terrorist financier by the name of Osama bin Laden had offices in Nairobi and that they were disrupting his operations. This sounded fine with me.

I took the oath to protect and defend the Constitution in front of a large group of family and friends in the elegant Benjamin Franklin Room of the State Department. Richard held the Bible, and George Moose swore me in. I focused my remarks on Foreign Service families and communities. Mom and Dad were in the audience standing proud.

We left in August. The CIA had been talking to Junior for two months. CIA director George Tenet later wrote: "By 1996 we knew that bin Laden was more than a financier. An al-Qaeda defector [Jamal al-Fadl] told us that [bin Laden] was the head of a world-wide terrorist organization with a board of directors that would include the likes of Ayman al-Zawahiri and he wanted to strike the United States on our soil."[13] They knew that Wadih el-Hage was involved in at least two murders in the United States and that the charities he was running in Nairobi were fronts for terrorist operations. The CIA was tapping his phones. They recognized bin Laden as a danger to national security, with links to the 1993 World Trade Center bombing, dead American soldiers in Somalia, and the conspiracy to blow up landmarks in New York City. They knew that Ali Mohamed, unindicted coconspirator in the Landmarks conspiracy case, had business in Kenya and visited el-Hage. As Junior continued to talk, they learned much more. All of that information was withheld from me as I was handed the responsibility for the safety of all American citizens in Kenya.

January–July 1997: Washington DC, Nairobi

Bill Clinton inaugurated his second term in freezing temperatures and talked about domestic reforms and the economy. The Republican Congress focused on a campaign finance scandal and reelected Newt Gingrich as Speaker of the House. Tony Lake's replacement as national security advisor, Sandy Berger, and the new secretary of state, Madeleine Albright, focused on those aspects of foreign policy that interested them. The press focused on the divorce of Prince Charles and Lady Diana and later on her death. Mad cow disease and El Niño shared the headlines.

The FBI focused on investigating the Oklahoma City bombing, the Khobar Towers bombing, the bombing at the 1996 Summer Olympics, and the explosion of TWA Flight 800. The I-49 Squad, NSA, and Alec Station focused on getting results from wiretaps on the likes of Wadih el Hage, Ali Mohamed, and bin Laden. The Alec Station team, composed mostly of women, also focused on being heard within the CIA. The more the team learned about bin Laden's network and efforts to buy weapons of mass destruction, the more it sounded the alarm, only to be rebuffed at senior levels. According to later reports, the CIA's top brass "started to view Scheuer as an hysteric, spinning doomsday scenarios." Some started referring to him and the bin Laden unit as "the Manson family," in reference to mass murderer Charles Manson and his female followers.[14]

There were other problems. Bin Laden's conversations were in Arabic, and translators were few. The raw data the NSA picked up would not be shared, provoking the CIA into building its own controlled ground station so they could directly intercept calls between bin Laden in Afghanistan and his operations center in Yemen. That gave them only one side of the conversation, however, so Michael Scheuer went to the NSA to analyze their half. Nothing doing.[15]

What bin Laden was doing in the meantime was putting into motion a plan to blow up the U.S. embassy in Nairobi; the embassy in Dar es Salaam made the list later. He called Wadih el-Hage to Afghanistan in February 1997. According to later trial transcripts, "Wadih el-Hage brought back with him a new policy, a policy to militarize . . . the cell that in 16 or 18 months thereafter would carry out the bombings in East Africa."[16] Soon after that, el-Hage's deputy, Haroun Fazul, left Nairobi to be trained in Somalia.[17]

The leadership of the Africa Bureau changed as George Moose left and Susan Rice came over from the NSC. She was pursuing a policy of cultivating so-called Renaissance men among English-speaking African presidents. President Moi was not among them. That meant the embassy was unimpeded by Washington interest, and we could interpret the policy of "peace, democracy, prosperity" ourselves. In addition to U.S. interests in Kenya, our mission ran assistance programs to southern Somalia, and we housed the tiny American staff of the U.S. embassy to Sudan. We had a large community and a reputation for poor morale.

I settled into my role as chief of mission, and Richard threw himself into his role as Top Spouse, immediately volunteering his accounting skills to the Employees Association, which ran the commissary and video club. I worked on establishing a constructive relationship with President Moi and had a breakthrough when I respectfully refused to be bullied. We were in his severe gray office at State House discussing Kenya's political culture—

and how much I did not understand, according to him—when he said accusingly, "I have never once heard you say anything nice about my political party."

"You have never once heard me say anything nice about any political party," I retorted.

"You are right," he admitted.

With that remark we turned a corner, and after a while he actually began to listen to me. Over time we disagreed aplenty. But I found President Moi a man of his word and helpful in many areas of mutual interest—unless it had to do with how he was running his country.

Security concerns permeated both policy and community discussions. Tranquil by comparison to some of its neighbors, Kenya nonetheless faced significant challenges: ethnic tensions, extreme poverty exacerbated by the floods and drought from El Niño, and a political class with a reputation for stealing. Nairobi's crime threat was "high." The embassy community struggled to find safe places for teenagers to hang out together, while our security team strained to maintain the balance between advising, dictating, and terrifying people, newcomers in particular. We implemented weekly checks of the handheld radios Americans received for security communications and gave every family the choice of its own call sign. The consular team reenergized the warden system, our communications link to American citizens, most of them missionaries. I held town meetings at my residence and opened the tennis court and pool to the American employee community.

The embassy was located at one of the city's busiest corners, across from the railroad station, a major bus stop, and a small college. As political demonstrations increased with the advent of political campaigns, I could stand at my window overlooking Moi Avenue and watch young people run by like gazelles, the police at their heels pursuing like predators. Behind them, the media, like the tourists, chased the game to snap the photos. Now and then, tear gas would seep into the first-floor Consular Section waiting room, and we counted the gas masks. Frequently we issued embassy radio-net announcements advising family members of alternate routes should they be coming for a medical appointment or grocery shopping. Once a colleague stopped the brutal beating of a protestor on the other side of our fence. We were in the thick of it, and I let my Washington colleagues know it.

August–December 1997: Washington DC, Nairobi

George Tenet became CIA director after a year as "acting" and began on a high note. A month earlier he had told an assembled and elated staff, "No terrorist should sleep soundly as long as this agency exists."[18] The rendition program was working: the gunman who had shot and killed CIA employees in 1993 was kidnapped into U.S. custody and was now on American soil. Why not "render" bin Laden? Dick Clarke later reported:

> By 1996 and 1997 the CSG was developing plans to snatch bin Laden from Afghanistan. One plan called for an Afghan snatch team to drive a bound-and-gagged bin Laden to a dirt strip on which a CIA-owned aircraft would briefly land and then head back out of Afghanistan. . . . The flaw that developed in the snatch was our inability to know when it would occur. . . . A variation on the plan was developed. The Afghan snatch team would not just wait for bin Laden to drive by, they would go pick him up at his "farm" at the same time that the CIA aircraft was flying into the country.[19]

Unfortunately, the farm was a fortress, and the CSG decided against the attempt. Tenet assured the 9/11 Commission years later that more than seventy renditions had been organized before 2001, but none got to bin Laden.[20]

Sudan's president, Omar al-Bashir, kept up efforts to persuade the U.S. government to cooperate. To pass his message along, he found a multimillionaire Pakistani American businessman personally acquainted with President Clinton and National Security Advisor Sandy Berger. Al-Bashir also wrote to Lee Hamilton (D-IN), the ranking Democrat on the House Foreign Affairs Committee: "We extend an offer to the FBI's Counterterrorism units and any other official delegations which your government may deem appropriate, to come to the Sudan and work with [us] in order to assess the data in our possession and help us counter the forces your government, and ours, seek to contain." Like the other offers, the letter was sent to the NSC and received no reply.[21]

On the more constructive side, months of interagency discussion about reopening the U.S. embassy in Khartoum finally came to a consensus. Yes, do it. The decision was endorsed by Secretary of State Albright and sent to the NSC for approval. The NSC advisor for Africa, Susan Rice—soon to be assistant secretary for African affairs at State—and Dick Clarke would have none of it, however, and asked Sandy Berger to overrule this decision. Albright withdrew her consent, and State announced that it was scrapping its own initiative.[22] American intelligence agents waited until 2001 to see the files Sudan kept on bin Laden.

On August 21 members of Alec Station and I-49 Squad arrived in Nairobi to raid Wadih el-Hage's house with help from Kenyan police. Like other joint ventures, it involved a kerfuffle. Michael Scheuer later reported:

> For most of a year the bin Laden unit prepared for an operation in a foreign city that was set to come to fruition in late-summer 1997. The unit's lead U.S.-based officer on this operation was an extraordinarily able analyst from [the FBI]; she knew the issue cold. Days before the operation occurred the [FBI] ordered her back to its headquarters. She protested, but was told that she would not be promoted if she balked at returning. I protested to my superiors and to the three most senior officers of the [FBI] who were then in charge of terrorism. All refused to intervene. The operation was much less well exploited because of the loss of this officer.[23]

I knew a joint CIA-FBI team was coming to talk with Wadih el-Hage, with Kenyan police in the lead. I knew he was a person of interest to the intelligence community because of his relationship with the terrorist financier, Osama bin Laden. I did not have the right to know the purpose, the substance, or anything else relating to the raid on his house lest "sources and methods" be revealed.

When the Kenyan-American group arrived at el-Hage's house, only his American wife was there to let them in. El-Hage was on his way back from another planning meeting with bin Laden in

Afghanistan, and el-Hage's deputy, Haroun Fazul, was on the coast visiting with another confederate, a man named Mohammed Odeh who ran a fishing business. The Americans left with el-Hage's computer, diaries, disks, and address book and went to the airport to meet el-Hage himself with the same message they had given his wife: return to the United States.[24] When he did just that, I was told, the al-Qaeda office was no more. That was not the case.

When el-Hage took the Americans' advice to return to the United States, the FBI was waiting for him. He was taken into custody when he got off the plane in New York City and offered a deal if he would switch sides. He declined and ended up in front of a secret grand jury questioned by Assistant U.S. Attorney Patrick Fitzgerald. El-Hage chose to lie repeatedly and was allowed to go on his way to Arlington, Texas.[25]

That left 1-49 and Alec Station with el-Hage's computer and the contents of his address book, which included Ali Mohamed's phone number. On the computer the FBI found a document indicating that he had been sent to Nairobi to prepare activists for a new policy.[26] Even more interesting was what el-Hage's deputy, Fazul, had written clearly in a state of panic.

Fazul had read an article in a British newspaper that bin Laden's chief financial officer had turned himself in to the Saudi Arabian authorities and was telling all. Further, Fazul had discovered that el-Hage's phone was tapped.

> We can now state that the security position in the cell is at 100 percent danger. In this report, I will try to explain the reasons that make us feel that danger. I will also try to offer my recommendation to honored and wise high command which I know understands everything and we hope is seeking the best. . . . There is an American-Kenyan-Egyptian intelligence activity in Nairobi aiming to identify the names and residences of the members who are associated with the Shaykh [bin Laden] since America knows well that the youth who lived in Somalia were members of the Shaykh's cell and the ones who killed the Americans in Somalia. They know that since Kenya was the main gateway for those members, there must be a center in Kenya.[27]

Fazul then described security measures he had taken and with whom, listing al-Qaeda cohorts in Qatar, Germany, and Sudan. He wrote that he and an associate collected el-Hage's files and put them in another location. The partisans from Mombasa called, he continued, and he told them never to call el-Hage's home number again, "as I am one hundred percent sure that the telephone is tapped." As to activities at hand, Fazul asked, "Are we ready for that big clandestine battle? . . . We, the East Africa cell members, do not want to know about the operation plans since we are just implementers." He did, however, ask that they be informed in a timely way to "prepare ourselves . . . or so that we may go underground for a while." Fazul ended the letter suggesting that future communications with the Nairobi cell be conducted by internet or fax.[28]

In front of the secret grand jury, Patrick Fitzgerald asked el-Hage about the files Fazul mentioned in the security letter. El-Hage gave detailed instructions and a map. When FBI investigators looked for them after the bombings in 1998, they found the boxes exactly where el-Hage had said they would be. "The hardest thing to understand in retrospect is why U.S. law enforcement did nothing to disrupt the activities of the Nairobi cell," wrote John Miller later. "When el-Hage left Kenya, Haroun Fazul simply stepped into the vacant leadership slot and seamlessly resumed preparations for the embassy bombings. A garden-variety robbery crew would show at least as much resilience. Did the CIA and the FBI still not yet understand that an al-Qaeda soldier was eminently replaceable?"[29]

A few weeks after questioning el-Hage in New York City, Patrick Fitzgerald and 1-49 Squad agents flew to Sacramento to have a conversation with Ali Mohamed. Over dinner Mohamed frankly admitted that he had been in Somalia in 1993 during the battle of Mogadishu and that he had trained bin Laden's bodyguards in 1994. Bin Laden's people, he said, were responsible for killing the U.S. soldiers. They did not need a *fatwa*, or religious edict, to make war on the United States, since it was obvious that America was the enemy.[30]

An agent present remembered, "He said that he was in touch with hundreds of people he could call on in a moment's notice that could be, quote, 'operational,' and wage jihad against the United States. Very brazenly, he said, 'I can get out anytime and you'll never find me. I've got a whole network. You'll never find me.'"

"This is the most dangerous man I have ever met. We cannot let this man out on the street," Patrick Fitzgerald was quoted as saying. But he did exactly that. Fitzgerald put a wiretap on Ali's computer and his phone, and that was that. An agent told author Peter Lance, "The Sacramento [FBI] office did a wonderful job in getting into his apartment, wiring it up, and exploiting his computer. So we were able to down a lot of stuff." After quoting the agent, Peter Lance wondered, "That stunning revelation, published here for the first time in print, raises an even bigger question: If Fitzgerald and the agents in his bin Laden squad had access to Mohamed's phone and hard disk, why didn't they come to understand his role as a key player in the embassy bombing plot?"[31] Instead, Ali Mohamed was free to fly to Pakistan a few weeks later to meet Ayman al-Zawahiri, who by now had become bin Laden's partner.

The threat from al-Haramain, the Islamist "charity" near the Somali border, came after the raid on el-Hage's house. I had no context in which to place the threat, and Washington provided none. It was only as President Moi was making good on his promise to disband the organization that I heard the FBI-CIA wanted to return to interview the men. I agreed with my colleague in Nairobi that we would not press the Kenyan officials if this proved difficult, which it did. We needed their support and willingness to go the extra mile for us. After the bombing, I read that these interviews could have been important. If so, someone should have made that point with me at the time.

In December I was in Washington listening to a colleague lecture me to "stop nagging" about security when a man named Mustafa Mahmoud Said Ahmed walked into our embassy in Nairobi with information that he knew of a group planning to detonate a bomb-laden truck inside our underground parking garage. It would involve several vehicles and stun grenades. The CIA in Washington said he had made up the story. It then issued two reports,[32]

neither of which I saw, and sent word to me that he was a "fabricator." On Christmas Eve, amid holiday festivities, I dispatched yet
another cable to Washington noting increased crime and political
violence, the al-Haramain threat, the walk-in warning of a bombing, and a personal threat against me from the Holy Spirit Movement in Uganda, predecessor to the Lord's Resistance Army. Let
my colleagues in Washington be irritated. The threats were real.

11

THE EXECUTION

U.S. unemployment was under 5 percent, and *Titanic* was bringing record-breaking crowds to movie theaters around the country. The Denver Broncos beat the Green Bay Packers in the Super Bowl, and the media followed reports of the president's relationship with a White House intern, Monica Lewinsky. Meanwhile, the special prosecutor of the Whitewater case, an investigation into the Clintons' financial dealings, began to issue subpoenas for White House testimonies and records. Concerns about foreign affairs focused on Iraq's weapons of mass destruction. The press gave President Clinton's statement," I did not have sexual relations with that woman, Miss Lewinsky," front page coverage.

In New York, Patrick Fitzgerald and the 1-49 Squad prepared charges against Osama bin Laden for murdering U.S. citizens in Somalia in 1993 and Saudi Arabia in 1995. A U.S. court sentenced Ramzi Yousef, mastermind of the 1993 bombing of the World Trade Center, to life imprisonment, and authorities unsealed an indictment against his uncle, Khalid Sheikh Mohammed, for the conspiracies of the Bojinka plot. A $2 million reward for his capture went with it.

In Afghanistan, bin Laden met with other top al-Qaeda leaders and issued a fatwa: it was the religious duty of all Muslims "to kill the Americans and their allies—civilians and military . . . in any country in which it is possible."[1] It was signed by representatives from Sudan, Saudi Arabia, Somalia, Yemen, Eritrea, Djibouti,

Kenya, Pakistan, Bosnia, Croatia, Algeria, Tunisia, Lebanon, the Philippines, Tajikistan, Chechnya, Bangladesh, Kashmir, Azerbaijan, and Palestine under the umbrella name the International Islamic Front for Jihad against Jews and Crusaders. Afghan and Pakistani jihadists contributed their own fatwas later. This was the first time such a large group of signatories publicly endorsed bin Laden's edicts. Iran was noticeably absent from the public eye, but apparently was heavily involved behind the scenes.[2]

Bin Laden continued to use the satellite phone that the NSA was tapping, and Ali Mohamed continued to use the phone that the FBI was tapping. Early in the year Mohamed called Wadih el-Hage, once again in Texas living with his family, to discuss the FBI's interaction. He later phoned other operatives who passed it up the chain to bin Laden.[3] No one who was listening in did anything.

From Nairobi my team and I kept pressing our case about our building's vulnerabilities. In January our security engineer sent to the department's Diplomatic Security Services office a detailed technical report, complete with photos, showing how easily a truck bomb could blow us up. The department later sent a security assessment team to Nairobi that never produced anything in writing.[4] What could they say? That we were not vulnerable to a truck bomb?

In Paris Zbigniew Brzezinski, whose excellent idea it was to fund radical Islamists to fight the Russians in decades past, was asked about any regrets for the consequences of his decision in an interview with Le Nouvel Observateur. "What is most important to the history of the world? The Taliban or the collapse of the Soviet empire? Some stirred-up Muslims or the liberation of Central Europe and the end of the Cold War?" The interviewer countered, "Islamic fundamentalism represents a world menace today." Brzezinski responded, "Nonsense! It is said that the West had a global policy in regard to Islam. That is stupid. There isn't a global Islam."[5]

Sudan made one last effort to share intelligence with the United States. Its director of intelligence wrote to the FBI head of counterterrorism: "I would like to express my sincere desire to start contacts and cooperation between our service and the FBI. I would like to take this opportunity with pleasure to invite you to visit our country. Otherwise, we could meet somewhere else." After months of arguments, the American agent responded in late June, a few weeks before the bombing. "I am not currently in a position to accept your kind invitation." The State Department had denied the FBI request to go to Sudan. The Sudanese later noted, "If they had taken up my offer in February 1998, they could have prevented the [U.S. embassy] bombings." If nothing else, U.S. authorities would have learned that el-Hage's deputy, Haroun Fazul, now living in Sudan, was making trips to Nairobi while the Sudanese were keeping track.[6]

Bin Laden issued the fatwa to kill Americans in late February. Within days Fazul purchased a ticket from Khartoum to Nairobi. His colleague on the Kenyan coast, Mohammed Odeh, was bringing in bomb parts.[7]

At the NSC Dick Clarke wrote more presidential directives about "Continuity of Government" and mandating a "national coordinator" for counterterrorism. As he put it, "The CSG would officially become not just a crisis response committee, but a policy formulation body with a budget and programmatic role. Moreover, the CSG would have oversight of the 10 programs they were running, the same way that a congressional committee had oversight of an Administration program. Predictably, most departments and agencies saw it as a White House power grab."[8] Within a year Clarke would "coordinate" an $11 billion a year enterprise, with a seat at the table during cabinet meetings.

In Nairobi we were still vulnerable. U.S. Central Command Gen. Tony Zinni, whose "theater" included Kenya, understood and shared my security concerns: force protection was a four-star issue in the military. Since Washington colleagues kept saying there was no money for anything, we agreed that Tony would offer his vulnerability assessment team for free. I followed up with my own cable endorsing a coordinated State-Defense assessment and received the fastest response to any security message I had ever sent. No, no, and no. Embassy security was the department's business, and General Zinni should mind his own. Back to square one.

Eric Boswell, assistant secretary for Diplomatic Security, later said:

> I can tell you right here . . . that one of the things I regret
> most from my time in DS is that I was absolutely convinced
> that building more secure embassies was the only way to go.
> Keep in mind that I had this conviction in the face of 10 years
> of virtually no assaults against a U.S. embassy so it was really
> a tough position to try to defend but I felt it and I still feel it. I
> never really got [this position] on paper. I never really wrote a
> memorandum to the secretary or the undersecretary for Man-
> agement saying that I thought our capital account was grossly
> underfunded. . . . I never did that because I thought it would
> be just hopeless; I thought it had no chance of success.[9]

In March Bin Laden sent a senior lieutenant to Kenya with a message to Fazul and Odeh: get your affairs and travel documents in
order to be ready to pull out of the country on command.[10] Alec
Station, in the meantime, was almost shut down.

"This was done, so far as I know, without the knowledge of the
DCI [Director of Central Intelligence]," Michael Scheuer reported.
"When DCI found out about this plan, he intervened in mid-May
1998. By doing so, the DCI preserved the unit and dodged the bullet
of having to explain to the American people why the CIA thought
bin Laden was so little of a threat that it had destroyed the bin Laden
unit weeks before two U.S. embassies were demolished. Needless
to say, the on-again, off-again signals about the unit's future status
made for confusion, distraction, and much job-hunting in the last
few weeks before al-Qaeda's August 1998 attacks in East Africa."[11]

Scheuer and his team were still pitching rendition plans. In
one, Afghan tribesmen would kidnap bin Laden and take him to a
commercial shipping container equipped with a dentist chair and
restraints that could fit into a large aircraft. The plane could drop
bin Laden off in Egypt, where he would be handed over to authorities. The FBI hated the plan, however, and the NSC would not authorize it. One plan after another was nixed for one reason or another.
CIA director George Tenet even asked for help from the Saudis,
but nothing materialized to bring bin Laden out of Afghanistan.[12]

The embassy team carried on with business as usual. The Kenyan presidential elections in December were fairly free and fair, a tribute to many efforts. Rather than funding international observers, we pushed resources into training more than 20,000 Kenyans about their voting rights as citizens, poll watchers, and independent election officials. The diplomatic community in Nairobi fanned out across the country to serve as the international observers. It did my American heart good to include ambassadors from former Soviet countries who wanted "in" to our local, international democracy group. Ethnic clashes nonetheless took place in the Rift valley, and tensions rose among Muslim communities along the Somali border and the eastern coast. Everyone was concerned.

I asked for Jessie Jackson, a popular figure who had visited Kenya months earlier. We went to the epicenter of the conflict where Reverend Jackson held a press conference at which he rhetorically asked why the president of Kenya was not there to make peace. The president of Kenya was at my doorstep the next day per an invitation to breakfast, clearly unamused by Jackson's call. In a masterful piece of theater, Jackson bounded out from the living room and landed on his knee, grinning brilliantly. "Bet you're really mad at me," he said to the astonished Moi. At breakfast Jackson led Moi and me in prayer, holding hands as he asked that the Lord provide his shepherd Daniel arap Moi with the courage to go into the valley and call for peace. We talked about it over omelets. President Moi, an evangelical Christian, promised to go and did so the following week.

With encouragement from the country team, I happily went into the Muslim communities, where women dressed me up in all sorts of covering garb. The practice of Islam I experienced in East Africa was more austere and less welcoming than the one I had found in West Africa. Centuries of Arab trade and culture had left a different mark from the French, English, and Portuguese. Kenyan Muslims were a minority in a largely Christian country, and many felt politically and economically marginalized. Postelection violence and rumors that the embassy was responsible for the government's decision to deport members of the "humanitarian" al-Haramain organization directed anger our way. It was my job to understand and confront it.

I met with Muslim political leaders in the neutral territory of a hotel conference room. No one would sit next to me, so I had one side of the table to myself while huddled male faces looked at me from the other. One by one they launched into a litany of concerns and complaints about the United States, working themselves into a virtual crescendo. "You hate all of us Muslims," they accused. I listened politely until I had heard enough.

"Do not tell me I hate you," I said firmly. "I have lived in Muslim countries about a third of my life. I have been cared for by Muslims, prayed over by Muslims, worked with Muslims, worked for Muslims, and danced with Muslims. I have done everything but marry a Muslim, so don't tell me I hate you. If you want to talk about my government or my embassy, you had better be specific." An awkward silence followed. We moved the discussion into ways the embassy could improve its relationship with their communities. As we said good-bye—most of them shaking my hand—one asked, "Ambassador, will you marry me?"

"I'll have to ask my husband," I replied, pleased with what I thought was an appropriate response to this man.

"Well," he said with a nice smile, "you said you had done everything but marry a Muslim, and I thought I would give you the chance." I took the remark as a gesture of friendship and smiled back. Muslim leaders and embassy officers persevered in creating relationships built on respect if not friendship. It helped greatly that one of our Foreign Service officers was Muslim. After the bombing, that respect proved crucial to keeping people safe as investigations took Kenyan police and American FBI agents into Muslim communities that became increasingly embittered.

In April I received my annual performance appraisal. In the Needs Improvement section was this: "Reflecting her strong managerial skills, in many instances over the past year Amb. Bushnell has been able to prevail over bureaucratic obstacles through persistence and the logic of her beliefs. On one or two occasions, however, she has tended to overload the circuits." I may have overloaded the circuits among my management colleagues, but I would not remain silent in the face of reality-based concerns in my community. When the director general of the Foreign Service, State's head of human resources, visited a few weeks later, he offered to take a personal note to Secretary Albright. This is what I wrote:

> Secretary, Skip Gnehm is in town and offered to pass on an issue you could use to further substantiate the need for additional funding for State. Our Chancery is in a dangerous part of town and does not meet Inman security standards. We receive lots of sympathy—and support from DS—but no resources to relocate. Other chanceries are in far worse shape, we are told, and I understand. But that doesn't mitigate our situation.
>
> Last summer we were under a credible bomb, then assassination, threat from a group with ties to a well-known terrorist organization. We were under surveillance, according to an informant with direct access, and when we learned the group had received weapons, I asked the GOK [government of Kenya] to move against them. Immediately, President Moi had his security service do so. I could breathe again, at least for the time being. Recently, I received a threat from the Holy Spirit Movement, predecessor of the Lord's Resistance Army in northern Uganda. The Chancery remains vulnerable, and I remain nervous.
>
> The fact that USG employees are endangered has nothing to do with the effectiveness or decision-making of our bureaucracies. Everyone is doing the right thing given resource constraints. The constraints are the problem. If you need an example of real impact, please feel free to use this one. (The solution is to address the security of chanceries around the world—that requires more money than FBO [Foreign Buildings Operations] has.)
>
> I follow your activities with interest and enthusiasm and hope to see you in Kenya sometime. You could do wonderful work here.

I followed up with a letter to Undersecretary for Management Bonnie Cohen. She wrote back that we were considered to be under a "medium" threat of a terrorist attack. Eric Boswell, who signed off on Nairobi's designation as "medium threat," later said:

> I think my response to Ambassador Bushnell was the last piece of paper I signed as assistant secretary for DS. It was on my last

day in the office, and it was "no." It was, "We are sending a team out to look at your situation and we will help you in every way we can but you are not high enough on the scale as a medium threat post to warrant a new embassy." What we didn't say was that nobody was high enough on the scale to warrant a new embassy because there simply wasn't any capital budget for embassy construction.[13]

As I was smarting over my performance appraisal, Haroun Fazul rented a house in the posh suburb of Runga Estates. The landlord remembered that Fazul insisted on an international telephone line.[14] Visitors began to come and go, among them Odeh from the coast, bringing in parts to build the bomb.

In May bin Laden hosted a press conference. "By God's grace, we have formed with many other Islamic groups and organizations in the Islamic world a front, called the International Islamic Front, to do jihad against the Crusaders and Jews. And by God's grace, the men . . . are going to have a successful result in killing Americans and getting rid of them." He predicted the results would be visible in a few weeks.[15] At the time, Ayman al-Zawahiri was sitting next to him, and the two sons of Abdel-Rahman, the Blind Sheikh, were distributing their father's fatwa to the audience.

From prison, the Blind Sheikh communicated to his followers:

Cut off all relations with [the Americans, Christians, and Jews], tear them to pieces, destroy their economies, burn their corporations, destroy their peace, sink their ships, shoot down their planes and kill them on air, sea, and land. And kill them wherever you may find them, ambush them, take them hostage, and destroy their observatories. Kill these infidels. Until they witness your harshness. Fight them, and God will torture them through your hands, and he will disgrace them and make you victorious over them, and the nation of the believers is on the verge of creation, and the rage will go from them. Your brother Omar Abdel-Rahman from inside American prisons.[16]

Two days later, bin Laden offered an interview to CNN reporter John Miller. At the interview, Miller was greeted by Ayman al-

Zawahiri and came away with a distinct impression. As Miller later wrote, "Zawahiri was to Osama bin Laden what Karl Rove is to the White House. I mean, he crafted the message, he called the tunes. Bin Laden seemed to be the inspirational leader, the front guy, you know the guy that they would put out on camera." On camera, bin Laden announced, "I predict a black day for America; a day after which America will never be the same." He continued: "I'm declaring war on the United States. I'm going to attack your country."[17] Dressed to the jihadi nines in camouflage fatigues and a turban, he sat in front of a large map of Africa in the company of two men who would be sent to Nairobi to kill us.

Also in May Dick Clarke was officially named national coordinator for counterterrorism, and FBI director Louis Freeh declared that his highest priority was to prevent, detect, and deter terrorism. Everyone else, government officials included, watched the unfolding of the so-called Monica Lewinsky scandal and the special prosecutor's energetic pursuit of President Clinton. Top Spouse and I went on vacation.

In June a New York City grand jury issued a secret indictment against bin Laden for his actions in Somalia. Richard and I, along with the rest of the world, were oblivious. But they were getting to know bin Laden. Ted Koppel's *Nightline* aired the Miller interview to Americans across the country. Later in the same program, National Security Advisor Sandy Berger commented that bin Laden was "the most dangerous non-state terrorist in the world."[18] In Washington the State Department issued a warning of his threats against Americans, but it did not include U.S. embassies in Africa on the list of addressees. In London the al-Qaeda public affairs guy rush-ordered four hundred additional minutes for bin Laden's NSA-bugged satellite phone.[19] In Dar es Salaam a man named K. K. Mohammed rented a house four miles away from the embassy.[20]

June–August 1998: Nairobi

Richard and I prepared ourselves for July 4 celebrations and summer turnover. I puzzled about how to diplomatically cope with the band that was to accompany President Moi, who had announced he would honor us with his presence. The band, which would strike up the Kenyan national anthem upon the president's arrival and departure, was known for alcohol abuse and disruptive conduct. I would have none of it. Official national day events are seldom happy ones for ambassadors, which were more of a protocol "must" than a celebration. The fun stuff occurs at the community events. Fortunately, we had lots of volunteers to help in the production, and we invited students of the American School of Kenya to sing the Kenyan anthem instead of the band. Problem solved. Moi loved it. The weather was cool and sunny, the turnout was great, and Moi and I were on our best behavior. It was a happy event for the community, the last one we had. Welcoming newcomers and a VIP visit from Treasury Secretary Robert Rubin took up my time for the rest of the month.

August 2

Mohamed Rashed Daoud al-Owhali, a Saudi veteran of the Somalia campaign, arrived in Nairobi on Sunday. I was pulling weeds in the residence garden. Al-Owhali took a taxi to a hotel, checked in, and waited for Fazul to pick him up. They went to Runga Estates where al-Owhali's friend and fellow perpetrator was already waiting. In Dar es Salaam another accomplice had also arrived.

I dug out weeds, transplanted flowers, had popcorn and beer for lunch, and enjoyed a restful afternoon. I had no idea that Iran had recalled its ambassador to Kenya as well as their so-called cultural attachés from Kenya and Tanzania.[21] I was tending my garden.

August 3

Gray winter skies chilled the air as the U.S. mission carried out another day of its obligations during the summer transfer season. A third of Americans at post were either coming in or leaving, and many who stayed in place were serving as "acting" in other positions to fill the gaps. I had lots of "check-in" meetings. Bill Daley was coming to town with a trade delegation, and members of his advance teams had already started working on the details. After conferring with them, I attended an early reception and went home. At the Runga Estates, Fazul and our killers reviewed their plans.

August 4

Fazul took al-Owhali and his partner-in-crime to the embassy to walk through the plan. Al-Owhali was to get the embassy guard to open the drop bar that separated the rear embassy property from the larger shared parking lot. His partner would drive the truck as close to the chancery building as possible and flick the switch.

I spent the day in courtesy calls with newcomers, like the incoming director of USAID. I chaired another planning meeting for Secretary Daley's trip and visited a Kenyan youth club.

August 5

Ayman al-Zawahiri issued a statement calling out the CIA for "rendering" his cohorts in Albania. The CIA had already started disrupting Islamist cells in Macedonia and Bulgaria, handing their Egyptian members over to Egypt for likely torture, imprisonment, and perhaps death. When they learned that al-Zawahiri's Islamic Jihad cell was planning to blow up the U.S. embassy in Tirana, Albania, a joint CIA-Albanian intelligence team swooped in to capture and "render" to Egyptian authorities four of al-Zawahiri's colleagues. After interrogations by the CIA, Egyptians flew them home to be brutally tortured. Al-Zawahiri had just set up the cell, and he took the kidnappings personally. He said in his statement, "We are interested in briefly telling the Americans that their message has been received and that the response, which we hope they will read carefully, is being prepared because, with God's help, we will write it in the language that they understand."[22]

That day I flew to Dadaab near the border with Somalia, one of the largest UN refugee camps in Africa, to "show the flag" and discuss women's security, an issue that would get short shrift unless an ambassador showed up. For the first time ever, Richard had a bad feeling about my safety.

August 6

I had more meetings—about embassy management, American business interests, and International Monetary Fund activities— and more courtesy calls from newcomers. The day ended with a reception hosted by the Dutch ambassador. Al-Owhali and his partner ended the day with phone calls and mental preparation.

August 7

At 4:30 a.m. GMT, the fax machine in bin Laden's London public relations office lit up. For days the office's satellite telephone had been devouring minutes, and now the fax would. Out came a statement signed by the Islamic Army for the Liberation of Holy Places taking credit for bombing two U.S. embassies in East Africa.[23]

In Nairobi I faced another easy day: more meetings with newcomers, a brown bag lunch with summer interns, and a working tea with the German ambassador. But first I had a meeting with the Kenyan minister of commerce about Secretary Daley's visit. The timing of this meeting meant I would skip our weekly country team meeting. Not a bad day and a Friday to boot.

At Runga Estates al-Owhali dressed in faded, baggy jeans, tucked homemade explosive devices into his pants, put a gun in the pocket of his blue jacket, and got into the truck.

I had finished one courtesy call and readied my notes for the meeting with the minister.

Fazul drove out of the walled compound in the lead vehicle. Behind him al-Owhali and his co-martyr-to-be, in the driver's seat, listened to religious poems and chants as they passed through the city's foothills and potholes to their downtown destination. The driver commented that al-Owhali might want to remove his denim jacket for easier access to the explosive devices in his belt, and al-Owhali took the suggestion.[24]

In Dar es Salaam, another attacker said good-bye to his host, K. K. Mohammed, and headed for the U.S. embassy.

10:15 a.m.

Duncan guided my Commerce Department colleagues and me through the rear parking lot to the correct entrance of the Commerce Bank Building. I teased him that he should be holding up the small American flag we flew from the car while on an official government-to-government call. Duncan left us at the door and took the burgundy, fully armored Cadillac with orange-red license plates to fetch a rare photo of President Clinton with President Moi. I was having it framed before presenting it. The minister of commerce and I said a few words to the press and settled in for tea and discussion.

10:28 a.m.

Fazul pulled to the side of the road at the traffic circle on the embassy's corner. He motioned to the driver behind him to keep going and then waited. The driver turned onto the side road, heading against traffic into the parking lot that was surrounded on three sides by the Commerce Bank Building, the Ufundi House, and the U.S. embassy. When the truck stopped at the drop bar, al-Owhali got out and started toward the guard shack. Then he remembered his gun was still in the pocket of his jacket in the truck. Too late. He improvised. He demanded that the guard lift the bar, and when the guard, Joash Okindo, refused, he pulled one of the stun grenades from his belt. Okindo ran, frantically trying to alert the marine on Post One as he did. Al-Owhali threw the grenade. The driver moved the truck parallel to the chancery.

10:30 a.m.

In the minister's office, the noise drew several people to the window. Yards below, al-Owhali decided against suicide and ran. His partner detonated the bomb. Two hundred and thirteen people died instantly; five thousand more were injured.

10:39 a.m.

In Dar es Salaam an al-Qaeda cohort drove his truck of explosives to one of the U.S. embassy's two vehicular gates. It was blocked. He detonated the bomb behind a water tanker. Eleven people were killed and more than eighty injured.

A Few Hours Later

In Washington CIA director George Tenet assured President Clinton, "This one is a slam dunk, Mr. President. There is no doubt that this was an al-Qaeda operation. Both we and the Bureau have plenty of evidence."[25]

In New York Assistant U.S. Attorney Patrick Fitzgerald told a colleague, "Now it begins."[26]

August 8, 1998–September 11, 2001: Nairobi, New York City

Within two days of the attacks, Odeh, the bomb maker from the coast, and al-Owhali, the would-be martyr who changed his mind, were in custody, and the FBI was on the phone to Ali Mohamed. He confirmed that al-Qaeda organized the attack but refused to give the names of the perpetrators. Yes, he had lived in Kenya in 1994 and, yes, he ran front companies for bin Laden there, and, yes, he saw a plan to attack the U.S. embassy in Kenya— but he "discouraged" the cell members from carrying it out.[27] The FBI searched his home a few days later and confiscated his computer. That was it.

Odeh from the coast was caught in Karachi, Pakistan, when he tried to bribe a Pakistani customs agent to ignore his passport photo, which bore no resemblance to the man in front of her. He ultimately ended up in FBI hands. Al-Owhali was picked up after a suspicious desk clerk alerted the Kenyan police. Once in the custody of the FBI, he was only too happy to tell his story.

Having tossed the stun grenade, al-Owhali figured his mission was fulfilled. Staying around would only mean suicide, against the precepts of Islam. As he ran away he was injured in the back. He disposed of the remaining grenades around his belt in a near-by trash can—a rarity in Nairobi—before he sought medical attention. At the hospital, he tried unsuccessfully to flush the bullets and the extra set of keys to the truck padlock down the toilet of a men's room. When that did not work, he left them on the windowsill, where they were later found. He was injured and broke, without travel documents or any familiarity with Nairobi. A good Samaritan taxi driver agreed to take him to the only place al-Owhali knew, the hotel where he had met Fazul on August 2. There he persuaded the clerk to give him a room and lend him money for the taxi and a phone call. Then he contacted his handler in Yemen, who wired him $1,000 and made plans to bring him new documents. Thanks to the desk clerk, the police got to him first.[28]

Among other things, Al-Owhali identified Haroun Fazul from

a videotape and described the person in Pakistan who issued instructions to go to Nairobi. Al-Owhali also disclosed that his operational leader told him, "There are targets inside the U.S. that could be hit but not everything was in place yet."[29] Unfortunately, by the time authorities had this information, al-Owhali's supervisor and the rest of the Nairobi perpetrators were long gone.

The information he gave about his Yemen contact and the phone number he used produced a better outcome—the discovery of a vital communications hub linking bin Laden in remote Afghanistan to his global network.

The man who walked into our embassy in November 1997 to warn of a truck bomb met with the CIA in Dar es Salaam within a week of the bombings and was arrested by Tanzanian authorities.[30] He was charged with participating in the Dar es Salaam attack, and months later he was deported to Egypt, never to be seen again.[31] The United States never asked for his extradition. Nor did U.S. authorities accept Sudan's offer to hand over two other suspected al-Qaeda operatives who had arrived in Khartoum after staying at the same Nairobi hotel as other perpetrators. Instead, they were sent to Pakistan and released.[32]

President Clinton signed a memorandum of notification to the CIA to use force if necessary to eliminate bin Laden. Over the next nine months, Dick Clarke and his CSG would review six plans, but none was implemented, each for a different reason.

On August 20, sixty-six American missiles landed in various training camps in Afghanistan and thirteen missiles hit a pharmaceutical factory in Sudan. None landed on bin Laden, and the factory proved legitimate.[33]

In September the FBI issued Ali Mohamed a subpoena to testify before a grand jury hearing in New York. He did so and planned to flee the country immediately thereafter. Just before he got into a cab to head for the airport, however, he was arrested on a secret "John Doe" warrant. Attorney Patrick Fitzgerald later blamed "the wall" for the difficulty in getting the arrest accomplished.[34] Ultimately Ali Mohamed pled guilty to five charges of conspiracy, received no sentence, and disappeared into the U.S. judicial system. Wadih el-Hage was also arrested in September and sentenced to life imprisonment in a maximum security facility in Florence, Colorado.

By that time Washington had moved on. Near simultaneous bombings of two U.S. embassies on August 7, 1998, provoked no interest in learning about how such an intelligence and security failure could have happened. Admiral Crowe's Accountability Review Board focused narrowly on perimeter security. A member of his board noted, "Despite strong and confirmed suspicions among several members that the ARB was barely scratching at the surface of the real issues—and lacking the kind of conclusive intelligence that the CIA and FBI chose to withhold—the ARB chose to adhere to its narrow mandate."[35]

Congress limited its review of the East Africa bombings to a request that the U.S. Government Accountability Office look into "Combating Terrorism: Issues to Be Resolved to Improve Counterterrorism Operations." The report indicated, "There was no interagency process in place to capture and share lessons learned and that a key part of any lessons learned process is preparing an after-action report (AAR). For counterterrorism operations, which are inherently interagency matters, the lessons learned process should also address the interaction between different agencies to highlight problems for resolution in interagency forums or by top national leadership."[36] No one did a thing. The NSC did not even comment on the report, and the fifteen agencies concerned ignored the recommendation to conduct after-action reviews.

The 9/11 Commission Staff report later noted, "The community had not institutionalized a process for learning from its successes and failures. We did not find any after-action reviews sponsored by the intelligence community after surprise terrorist attacks such as the embassy bombings of August 1998 or the USS Cole attack of October 2000. . . . We did not find an institution or culture that provided a safe outlet for admitting errors and improving procedures"[37]

In December 1999 the White House received a presidential daily briefing (PDB) headlined: "Bin Laden Preparing to Hijack U.S. Aircraft and Other Attacks." Tenet issued a memo declaring war on bin Laden and held a meeting.[38] In the meantime, bin Laden took responsibility of a sort for the bombing.

As New Year's Eve approached, the NSC learned of possible jihadist attacks on the Boston and Los Angeles airports, a hotel in Jordan, and a naval ship in Yemen. National Security Advisor Sandy Berger told his senior interagency group: "We have stopped two sets of attacks planned for the Millennium. You can bet your measly federal paycheck that there are more out there and we have to stem them. I spoke with the President and he wants you all to know"— Berger looked at Janet Reno, Louis Freeh, and George Tenet—"this is it, nothing more important, all assets. We stop this fucker."[39] None of the attacks took place. A shared goal, a demonstration of leadership, and an expectation of accountability worked. Dick Clarke called for an after-action report that produced twenty-nine recommendations, most concerning al-Qaeda sleeper cells in the United States.

Over the following year, the FBI added Osama bin Laden to its 10 Most Wanted List with a $5 million reward for his capture. The CIA issued three warnings to Congress of possible attacks on the United States. The NSC made capture plans that never materialized. "I still to this day," Dick Clarke later wrote, "wonder why it was impossible for the United States to find a competent group of Afghans, Americans, third-country nationals, or some combination, who could locate bin Laden in Afghanistan and kill him."[40]

Michael Scheuer was removed from Alec Station and replaced by someone who continued a poisonous relationship with the FBI. The FBI and the White House continued to mistrust one another, and the NSA continued to refuse raw data of its intercepts to the CIA. As al-Qaeda used its regional communications hub in Yemen to plan an attack on an American ship, NSA listened in but did not report the substance until it was too late.

On October 12, 2000, in the Port of Aden, Yemen, two al-Qaeda suicide bombers detonated a small fiberglass boat filled with explosives next to the missile destroyer, USS *Cole*. They killed seventeen sailors and wounded thirty-nine more. Two months later Dick Clarke asked Condoleezza Rice, national security advisor for the incoming George W. Bush administration, for an urgent meeting to discuss what he at the time called "al Qida" and the U.S. response to the *Cole* attack. He recommended the policy of responding in a "time, place and manner of our own choosing" and urged a discussion of a larger strategy of dealing with al-Qaeda after listing regions of the world affected by its activities. He left off sub-Saharan Africa and North America.[41] The meeting he requested finally happened on September 4, 2001.[42]

On September 11, 2001, al-Qaeda jihadists flew three hijacked planes into the two World Trade Center towers and the Pentagon. Others crashed a fourth plane into the ground in rural Pennsylvania; its target was believed to have been the U.S. Capitol. At least 3,044 people were killed in the attacks. At the insistence of family members, a 9/11 Commission was convened. This is what it said about August 7, 1998. "The tragedy of the embassy bombings provided an opportunity for a full examination across government, of the national security threat that Bin Laden posed. Such an examination could have made clear to all that issues were at stake that were much larger than the domestic politics of the moment."[43]

3

SO WHAT?

12

THE OUTCOMES

2005–2008: Falls Church, Virginia

The second term of George W. Bush coincided with his continuing global war on terrorism—our "long war"—and my retirement. I transitioned from full-time employment to self-employment while he shifted downward in opinion polls. The war in Iraq was escalating, with the invasion proving to be expensive and ill-conceived. In Afghanistan, Americans and NATO allies kept the Taliban at bay as elections took place. President Bush took heat for misleading the public about Iraqi weapons of mass destruction and for the administration's response to the devastation of Hurricane Katrina, which left in its wake more than 1,800 dead and billions of dollars in damages. Our vocabulary grew to include words like "enhanced interrogations," "code orange," and "WikiLeaks" as the war against a tactic called "terrorism" proved to be more than the promised cakewalk. Prisoner abuse at Abu Ghraib in Iraq and surveillance activities in the American homeland sparked conversations about the toll that national security was taking on civil liberties and traditional values. The trillion-dollar cost of the conflicts sparked concerns about the deficit. The Congress passed "No Child Left Behind" education legislation while it debated immigration reform and privatizing Social Security. The year 2008 brought the worst financial crisis since the Depression. People saw their stock portfolios and retirement savings plummet and watched helplessly as Congress passed the administration's initiatives to use billions of taxpayer dollars to bail out the financial industry that caused the crisis.

The mood of the country matched mine as my research into August 7 produced not just a sad story but a keen sense of betrayal. The 9/11 Commission had noted the tragedy of ignoring issues at stake that were larger than domestic politics—e.g., the Clinton sex scandal—but it did not clarify what those issues were. I did.

Strategic and tactical failures within our intelligence agencies and the FBI to discern bid Laden's intentions, given information available to them at the time.

Refusal among government agencies and officials to share vital information with those who needed it to mitigate or prevent al-Qaeda attacks, in this case the State Department and U.S. ambassadors charged with the responsibility of keeping American citizens safe.

Dismissal and degradation of anyone who challenged group think or Washington policies.

Unchecked Washington-based assumptions and attitudes— this time concerning events and leaders in East Africa—that blinded policy makers to realities and opportunities at the cost of hundreds of lives.

Disinterest of political leaders, political appointees, and senior career officials in placing their responsibility to protect civilian employees overseas above their personal, policy, and budget agendas.

Reliance on a secretive, insular, and apparently dysfunctional National Security Council coordinating group that was constantly planning covert and military activities as the only means to control and stop bin Laden from harming civilians.

Serious tactical mistakes. The information found on el-Hage's computer about al-Qaeda operatives in Mombasa, Kenya, was ignored. It revealed "engineers" who would arrive imminently to help the cell prepare for the "big battle" and "that we may go underground for a while."

Mistakes were made in vetting others, starting with the CIA's asset in Sudan who said the embassy was under threat and causing the removal of American eyes and ears from Khartoum

The FBI's naïve faith in Ali Mohamed, enabling him to plan our deaths as he openly discussed his links to radical jihadist activities and bin Laden. A former agent who worked in the FBI's New York office later wrote, "There is zero doubt if Ali Mohamed had been properly vetted, his inside knowledge of the embassy-bombing plot, coupled with the intel the Bureau had, could have interdicted that event."[1] As to the walk-in who warned us about an attack, he was the real thing, not a flake.

A former CIA employee wrote, "CIA's Counterterrorism Center knew there had been an intelligence failure. There were so many indicators that an attack was in the works; the dismissed walk-in was only an important one of them. The pre-attack pattern of activity was documented thoroughly, and it would serve as an accurate template to predict later attacks."[2] But the sad fact was that the CIA's Office of the Inspector General did not get around to reviewing the agency's pre-9/11 performance until 2005. Then it concluded that "the agency and its officers did not discharge its responsibilities in a satisfactory manner."[3] What does that mean? I wondered.

A group of former national security officials studied the East Africa bombings as a case study in dissent. They underscored "the chronic challenges the U.S. government faces in fostering responsibility, leadership, and 'ownership' of problems among officials in a culture where hierarchy, bureaucracy, and conformity can rob individuals of the incentive to accept responsibility for policy outcomes."[4] Their conclusions changed nothing.

Eric Boswell, head of Diplomatic Security in the mid-1990s, revealed in his oral history, "I think all of us in DS knew that something like Nairobi and Dar would happen at some point. We didn't know it would be Osama bin Laden and we didn't know it would be Nairobi, but we knew that particular hammer was going to fall somewhere because we were just so vulnerable in so many places."[5] But no one did anything.

I accepted the mistakes that had occurred before we were blown up. I understood the dynamics of the national security interagency, and I knew that Washington's political culture did not tolerate pushback from career types requesting funds adequate to run an international organization safely and effectively. I did not understand, or accept, the government's indifference after the bombing to what needed changing in order to prevent al-Qaeda from killing more of us. The embassy bombings were so little valued—"only" twelve Americans died and "stuff" happens—we did not warrant spending the time to learn something. Was there something else I could have done? Would anything have been different had I been a man? I struggled with "commander's guilt" and eventually backed away from futile questions.

Instead, I got up from the desk and got out of the house. I found work. Sometimes I volunteered and sometimes I got paid. I laid bathroom tiles for a general contractor friend and found myself grouting the floor as a Salvadoran man primed the wall on a nearby ladder. He commented on my conversational Spanish and, looking up from the floor, I explained that I had served as U.S. ambassador to Guatemala. "Ah," he said amiably, "my mother says that it is good to always keep on working." His mother was right. I volunteered to teach literacy to a Pakistani woman who had for years managed a car and a job without knowing how to read.

I learned to train fostered rescue collies to walk on a lead so they would be ready for permanent adoption. "Throw your shoulders back," instructed the dog expert. "Thrust your chest out and declare authoritatively *my walk*." That attitude worked for my third age transition in general.

I worked with a clinical social worker to diminish my posttraumatic stress and worked with Richard to stay in good physical shape. I knitted and read, and I allowed time, life, community, and family to nudge me away from anger. I learned new things. Three years on the board of the Oklahoma City National Memorial Museum taught me how members of a stricken community could turn an act of terrorism into a meaningful opportunity, in this case to address violence. I began speaking publicly about what happened in Rwanda and Nairobi, and over time I trained myself to say what I really thought. I reexamined my experiences through a prism of "management" and "leadership."

Peter Drucker, a leading management guru, has written that management is "doing things right" and leadership is "doing the right thing."[6] When we are managing, we are bringing order, consistency, and control to organizations. When we are leading, we are bringing value, direction, and change to organizations. In Washington, presidents have long political agendas and a four-year time frame to do things right. Political officials need others to manage so they can get their guy and their political platform either reelected or historically well regarded. President Woodrow Wilson "fathered" public administration for just that purpose.

It was always assumed that the political appointees and their senior career colleagues would provide the leadership. I challenge that assumption. In my experiences, senior career people managed all the way up the chain—"doing things right"—to impress political officials who were themselves focused on advancing their own policy agendas. Leadership—"doing the right thing"—was apparent overseas but not in Washington. After all, every ambassador has a letter from the president spelling out chief of mission responsibilities, explaining bureaucratic obligations to present a mission program plan complete with budget implications, and directing a country team of ambitious professionals who are overseas to get things done.

I thought about the tensions between "doing things right" and "doing the right thing" in the context of two crucible events, the Rwanda genocide and the Nairobi attack. I started talking to federal audiences about my lessons learned and later wrote in the *Foreign Service Journal*. My conclusions:

Leadership is not about you. I already knew before Nairobi that practicing leadership was more than showing up and issuing brilliant commands. But soon after the bombing, that lesson—leadership is not about you—became particularly stark. A bereaved family changed an earlier decision to forgo a memorial service and expected me to speak when they suddenly decided to hold an event. I was burned out from funerals, memorial services, anger, and sadness. Physically and emotionally exhausted, I actually felt a stab of resentment. Then, "Whack! This is not about me."

During the Rwanda genocide, in contrast, it was all about us. Washington policy makers acknowledged that we were the "world leader" in the international arena, but when it came to addressing this crisis, practicing leadership was the last thing we did. We spent almost all of our time talking about us—what the U.S. government could/should/would not do, instead of harnessing our considerable brainpower to come up with innovative ways of halting a genocide absent military boots on the ground—if such a thing were possible.

The best strategies come from asking good questions and listening, especially to dissent. I learned the importance of good questions while assisting in evacuations and leading crisis task forces in the Africa Bureau. When we were bombed, I had no idea what people needed in order to survive at ground zero. I was in the building next door and then at our crisis control center. The survivors who turned themselves into first responders were the ones with the information. My job was to understand their reality and represent their needs. That part never stopped over the next ten months. To move forward, I needed to get accurate information and honest feedback. No one seemed to have a problem with that, and as a result we avoided important mistakes. The physical memorial to honor the dead and the resilience of the living in downtown Nairobi is there because someone said, "You can't do that."

Could we have picked up warning signs of a pending genocide in Rwanda had we asked good questions and listened? Perhaps. For my part, I was delivering démarches in the country until two weeks before the slaughter began, and I can attest that we and other foreign governments were talking, not listening.

Grow teams and develop trust through meaningful goals. When violence erupted in the streets of the Rwandan capital, Kigali, the interagency crisis team in Washington worked night and day to help American citizens leave Rwanda safely. We had concrete goals, realistic evacuation strategies designed by the people on the ground, and a worldwide team. Once Americans were out and U.S. interest evaporated, we morphed into a cantankerous policy working group without goals, direction, or authority. As hundreds of thousands of people died, we tasked one another with reports.

In Nairobi before the bombing, the country team set challenging goals to address corruption and promote peaceful presidential elections in 1997. The experience of interagency and Kenyan and American work teams pursuing those goals together literally saved lives on August 7 and 8 when we were on our own. Over the following days, weeks, and months, we understood in our heads, hearts and guts what needed to be done, but it was important to articulate it. Commitment and shared understanding of our goals made it easier to incorporate the help of newcomers and kept us focused during some very challenging times.

Nurture a culture of leadership and mind your leadership business with integrity. My leadership business was to transparently direct and effectively multitask our way forward. If I got my job right—from getting the resources to overseeing the many moving parts of our reconstruction, policy, and law enforcement efforts—everyone else did, too. Decisions got pushed down, and leadership emerged at every level. I could not heal a wounded community, but I could help create an environment in which healing was possible. That was a good part of my business. So was visibility. I could not take away anyone's anger or loss, but I could accompany. That meant showing up. Offering feedback about what we were accomplishing and celebrating milestones helped. When I was in leadership mode, I was thinking strategically, acting intentionally, and behaving with the integrity people demanded. Nothing just happened.

During the Rwanda genocide, if someone had put a gun to my head demanding to know the leader of our interagency community and chief policy decision maker, I would have been shot. Neither the goals nor the leaders were apparent, and it took twenty years to determine exactly who had initiated the directive to withdraw the peacekeepers from Kigali—it was Dick Clarke.[7] The advantage of secretive decision making and diffused or absent leadership is the absence of accountability. It would not have worked in healing a community or achieving visible success.

Take care of your people, and the rest will take care of itself. This advice, from a former boss and mentor at the Foreign Service Institute, popped into my head twenty-four hours after the attack. It became my mantra and leadership philosophy. It was not easy. It meant addressing poor performance and people suffering PTSD, challenging archaic department traditions and regulations, and making waves to create change. Ambassador Don Leidel was right on the mark with his advice. We overcame extraordinary challenges, and we did it together.

I saw what can happen when we do not take care of people, in particular the people we employ locally, when I returned to Rwanda shortly after the killing had stopped. As I spoke at a memorial service for our fallen Rwandan colleagues, I became keenly aware of a sense of betrayal. We had barred all Rwandan citizens from our evacuating diplomatic convoys in order to ensure safe passage for U.S. passport holders. I now understood their reaction.

Take care of yourself. My body needed rest and exercise, my mind needed distraction, and my spirit needed healing. I was a good role model, intentionally taking time out and demanding that others do so as well. Stiff upper lips, overworking, and sleep deprivation could not produce the leadership style of energy and optimism I wanted to convey and nurture. It took discipline.

Persevere. During the early days of the Rwanda genocide, I spoke several times with one of the senior perpetrators, demanding that the killing stop and eventually advising him he would be held personally accountable for his role. He did not listen, and Washington colleagues mocked me for my attempts. But at least I was doing something, and I never regretted the effort. That perpetrator is now serving a life sentence in prison. Rwanda taught me to leave no stone unturned or cage unrattled if I wanted to understand local events or get unpopular decisions made in Washington. My efforts to get attention paid to the security vulnerabilities of our chancery in Nairobi, albeit a failure, allowed me to forgive myself.

We managed in Rwanda. We did things right for us, by removing most peacekeepers from harm, remaining on the sidelines, wasting no treasure, and taking no risks. But a few years later when President Clinton flew to Kigali to apologize, he admitted we had not done the right thing. In the case of our security in Nairobi, colleagues on the management side of the department also did things right. They stayed within budgets by waiving their security regulations, while in Nairobi we were trying to do the right thing by relentlessly demanding attention both before and after the bombing. As I speak about these tensions of headquarters/field and management/leadership, audiences nod their heads with understanding. Sometimes people come up at the end of my speech to whisper: "Thank you for saying what we cannot."

In 2008, on the tenth anniversary of the East Africa bombings, the State Department held a remembrance ceremony. By then Secretary Condoleezza Rice had realigned the Foreign Service personnel system to support military efforts in the global war on terrorism. Foreign Service colleagues were serving in conflict zones in Iraq, Afghanistan, and Pakistan, living in walled compounds under the protection of armed security guards, in places we would have evacuated in other days and regions. In other parts of the world, colleagues worked in fortress-like chanceries, the legacy of Secretary Colin Powell's program of building safely out of downtown areas, and increasingly focused government-to-government discussions on the war on terrorism. Meanwhile, al-Qaeda's influence and tactics spread from Pakistan, Afghanistan, and Iraq through the Arabian Peninsula to North, East, and Central Africa and as far away as Indonesia. There was much to manage.

I participated in a few telephone conversations during the

planning stage of the 2008 commemoration. A person asked if anyone was considering sponsoring a special event to bring together the communities of Nairobi and Dar es Salaam. We had gone our separate ways in the intervening ten years. The conclusion: "Not a good idea. They will think we are going to do something for them and we are not."[8]

2008–2012: Falls Church

President Barack Obama promised hope and change and won the presidency in 2008. Domestic intentions touched a broad range—from the economy, health care, and education to Social Security, energy independence, and climate change. Waiting for his team on the international front were wars in Iraq and Afghanistan and the threat of nuclear weapons in Iran. Like his predecessors, he appointed thousands of people to positions around government, and they surrounded themselves with like-minded folks. Senator Hillary Clinton became secretary of state.

The president was unable to deliver on the promise of bipartisan cooperation, however, and as his policies struggled to become reality, divisiveness in Washington and around the country grew, exacerbated by the crippling effects of the 2008 "Deep Recession." By the 2010 midyear elections, when the Republicans won a majority in the House and Senate, it looked as though Senate Republican leader Mitch McConnell's strategy to make the president a one-term president was working.

Economic recovery was too slow for too many Americans, and too many bodies of American soldiers returned in coffins from Iraq and Afghanistan. By the time bin Laden was killed in 2011, we were spending up to $5 trillion supporting 65,000 troops.[9] Eighteen hundred soldiers had died.[10] Among Afghan, Iraqi, and Pakistani civilians, the number of children, women, and men killed was reaching 1.3 million.[11] The conflicts had deprived another 7.9 million people of their homes, making up almost half of the refugees and internally displaced people in the world.[12] Furthermore, there was no victory in sight. Unrest in Syria was spiraling out of control, and North African countries like Tunisia, Egypt, and Libya were seething with political discontent.

When Osama bin Laden was finally killed in Pakistan, I was relieved that we had one less mass murderer on this earth, but otherwise I was surprisingly unmoved. I was, however, aghast at the amounts of troops, treasure, and casualties it was taking to sustain a war against a centuries-old political tactic of influencing governments by killing civilians.

Additional diplomats and economic development professionals went to support or sustain our armed forces and the elusive goals of the conflicts. One-year unaccompanied (by family) tours had become mandatory for a successful career in the State Department. State dealt with the stress of returnees from dangerous and hardship posts by sending them to the Foreign Service Institute for debriefings. A program dedicated to resilience raised awareness of the need for a shift in culture. The behavior of senior people in those posts came under increasing scrutiny as recognition of the link between leadership, morale, and output became evident.

I kept up my talks about "doing things right" and "doing the right thing" because I wanted to promote leadership in the federal sector and the topic resonated with audiences. After a discussion with a national security interagency group in the spring of 2012, a participant approached me. "I just want you to know that nothing has changed. We are going through exactly the same thing you did in Nairobi. We have been trying to get attention to the vulnerabilities of the compound where we work and live in Benghazi and no one will listen to us. All we get is 'you're not even a real diplomatic mission, so don't even ask.'"

A few months later, on September 11, 2012, Ambassador Chris Stephens, Sean Smith, Tyron Woods, and Glen Doherty died in an assault on the Benghazi compound and its annex. Stephens died of smoke inhalation. I had my first flashback in years: no longer was I in leafy northern Virginia. I am in a smoky stairwell of the Cooperative Bank Building in Nairobi. People are glued to one another moving slowly down one step after another. Then we stop. Someone yells, "Fire!" I think I'm going to die. But at least I will die of smoke inhalation and not burn to death.

The cell memories were vivid, and it took a few hours to shake them. All the time I was keenly aware that I was alive to feel them.

I knew leadership practices were expanding among some ranks and bureaus. Secretary Clinton was even initiating a long-term policy planning process. Had things changed in Diplomatic Security? Yes and no. The Benghazi "special mission compound" was not a diplomatic facility in the formal sense of the word, and it received no protection from the Libyan government. It was a temporary installation that kept getting temporarily approved for a limited number of Americans. Diplomatic Security people, among others, would rotate in and out. Ambassador Stephens was among the visitors on an overnight trip when a large group of violent Islamists broke into the compound, opened the gates, and set fire to the buildings. Stephens and Sean Smith, a communications specialist, took refuge in a "safe room" and died of smoke inhalation. Later, attackers moved on to an annex where two more Americans were killed. Before the smoke cleared, the Republican members of Congress were accusing Susan Rice, our ambassador to the United Nations, of having misled the public with her early statements about the timing and nature of the assault.

The House Committee on Government Oversight and Reform and the Senate Committee on Homeland Security and Governmental Affairs initiated investigations as an Accountability Review Board was convened. Undersecretary Pat Kennedy's testimony at the initial hearings had a familiar ring.

> I have been a Foreign Service officer for nearly forty years. I have served every President from Nixon to Obama. No one is more determined to get this right than the President, the Secretary, and the men and women of the State Department. And nobody will hold us more accountable than we hold ourselves. The men we lost were our friends and colleagues, a cross section of the men and women who put their lives on the line every day in the inherently dangerous work of diplomatic service to our nation.[13]

When the Accountability Review Board, led by former undersecretary of state Tom Pickering and former admiral Mike McMullen, released its findings, I found more echoes of the past:

Systemic failures and leadership and management deficiencies at senior levels within two bureaus of the State Department (the "Department") resulted in a Special Mission security posture that was inadequate for Benghazi and grossly inadequate to deal with the attack that took place.

Security in Benghazi was not recognized and implemented as a "shared responsibility" by the bureaus in Washington charged with supporting the post, resulting in stove-piped discussions and decisions on policy and security.

Overall, the number of Bureau of Diplomatic Security (DS) security staff in Benghazi on the day of the attack and in the months and weeks leading up to it was inadequate, despite repeated requests from Special Mission Benghazi and Embassy Tripoli for additional staffing. Board members found a pervasive realization among personnel who served in Benghazi that the Special Mission was not a high priority for Washington when it came to security-related requests, especially those relating to staffing. The Board found that certain senior State Department officials within two bureaus demonstrated a lack of proactive leadership and management ability in their responses to security concerns posed by Special Mission Benghazi, given the deteriorating threat environment and the lack of reliable host government protection. However, the Board did not find reasonable cause to determine that any individual U.S. government employee breached his or her duty.[14]

Four people were dismissed from their jobs, including Eric Boswell, who had returned from retirement to serve again as head of Diplomatic Security. Pat Kennedy vowed to get things right. Some members of Congress complained that no one at his level or higher would be held accountable.[15]

The NSC, under the leadership of Susan Rice, brought the function of deciding the size of embassies in dangerous places into the White House. Senior and midlevel officials from at least five agencies trooped to the White House every week to discuss the security of U.S. facilities and personnel overseas. "It used to be that State ran foreign policy," a *Washington Post* article quoted a former White House official. "Now, everyone's got a hand in it. Go around the table, and they've all got equities, they've all got personnel out in the field, and all that needs to be managed."[16] State had lost its lead on counterterrorism issues years ago, and now its influence was diminishing even further.

An Independent Panel of Best Practices, recommended by the Accountability Review Board, took another stab at getting things right in the department by reviewing management weaknesses dating to the 1990s. It made forty recommendations in twelve areas. The "clear and overarching recommendation" was the creation of an undersecretary for Diplomatic Security, taking it out of the "management" family.[17] It never happened. The Panel also recommended that State establish a formal "Lessons Learned" process. Management failed to implement this important recommendation. Meanwhile, eight separate committees of Congress held a parade of hearings—thirty-two as of late 2015 costing $20 million—to sustain Benghazi-related investigations. I was asked to be interviewed on Fox News and to testify before a "gotcha" congressional subcommittee and refused both.

As the hype over Benghazi heated up, I wrote for the *New York Times* opinion page an article titled "Our Diplomats Deserve Better." This produced an invitation to join a special committee of Secretary Clinton's advisory Foreign Affairs Policy Board. Our task was to present suggestions for improving risk management in the wake of Benghazi. Our findings—the need for more shared information, more resources, better access to senior leadership in Washington—were to be briefed to Secretary Clinton. I was disappointed by such pedestrian suggestions but was pretty certain nothing would come of the report anyway. I also knew this was my best and biggest chance to speak up about leadership responsibilities and security. For years I had encouraged participants of the federal Women's Leadership Seminar to exercise strategies to be heard in male-dominated cultures. Here was a chance to practice what I was preaching.

I brushed past ghosts as we walked toward the square meeting table under the elegant crystal chandeliers of the huge Benjamin Franklin Room. I had taken the oath of office as ambassador to the Republic of Kenya in front of proud parents, family, and colleagues in this room. I had also attended the memorial service for our dead in this room. I literally felt the past.

I recognized some of the policy board members from President Clinton's administration and bombing days. I knew that our subcommittee chairperson would summarize our deliberations and then ask each member to comment. Secretary Clinton was ill and unable to attend, but other influential people were present. When I was asked for my comments about the report, I responded, "I have been waiting fifteen years to say this." That got attention! "The exercise our group just completed has convinced me again that Washington has smart, caring people who could probably come up with the solutions to keep people safe in very short order, especially since many of them have written past recommendations themselves." I looked at Tom Pickering and Mike Mullen, the Benghazi Accountability Review Board chairmen, when I quoted their concern about systemic failures and leadership and management deficiencies at senior levels. I asked the group at large if anyone thought that "firing" four people really solved the problem. "If not, when are you going to do something?"

I suggested the formation of a discrete, bipartisan group of interested people to discuss the mission and purpose of the State Department and perhaps move toward a new Foreign Service Act. The last one came out in 1980 when big hair was in vogue and we were fighting the Cold War.

When I stopped, our chairman turned to the next person, who said this: "I want to get back to what Jim/John/Whoever said earlier." Such a hackneyed way to disparage me. I almost smiled. As the men in the room continued as if I had never uttered a word, I wondered if I actually had. In the later question-and-answer period, a former member of Congress, Jane Harman, acknowledged my "unflinching candor," but no one said a thing about my ideas. At the break, I shook lots of hands, had pleasant conversations, and everyone went back to business as usual.

The New York Times opinion piece also produced an invitation to speak as "Newsmaker" at the National Press Club. I prepared for days, invited my knitting group and other friends to the sur-

prisingly small room, and spoke before a camera. David Ignatius, a prominent *Washington Post* columnist, had just written,
"How can America shape events in an unstable world without
putting boots on the ground or drones in the air?" and concluded,
"Cabinet members and agency heads look awkwardly at each
other—because nobody has a good idea."[18] Well, I had one, and
I gave it: create an appropriate mission/purpose for the people
who shape events in an unstable world without requiring boots
on the ground or drones in the air; then shape a culture of leadership at the State Department that would enable people to get
the job done. My friends, a few strangers, and knitting classmates gave me warm applause, and we all went back to business as usual. Had I actually spoken?

2013–2016: Falls Church

American toddlers belted out the song "Let it Go" from the movie
Frozen, while parents, relatives, and other adults digested news
about Lance Armstrong doping himself through Tour de France
victories and growing allegations of sexual assault by comedian
Bill Cosby. President Obama worked through his second term.
Colorado legalized marijuana, Russia annexed Crimea, Scotland
narrowly voted to remain within the United Kingdom, and the
United Kingdom narrowly voted to leave the European Union.
Concerns of the rising gap between "haves" and "have nots" in
the United States followed news that the slowly recovering economy was producing fewer jobs than desired. The movement Black
Lives Matter began in protest to the acquittal of George Zimmer-
man in the shooting death of African American teen Trayvon Martin. Millions of Americans signed up for "Obamacare" as a means
to gain health insurance while Republican Party leaders vowed to
get rid of it. We were polarized as a country, we were told. A comprehensive climate change agreement was signed in Paris, and
a Republican majority retained congressional seats in Washington. Another presidential campaign season began, and hearings
into Secretary Clinton's email server morphed into more general
attacks on her from her all-male competition for the presidency.

I returned to obscurity after my brief interventions post-

Benghazi, researching and writing the book. I found common ground with psychiatrists exploring disasters' impacts and post-traumatic stress disorder, PTSD, and I coauthored an article about the leadership–mental health connection. I continued to give leadership talks and training sessions, adding students at Hamilton College in Clinton, New York, to my list of favorite audiences.

An invitation to host a seminar about Africa in 2010 had introduced me to young people seriously interested in leadership at Hamilton. The Arthur C. Levitt family generously funded a subsequent proposal to create a leadership training institute. In 2012 the Levitt Leadership Institute launched a week's training on campus in the last week of winter break and a week in Washington during the first week of spring break. The program was aimed at second-year students with some first-, third-, and fourth-year cohorts to enlighten the discussions. It attracted international students who could not go home over break and women who always formed the majority of participants. All of them wanted to learn "transformational" leadership.

This style of leadership, which was introduced in the 1970s by James McGregor Burns, an authority on leadership studies, highlights shared values and intrinsic rewards to achieve goals, rather than external incentives. Leaders and followers who are focused on achieving a positive goal together and who reinforce one another's sense of purpose may find themselves to have changed for the better as a result of the effort. That, I realized, is what we were practicing in Nairobi after the bombing. No one who made it out of the building alive was offered a pay increase for going back into a deathtrap to save colleagues. We who struggled to pick up the pieces and help one another over the next weeks and months did so in the shared belief that we could do things right by doing the right things. Hamilton students wanted to focus on the latter even though they had learned to excel in the transactional environment of a college classroom. They knew how to get good grades, but they wanted to learn how to better influence.

We added recent Hamilton and Levitt Leadership graduates to the training team to become diverse in age, race, culture, and gender. We practiced teamwork, effective leadership, and good "followership." In the process we addressed issues of gender, race, class, culture, and authority, and we practiced difficult conversations. During the six years I worked with the students, I promoted the word "woman," urging both young women and men to use it when referring to females over eighteen. I, for one, did not consider myself to be a "guy," "girl," or "gal," or even always a "lady." In return, I learned it was a compliment to be called a "badass" and "kickass" woman.

Many participants were interested in social entrepreneurship— enterprises that create social change using business models. All of them committed to engage in a project that would make a measurable and positive change within two years. The results included innovative urban vegetable growing in Utica, New York, a student-led leadership program for first-year students at Hamilton College, three high school leadership programs in Addis Ababa, Ethiopia, and a water-disease prevention program using cell phone technology in the Pokot region of Kenya.

Like generations before them, participants were concerned about where to go next in their lives, how to deal with competing ambitions, and ways to eliminate student debt. The war on terrorism was not a topic. While most could not remember the time before September 11, 2001, when we were not at war, the conflicts in which we were currently engaged were far away and fought by others. Although few noticed, President Obama had actually declared an end to the global war on terror in May 2013, indicating that our military and intelligence communities would focus on specific groups, not a general tactic. There was no victory parade. Some of the victims and family members of the deceased in the Nairobi bombing were finally awarded compensation for al-Qaeda's attack in 1998, but meanwhile the number of jihadist groups around the world increased. Al-Qaeda expanded and splintered into the chaos of the civil war in Syria. The Islamic State in Iraq and Syria (ISIS) won enough territories through brutal conquest to impose a caliphate so cruel that even bin Laden's successor, Ayman al-Zawahiri, denounced it.[19]

The 2016 presidential candidates and the media drilled down on Hillary Clinton's use of a private email server when she was secretary of state. Investigations into Benghazi events had led to tentative conclusions that classified material could possibly have been compromised. The Justice Department investigated, and the opposition party went wild. The Congress held more public hearings, and Republican candidate Donald Trump led his followers in yelling, "Lock her up!"

Richard and I tended our house and large garden in Falls Church, one of our beloved and well-traveled Kenyan cats died, and I kept knitting sweaters. I joined and then left a variety of boards after learning that I was ill-suited to their needs. Someone had warned me that serving on a board was helping someone else's dream come true. What I should have known is that around Washington, the "someone else" would more than likely be a tradition-bound man, usually older, with a dream that had nothing to do with transforming systems that made it so difficult for women to lead and create change. I had spent decades in patriarchal cultures, and I had no intention of spending my third age in it. I did, however, choose to revisit history when the 1994 genocide in Rwanda returned to my life.

A joint initiative of the National Holocaust Museum and the National Security Archive at George Washington University sought and examined declassified official documents and interviewed their authors as part of the commemoration of the twentieth anniversary. The steno pad I used during those months had notes detailed enough to transport me to the meetings in which Defense Department colleagues demanded to know who was the enemy and what was our exit plan, looking smug when we could not come up with the answer. The project culminated in a conference of key players of the day: former government officials, human rights advocates, journalists, and members of the United Nations and peacekeeping operations. Each reported on what he did, and a few participants even read from speeches they had given in the day. Only a few of us were interested in the lessons we had learned. The Americans were among them. I had already spoken of my observations of U.S. actions to other audiences and had no problem describing them again to this one.

I had not met Canadian Gen. Roméo Dallaire before. He had

led the UN peacekeeping force in Rwanda. When at the U.S. government's initiative the Security Council ordered the peacekeepers to leave, Dallaire did the right thing—he refused to remove the troops on whom thousands of Tutsis were depending to save their lives. He and his Ghanaian deputy, Gen. Henry Kwami Anyidoho, were among the few international heroes during the genocide. After a session at which my colleagues Ambassador Joyce Leader, former assistant secretary John Shattuck, and I had spoken frankly about U.S. policy decisions, discussions, and lessons learned, Dallaire approached me. "Pardon my language. I usually don't talk like this in front of ladies. But you, lady, have a pair of balls." I was not sure he was referring to the actions I took in 1994 or the frank conclusions I laid out at the conference. I also wondered what a gender-neutral version of his compliment would be. I still had not discerned another word for kickass or badass woman. Courage, I decided. A woman of courage suited my self-image better than a badass/kickass woman with a pair of balls. I decided to interpret General Dallaire's words as "You, lady, have courage." I was touched.

Later, at dinner, I sat next to a member of the Rwandan government delegation who had also heard Joyce, John, and me speak. I had known Charles Murigande as the diplomatic representative of the Rwanda Popular Front in Washington during the genocide. He remembered that he had tried unsuccessfully to see me, and while I had no memory of ever refusing, I acknowledged I should have met with him. He was unaware of the tense discussions within the Washington interagency group and the late-night phone calls to one of the senior Rwandan government perpetrators. At the end of the dinner, Charles said sincerely, "I am very sorry for the pain the genocide caused you." His words produced a sudden memory: It was a few months after the genocide. I was in the deputy secretary of state's stately conference room sitting between two senior political appointees, across from the president of Rwanda, Pasteur Bizimungu. My colleagues sat silent as he bitterly accused me of partial responsibility for the genocide because I had not listened to the warnings during my final trip before the killing started. I was as stunned by his words as I was at the silence of my policy-making bosses looking on aloofly. I did not recognize how those words had penetrated until I heard Charles voice a message of empathy. As I reconnected with other African associates from the past, I remembered why I had found my years among the people in the sub-Sahara so meaningful, notwithstanding the man-made and natural disasters I had witnessed. They taught me how resilience, reconciliation, and perseverance accompany great tragedies.

In Washington, talks with former colleagues convinced me that a culture of leadership was growing within the State Department. Secretary Clinton had instituted a long-term planning mechanism for diplomacy and development, which her successor, John Kerry, continued. The mandatory leadership training at middle and senior levels that had been in place for a decade was slowly driving change. Colleagues who created a Leadership Roundtable in 2004 pressed for more leadership and additional professional development opportunities. The Bureau of Consular Affairs, charged with adjudicating visas and serving American citizens overseas—a source of revenue for the department—established their own principles. Among them were to model integrity, be self-aware, and foster resilience. Other bureaus followed suit. In 2014 Secretary Kerry had department-wide leadership principles incorporated into the Foreign Affairs Manual, 3FAM 1214. Now they were official.

The Office of the Inspector General made the principles part of its inspection process so that people in positions of leadership could now be evaluated against specific criteria. The Leadership and Management School at the Foreign Service Institute further energized discussions with "webinars" and seminars. Most important, a group called "iLead" became an active force to promote a positive leadership culture by working with the human resources bureau to more closely connect promotions and assignments to leadership principles. The department was finally demonstrating a recognition that good leadership and management have a place in diplomacy and development. The focus on people, including recognition of the rights and needs of LGBTQ members, and its effect on performance and morale moved State into the top five of "The Best Places to Work in Government."

The positive energy within parts of the department could not make up for its continued loss of influence within the national security policy process. The funding told the story. In 2016 the White House requested almost $600 billion for the Defense Department and just a little over $50 billion for all other foreign policy activities, diplomacy and development included. Pundits complained about the growth and overreach of the NSC and the eyebrow-raising number of politically appointed special envoys. The American Academy of Diplomacy, an organization of former ambassadors, reported: "America's diplomacy—the front line of our defenses—is in trouble. Increasing politicization undermines institutional strength; almost no career officers serve in the most senior State positions, while short-term political appointees penetrate ever deeper into the system. The Foreign Service lacks the professional education and standards to meet its current heavy responsibilities and to create its necessary future senior leaders. The Civil Service is mired in an outdated system with limited coherent career mobility."[20]

No one paid much attention because investigations into the emails sent through Clinton's private server continued to dominate the headlines. The public image of the department's senior career managers took another hit as Congress and the media turned the spotlight on Undersecretary Pat Kennedy and his management team (M). Why did they enable Secretary Clinton's request for a private server instead of advising her to stick within the rules? *Diplopundit*, a popular blog in the American diplomatic/development community, echoed concerns.

> If anyone at M . . . was shipped to Timbuktu for bringing up an inconvenient regulation, we'd like to hear about it.
>
> Make no mistake, the perception that the Service had picked a side will have repercussions for the Foreign Service and the State Department. If there is an HRC White House, we may see old familiar faces come back, or those still in Foggy Bottom may stay on and on and just never leave like Hotel California.
>
> But if there is a Trump or a Whoever GOP White House, we imagine the top ranks, and who knows how many levels down

the bureaus will be slashed gleefully by the incoming administration. And it will not be by accident.[21]

Friends of the Foreign Service worried, leaders in Congress held
more hearings, and the American public witnessed the spectacle
of the 2016 presidential campaign. Meanwhile, the no-longer-war-
but-conflicts-against-Muslim-terrorist-groups continued unabated.
We were still fighting in Afghanistan, using drone warfare in Pakistan, Somalia, and Yemen, engaged in the anti-isis campaign in
Iraq and Syria, and "advising" efforts to counter Islamist groups
in Cameroon, Mali, Nigeria, and Uganda.[22] Syria had degenerated
into a proxy war between Russia supporting President Assad, Iran
assisting Shia militias, and the Gulf States backing the Sunni rebels, with sometime and selective help from the United States. Casualties among Syrians reached 470,000 dead, 1.9 million injured,
and 45 percent of the population displaced from their homes.[23]

The direct costs of the war on terrorism were significant. By
2016, the United States had lost almost 7,000 service members
and around 3,000 civilians for a war costing more than $4 trillion
and counting.[24] We were deploying and redeploying a volunteer
force of men and women who returned to find the Department of
Veterans Affairs woefully unable to meet their health and other
needs. Leaks of nsa documents by contractor Edward Snowden
revealed the extent of government snooping on private citizens,
and another debate about constitutional and civil rights flared
briefly. Yes, we were safer from terrorist attacks. Cooperation up,
down, and around the intelligence and law enforcement communities helped to keep the number of Americans killed by jihadists in the United States since 9/11 to less than two hundred.[25]
The chances of winning the lottery in the United States were
better than becoming a victim of Islamist terrorism. But Americans were still afraid, and the attacks in Boston, San Bernardino,
Orlando, and New York fueled those fears. Trust in government
fell to historically low levels.[26]

While presidential candidates and the media howled about
threats to the Americans, no one looked at the world map and
noticed that most terrorist activities were taking place in Iraq,

Afghanistan, Pakistan, Syria, the Horn of Africa, and Nigeria, perpetrated by only a few groups. That did not mitigate the tragedies these murderers imposed. Since 2002, Kenyans had endured a hotel bombing, a missile attack on a commercial airplane, assaults at an urban mall, raids on small towns and villages, a variety of grenade and explosive incidents, and an attack on a university that left 147 students dead. But none of the candidates in the U.S. presidential campaign spoke about human security, only national security. Nor did any of them speak of the tragedies the United States and various allied forces were inflicting on civilians in Iraq, Pakistan, and Afghanistan.

When Gen. Stanley McChrystal took command of the mission in Afghanistan in 2009, he said, "I believe the perception caused by civilian casualties is one of the most dangerous enemies we face."[27] He was proved right. Islamist-inspired terrorist organizations grew from thirteen to thirty-seven between 2001 and 2016, while overall membership in all groups tripled.[28]

Europe fared better than other regions in the number of attacks it had experienced, most of them perpetrated by homegrown terrorists. But few in the West would take comfort. The consistency of terrorist bombings in urban areas and capitals made it difficult to believe that the war on terrorism was headed for victory. Lurid media reports and images from England, Belgium, France, Turkey, and Germany nurtured panic and anxiety. So did the influx of refugees.

More than a million migrated from their homes into Europe in 2015.[29] Within the first few weeks of 2016, at least 80,000 more refugees joined them, many fleeing by boat.[30] The region had not experienced this number of refugees since World War II, and some countries began to designate themselves "no go" zones. Anti-immigrant politicians with nationalist and populist right-wing agendas started to get voters' attention.

In the United States, Donald Trump promised to ban the travel of Muslims into this country and to build a wall on the Mexican border to be paid for by the Mexicans. No one talked about ending terrorism any time soon. Few talked about the toll it was taking on our armed services members, and even fewer talked about ways other than armed combat to confront it. In a 2016 opinion piece, the co-chairmen of the 9/11 Commission, Tom Kean and Lee Hamilton, did:

> The approach of the past 15 years, dominated by military counterterrorism operations, will not suffice. In the 9/11 Commission Report, we warned that terrorism would menace Americans and American interests long after Osama bin Laden and his cohorts are killed or captured. We stressed that our strategy must match our means to two ends: dismantling the al-Qaeda network and prevailing in the longer term over the ideology that gives rise to Islamist terrorism. We have yet to match our military might with an equal focus on the ideological aspects of the struggle. Until we do, this threat will not diminish.[31]

In November 2016 Donald Trump won enough electoral votes to become president. He became the fourth to cope with the jihadist terrorism.

EPILOGUE

2017: Arlington, Virginia

In January Donald J. Trump was inaugurated the forty-fifth president of the United States. He vowed to stop "carnage" in America, give the country back to the forgotten people, and put America first. To help he had a Republican majority in both houses of Congress. The budget he proposed bulked up the Defense Department, created a wall along the border with Mexico, left Medicare and Social Security alone, assuaging the taxpayer by "deconstructing" the rest of the federal government and increasing the national debt. Efforts to repeal and replace the Affordable Care Act, aka Obamacare, began immediately and floundered. The Congress then turned to tax reforms. The president's tweets on social media, which ranged in topics from North Korea and the nuclear agreement with Iran to personal taunts and insults, flummoxed policy makers, outraged many Americans, and reportedly delighted his base. The investigation into Russian meddling in the 2016 campaign resulted in legal indictments against former Trump campaign advisors. Two Republican senators and many in civil society and the media wondered aloud if the president was fit for office. A poll revealed "a starkly pessimistic view of U.S. politics, widespread distrust of the nation's political leaders and their ability to compromise, and an erosion of pride in the way democracy works in America."[1]

Americans reacted in horror to news of the violence at a white nationalist rally in Charlottesville, Virginia, in August. Also in

August, we celebrated the Great American Eclipse. In September we shuddered at the strength of hurricanes in Texas, Florida, Puerto Rico, and the Virgin Islands and watched with admiration the resilience of local communities confronting utter devastation. In October we turned our concerns to wildfires in California. We also recoiled in shock at a mass shooting when a man aimed military weaponry from a hotel window in Las Vegas into a crowd of 22,000 people attending a country music concert. He killed 58 as they tried to flee and wounded at least 500 more. In November we learned that another man had opened fire in a rural church in Texas, killing 26. Neither gunman was Muslim, so the events turned into quickly smothered debates about gun control and alarm at the president's tolerance of right-wing fringe groups. A genuine homegrown jihadist attack did take place in October, when a heavily bearded immigrant bent on murder careened down a New York City bicycle path in a rented truck, killing eight people and badly wounding twelve others before he was caught. The killer said that he represented isis, and the president immediately declared he should get the death penalty.

North Korea tested missiles; Catalonia tried to leave Spain; England tried to implement Brexit; and Cuba was accused of using sonic devices to attack American diplomats. A Hollywood mogul's decades of sexual assaults on women provoked the hashtag #MeToo, to which women around the world responded, ending the silence about hostile workplaces.

The war on jihadist terrorism continued. President Trump explained his view before a Polish audience:

> This continent no longer confronts the specter of communism. But today we're in the West, and we have to say there are dire threats to our security and to our way of life. You see there are threats. We are confronted by another oppressive ideology— one that seeks to export terrorism and extremism all around the globe. America and Europe have suffered one terror attack after another. We're going to get it to stop. . . . We are fighting hard against radical Islamic terrorism, and we will prevail. We cannot accept those who reject our values and who use hatred to justify violence against the innocent.[2]

To pay for the war and the strategies of his predecessors, President Trump requested more than $600 billion for the Defense Department and slashed by a third the budgets of the people who manage diplomacy, eradicate poverty, provide disaster relief, nation-build alongside military colleagues in conflict zones, adjudicate visas, and take care of all Americans and their business interests overseas. Congress restored some of the funding to international affairs but increased defense spending even more.

By the time the new administration was shaking up our world, Richard and I had already moved into new space. We had each celebrated another "decade" birthday, relatives who gathered at our spacious single-family home in Falls Church, Virginia, had aged, and children had grown and started their own families. Our fabulous house became too isolated and our drop-dead-gorgeous garden too time-consuming. We were ready for a less suburban environment and a place within walking distance of a Metro stop. We leased an apartment on the top floor of a large building next to Arlington Cemetery, overlooking the Iwo Jima Memorial, the Potomac River, and Washington DC.

The move made a significant difference. I left behind the books, memoirs, testimonies, and press statements from protagonists and investigators of 9/11. I finished writing this book, and our last beloved Kenyan cat died two days later. Saba and her brother, Sam, came into our lives as healing cats. Nineteen years and six moves later, she clearly considered her work to be done. I did not find closure from completing the narrative, but I did find meaning and perspective.

As I look down on the enormous statue of U.S. Marines planting our flag in Iwo Jima soil, I think of the flag we placed in the Athi Plains near the Nairobi Wildlife Park. Richard and I walk the hilly parts of Arlington Cemetery under canopies of old oaks. I wonder about the stories of people from past wars, especially the African Americans whose grave markers indicate only their military troop affiliation and date of death, or simply "citizen" or "civilian" in Section 27. What were their stories? How did they overcome betrayal and survive, hopefully thrive? On the last part of our walk, we go by the marker commemorating those who died in Kenya and Tanzania on August 7, 1998. We usually do not go up to it, but we do check on how well "our tree," the tulip poplar, is doing; it is almost twenty years old.

The graves of those who have died in the war on terrorism are in another part of the sprawling cemetery. It is a different experience to walk in that part of our military graveyard. The trees are still young, and so is the grief of many visitors.

I find it ironically fitting that our marker is so far away from those graves. After all, by the time President Bush declared war on al-Qaeda's tactics in 2001, vowing to find, stop, and defeat every terrorist group within global reach, we had already been casualties of the war Osama bin Laden announced in his 1996 "Declaration of War against the Americans Occupying the Land of the Two Holy Places." The Foreign Service is the first line of defense, so we got hit first.

What has changed after twenty years? Are we close to winning—finding, stopping, and defeating every terrorist group? How is the military strategy working? As the ambassador bin Laden targeted because I was a woman whose death would generate more press, I raised six issues I wanted addressed back then. Here is my take on them twenty years later.

Refusal to share information with the people who need it to keep others safe. Information sharing has greatly improved, according to many counterterrorist practitioners. Government agencies and personnel exchange vital data and threat analyses far more freely and effectively than before. National and local task forces have thwarted ninety-seven plots since 2001.[3] Kudos! What remains unclear, even hidden, is the impact of Defense Department activities: estimates of combatant deaths, civilian casualties, or even what eight hundred U.S. troops are doing in the Lake Chad area of Africa. Members of Congress, seemingly inured to the cost of the war, its contributions to the deficit, and its impact on civilians, started asking questions in 2017 when a Navy SEAL died in Yemen, another in Somalia, and four soldiers were killed in Niger. Some members suggested reauthorization hearings on the 2001 legislation that sanctioned military operations against terrorist groups. That would encourage the generals, current and former, in the Defense Department and the White House to explain who is the enemy and what, if any, is the exit strategy. These were the same questions my defense colleagues asked during the 1994 genocide. The administration argues that a new law is unnecessary.[4] The president has already decided to send more troops to Afghanistan.

The dismissal and degradation of people who challenge policy. One thousand Foreign Service officers signed a memo warning the incoming Trump administration that refugee bans and visa suspensions from seven Muslim-majority nations would betray our values, alienate those countries, and make America less safe. The White House spokesman had only one thing to say. "These career bureaucrats have a problem with it? I think they should either get with the program or they can go."[5] Scientists at the Environmental Protection Agency and other government departments around town have been gagged. Trump's disparaging tweets and off-handed slurs became so frequent that the *New York Times* started counting the "People, Places, and Things Donald Trump Has Insulted on Twitter: The Complete List."[6]

Indifference among elected and senior officials to placing the security of civilians overseas ahead of their agendas. The current administration is not just indifferent to civilian employees. It is actively sabotaging many of them. The State Department, along with the Departments of Education, Energy, and the Interior, are headed by appointees who seek to "deconstruct" them. That is a word I use to describe unraveling my knitting. Unlike the automatic "reconstruction" I perform on my knitting in short order, these appointees show no interest in achieving anything constructive for the organizations they lead. At the State Department, hiring has been frozen, hundreds of positions remain unfilled, promotions have been cut in half, and retirement buy-outs to encourage folks to leave have been put in place. Policy priorities have evaporated, and foreign governments' complaints that "there is no there there" become louder. Overseas, colleagues carry on with policies difficult to explain and futures difficult to anticipate. Fortunately, Ambassador Barbara Stevenson, president of the American Foreign Service Association, and her team are connecting with members of Congress and exhorting leadership from their Foreign Service colleagues, active and retired. They are doing the right thing by pressing for attention and resources. When the Republican chairman of the Senate Appropriations Subcommittee on the State Department and Foreign Operations looked at Secretary Rex Tillerson's proposed budget, he concluded it could cause more Benghazi-like situations.[7] In other words, the administration's budget request put thousands of civilians serving their country overseas needlessly at risk. Congress did increase the funding that one hopes will prove adequate to keep people safe. It certainly is not enough to position State and USAID to bring about the strategies and outcomes we need to reduce threats from jihadists.

Unchecked Washington assumptions and attitudes that ultimately cost lives. In his speech in 2017 to the Polish people, Trump implied that the threat of radical Islam is akin to the Communist threat of the past, and he assumed that the United States will confront the threats and the ideology and win. He implied that we have a right to kill people who reject our values and assumed that only they use hatred to justify violence against the innocent. The president's actions in giving his generals more money and latitude assumes that sending more treasure and troops to confront ISIS in Syria and Iraq, the Taliban in Afghanistan and Pakistan, and a variety of nasty groups around Africa will decrease the risk of terrorist attacks in the United States.

The Cato Institute, among other think tanks, disagrees: "The lessons from the War on Terror indicate that it is time for the United States to take a different approach. Policymakers need to acknowledge that although terrorism is a serious concern, it represents only a modest security threat to the American homeland. Further, the United States should abandon the use of military intervention and nation building in the War on Terror. Instead, the United States should push regional partners to confront terrorist groups abroad, while the U.S. returns to an emphasis on the intelligence and law enforcement paradigm for combating the threat against the American homeland."[8]

In the 1990s Washington assumed that bin Laden would not strike in East Africa because it was a backwater. Now Washington assumes it can transform the Middle East and parts of Africa through military means without blowback. Washington assumptions in the face of evidence to the contrary have literally been the death of us.

The reliance on secret, insular groups that considered only military and covert actions to control and stop al-Qaeda. The *Daily Beast* observed in 2016 that it is unprecedented in American military history to entrust a single command, Special Operations Command (socom) and its commandos, trainers, and advisors, with spearheading and orchestrating the war against isis along with other conflicts. And this, the article said, is only part of a larger secretive effort by "shadow warriors" to address instabilities and crises when and where American vital interests are at stake.[9] It used to be that American diplomats did that without guns.

Andrew Bacevich, a military historian, agrees that the war has largely been delegated to an all-volunteer military force (avf), which he likened to the French Foreign Legion. "Ours is like an imperial army," he writes. "Through hard-won experience it has acquired—in Afghanistan and Iraq—and continues to acquire the wherewithal appropriate to the sort of punitive expeditions and constabulary obligations that the management of an empire entails. . . . Whatever its other merits, the present-day professionalized force is not conducive to this civil-military intimacy. Indeed, to the extent that the members of the avf see themselves as professionals—members of a warrior caste adhering to their own distinctive code—they have little interest in nurturing a close relationship with civil society."[10]

At the State Department, Secretary Rex Tillerson kept his policy discussions limited to a small group of political appointees while he pushed career professionals with knowledge and experience out the door. At the White House, the president claims that when it comes to foreign policy, "The one that matters is me. I'm the only one that matters because when it comes to it, that's what the policy is going to be."[11] The former generals who are now the president's chief of staff, national security advisor, and secretary of defense have shown little interest in any public analysis of the costs/benefits of our current war strategy, which relies primarily on armed interventions.

Strategic and tactical failures. In 2004 Osama bin Laden commented on his own strategy. "All that we have to do is to send two mujahedeen to the furthest point east to raise a piece of cloth on which is written al-Qaeda, in order to make generals race there to cause America to suffer human, economic, and political losses without their achieving anything of note other than some benefits for their private corporations."[12] Seven years later, as the United States continued doing just that, the National Consortium for the Study of Terrorism and Responses to Terrorism concluded that not only was the United States not achieving outright success by its own measures but it was arguably empowering its enemy. Both Arab and western publics shared negative views about U.S. conduct, although their media offered different causes of the conflict and conflicting ideas of success and failure. The Arab public disparaged the perceived overreaction and the attempt to undermine Islam in order to exert U.S. hegemony over large parts of the Islamic world. In the West, people criticized the tendency toward unilateralism and denounced human rights violations. The western media argued that America's military project led to a degradation of power, loss of international standing, and betrayal of the standards the United States wished to import to other countries. The Arab press highlighted misdirected power and faulted decisions to choose military responses over peaceful options to accomplish social and political change.[13]

In 2016 an Army War College study used a statistical model to measure the impact of money spent and troops dispatched. It showed that for every additional billion dollars spent and additional thousand American troops sent to fight, the number of terror attacks worldwide increased by 19. Countries the United States invaded had 143 more terror attacks per year than countries the United States did not invade. Similarly, countries in which the United States conducted drone strikes suffered 395 more terror attacks per year than those where the United States did not. Results showed that the more money spent and soldiers sent, the worse the situation became.[14]

A year later, the Bipartisan Policy Center initiated a task force on "Defeating Terrorists Not Terrorism," co-chaired by Tom Kean and Lee Hamilton of 9/11 Commission fame. It reported that despite tactical successes on the battlefield, it is hard to conclude that we are winning. We have pummeled the terrorists, but we have not defeated their ideas, which still remain attractive to many, including Muslims in the West. Thousands of foreign fighters from across the world responded to the ISIS call for jihadists in 2014. By 2017, even as the caliphate lost territory, ISIS-inspired homegrown terrorists conducted attacks in Europe and the United States. As long as jihadists can replenish their ranks as fast as we can take them off the battlefield, the threat will persist. The Council committed itself to pursuing important questions: What role does ideology, as opposed to political, social, or economic grievances, play in driving people to terrorism? What is the relationship between Islamist terrorism and other strains of Islamist thinking? Can the United States and other non-Muslim actors meaningfully influence cultural and religious currents in the Islamic world? Which Muslim partners are most credible and effective in reducing the appeal of jihadism?[15]

I would add more questions: What contributions do we need from USAID, Foreign Service, and other representatives overseas to confront jihadist influences, and what resources do they need to accomplish the task?

Domestically, what strategies do we have to strengthen resilience, build bridges, and assist our communities so we can better cope with mass violence when it happens in any form?

In the long term, how does the United States rebuild its reputation for promoting peace, prosperity, and other benefits for the worldwide community and not just for ourselves?

I grew up in Germany, France, Pakistan, and Iran, when "America First" meant we would be among the first to feed the hungry, as we did in blockaded Berlin and many other places. We would be the first to launch a "Kennedy Air Lift" that brought young Kenyan men (including Barack Obama's father) to American universities so a new nation would have a larger cadre of educated people. We would be the first to urge volunteers of all ages to join a Peace Corps to show that Americans are as interested in learning from as they are in contributing to the lives of impoverished people around the world. In Senegal, Kenya, and Guatemala, we were among the first within the diplomatic communities to initiate projects to encourage regional peacekeeping, stem government corruption, take on disasters, and enhance women's lives. Our strength came from practicing leadership.

In the short term, we appear condemned to live with the policies of a different America. There is the strategy to confront jihadist terrorists through military might alone and to do away with diplomats and development professionals. Nothing in history is predetermined, however, and every problem presents a leadership opportunity.

I end my talks with graduate students in the international relations and national security fields with a smile even as I recount the unfinished business my generation is leaving young people. The list of what needs doing is meaningful and compelling, and it is not too early to start doing something. Go craft smart policies to address Muslim alienation in western countries. Start researching how to address the terror of mass shootings in our own country. Design the reconstruction of the State Department and USAID with clear missions and cultures of leadership. Strengthen the authorities of ambassadors along with the support and development of professional staff. The list goes on.

"Over to you. Let me know if you need help," I tell them. Twenty years ago, a rattling teacup signaled a deep peril. And then I had to take charge. Not anymore. I happily give to others the opportunity of making things happen to improve our global world. I have an afghan to knit for Richard, family and communities to enjoy, and a story to tell.

NOTES

1. The Bombing

1. *U.S. v. Usama bin Laden et al.*, George Mimba testimony, trial transcript, day 14, March 7, 2001.

2. Vandenbroucke, "Eyewitness to Terror: Nairobi's Day of Infamy," 32.

2. The Past as Prologue

1. *Operations Vittles*, 21.

2. Bodansky, *Bin Laden*, xiii–xiv.

3. Bruno, *Foreign Circus*, 4.

3. The Response

1. USAID, "Up from the Ashes."

2. Patrick F. Kennedy, "Transcript: Foley, Kennedy Brief on Bombings in East Africa," August 14, 1998, USIS *Washington File*.

3. Thomas Pickering interview, PBS *NewsHour*, August 12, 1998.

4. The Impact

1. H. S. Onyango, "Relocate Embassy," *East African Standard*, August 22, 1998.

2. Radmacher-Hershey, "Courage," 1995.

3. Charity Ngilu, "Adding Fuel to the Fire," *Nation Weekly Review*, August 21, 1998.

4. Bonnie R. Cohen, statement before the Senate Task Force on Function 150.

5. USAID, "Up from the Ashes."

6. Baranowsky, "Psychological Response Stages of Post-Trauma/Disaster."

7. Edward W. Gnehm Jr. to Bushnell, May 8, 1998.

8. Bonnie Cohen to Bushnell, June 1, 1998.

9. *U.S. v. Usama bin Laden et al.*, "U.S. Grand Jury Indictment against Usama bin Laden and Others," USIS *Washington File*, November 6, 1998, https://fas.org/irp/news/1998/11/98110602_nlt.html.

5. The Turning Point

1. Ross, "Voice: We Are Asked to Do Anything and Everything Except Be Victims," 242.

2. James Risen and Benjamin Weiser, "Before Bombings, Omens and Fears," *New York Times*, January 9, 1999.

3. Accountability Review Board, *Bombings of the U.S. Embassies in Nairobi, Kenya, and Dar es Salaam, Tanzania, on August 7, 1998*.

4. Vandenbrouke, "Nairobi: Remembering the Sacrifice."

6. The Consequences

1. Andrea Koppel, "Some Argue U.S. Must Spend More to Protect Its Embassies," *New York Times*, July 13, 1999.

2. Independent Task Force on State Department Reform, *State Department Reform*.

7. The Proxy War

1. Independent Task Force on State Department Reform, *State Department Reform*, 23.

2. Sick, *All Fall Down*, 92.

3. Interview with Elizabeth Ann Swift, Foreign Affairs Oral History Project, the Association for Diplomatic Studies and Training, December 1992. Foreign Affairs Oral History Collection, Association for Diplomatic Studies and Training, Arlington, www.adst.org.

4. Brzezinski, "How Jimmy Carter and I Started the Mujahideen."

5. Trento, *Prelude to Terror*, 167–68.

6. Brzezinski, "How Jimmy Carter and I Started the Mujahideen."

7. Coll, *Ghost Wars*, 129.

8. Armstrong, *Islam*, xi.

9. Dreyfuss, *Devil's Game*, 20.

10. Cooley, *Unholy Wars*, 110–11.

11. *The 9/11 Commission Report*, 94.

12. Coll, *Ghost Wars*, 155–56.

13. Miller, "Greetings, America: My Name Is Osama Bin Laden."

14. Wright, *Looming Tower*, 142, 169.

15. Lance, *Triple Cross*, 35.

16. Lance, *1,000 Years for Revenge*, 42.

8. The Blowback

1. Lance, *1,000 Years for Revenge*, 42.

2. Lance. *1,000 Years for Revenge*, 29–32.

3. Friedman, "The CIA's Jihad."

4. Lance, *Triple Cross*, 61–62.

5. Lance, *1,000 Years for Revenge*, 34–37.

6. Soufan, *The Black Banners*, 45–46.

7. Lance, *Triple Cross*, 95–96.

8. *9/11 Commission Report*, 74–78.

9. *9/11 Commission Report*, 57.

10. Waugh, *Hunting the Jackal*, 121–23.

11. Waugh, *Hunting the Jackal*, 133.

12. Miller and Stone, *The Cell*, 148–49.

13. Lance, *Triple Cross*, 77–78.

14. *U.S. v. Usama bin Laden et al.*, trial transcript, day 2, February 6, 2001, 265–68.

15. Benjamin Weiser and James Risen, "The Making of a Militant: A Soldier's Shadowy Trail in U.S. and in the Mideast," *New York Times*, December 1, 1998.

16. Scheuer, *Through Our Enemies' Eyes*, 139.

17. Casper, *Falcon Brigade*, 10.

18. Scheuer, *Through Our Enemies' Eyes*, 147

19. Conwill, *Dream a World Anew*, 18.

9. The Plots

1. Weiser and Risen, "The Making of a Militant."

2. *9/11 Commission Report*, 109.

3. Miller and Stone, *The Cell*, 144–46.

4. Clarke, *Against All Enemies*, 78–79.

5. Clarke, *Against All Enemies*, 87–88.

6. Lance, *Triple Cross*, 142.

7. Scheuer, *Through Our Enemies' Eyes*, 149.

8. Bergen, *The Osama bin Laden I Know*, 143.

9. Clarke, *Against All Enemies*, 88.

10. Tenet, *At the Center of the Storm*.

11. Waugh, *Hunting the Jackal*, 139.

12. Benjamin and Simon, *The Age of Sacred Terror*, 231.

13. Freeh, *My FBI*, 186–87.

14. Clarke, *Against All Enemies*, 93.

15. Bergen, *The Osama bin Laden I Know*, 150.

16. Bergen, *The Osama bin Laden I Know*, 143–44.

17. Colin Miner, "Sources Claim CIA Aid Fueled Trade Center Blast," *Boston Herald*, February 24, 1994.

18. Miller and Stone, *The Cell*, 147–48.

19. Lance, *Triple Cross*, 173–74.

20. Lance, *Triple Cross*, 151–52.

21. Mahle, *Denial and Deception*.

22. Clarke, *Against All Enemies*, 96.

23. Clarke, *Against All Enemies*, 96.

24. David Kocieniewsky, "Terrorism Evidence Destroyed," *Newsday*, April 16, 1995.

25. Clarke, *Against All Enemies*, 127.

26. Youssef M. Ibrahim, "Egyptian Group Says It Tried to Kill Mubarak," *New York Times*, July 5, 1995.

27. Miniter, *Losing Bin Laden*.

28. Mahle, *Denial and Deception*, 247.

29. Clarke, *Against All Enemies*, 92.

30. Clarke, *Against All Enemies*, 141.

31. Jane Mayer, "Outsourcing Torture," *New Yorker*, February 8, 2005.

32. Lance, *1,000 Years for Revenge*, 233–35.

33. Zeman et al., "The Path to 9/11: Lost Warnings and Fatal Errors."

10. The Plans

1. Miniter, *Losing bin Laden*, 114.

2. Miniter, *Losing bin Laden*, 114

3. Interview with David Shinn, Foreign Affairs Oral History Project, Association for Diplomatic Studies and Training, July 5, 2002, 71, www.adst.org.

4. Clarke, *Against All Enemies*, 142.

5. Barton Gelman, "U.S. Was Foiled Multiple Times in Efforts to Capture Bin-Laden or Have Him Killed; Sudan's Offer to Arrest Militant Fell Through after Saudis Said No," *Washington Post*, October 3, 2001.

6. Lance, *Triple Cross*, 218–20.

7. "Judge Says Illegal Phone Taps Can Be Used in Bomb Trial," Associated Press, December 19, 2000.

8. *9/11 Commission Report*, 479.

9. Zeman et al., "The Path to 9/11: Lost Warnings and Fatal Errors."

10. Clarke, *Against All Enemies*, 116.

11. Scheuer, "How Not to Catch a Terrorist."

12. Bodansky, *Bin Laden*, 177.

13. Tenet, *At the Center of the Storm*, 102.

14. Tenet, *At the Center of the Storm*, 102

15. Scheuer, "How Not to Catch a Terrorist."

16. *U.S. v. Usama bin Laden et al.*, day 37 (May 1, 2001) and day 39 (May 3, 2001).

17. *U.S. v. Usama bin Laden et al.*, day 24 (March 19, 2001), 5315–22.

18. Coll, *Ghost Wars*, 374–75.

19. Clarke, *Against All Enemies*, 149.

20. *9/11 Commission Report*, public hearing, March 24, 2004.

21. David Rose, "The Osama Files," *Vanity Fair*, January 2002.

22. Miniter, *Losing Bin Laden*, 148.

23. Scheuer, *Imperial Hubris*, 191–92.

24. Wright, *Looming Tower*, 243–44.

25. *U.S. v. Usama bin Laden et al.*, trial transcript, day 36, April 30, 2001.

26. Benjamin Weiser, "Prosecutors Portray the Strands of a Bin Laden Web of Terror," *New York Times*, January 22, 2000.

27. Miller and Stone, *The Cell*, 203.

28. *U.S. v. Usama bin Laden et al.*, trial transcript, 5347–58.

29. Miller and Stone, *The Cell*, 202.

30. Lance, *Triple Cross*, 274–75.

31. Lance, *Triple Cross*, 276.

32. Miller and Stone, *The Cell*, 204.

11. The Execution

1. Bergen, *The Osama bin Laden I Know*, 196.

2. Bodansky, *Bin Laden*, 220.

3. Benjamin Weiser, "In Terrorism Case, a Plea Bargain Secretly 2 Years in the Making," *New York Times*, October 24, 2000.

4. Richard Norris, notes of telephone interview with members of the Accountability Review Board, October 13, 1998.

5. Brzezinski interview with *Le Nouvel Observateur*, Paris, January 15, 1998.

6. Sudan director of intelligence interview, *Vanity Fair*, January 2002.

7. *U.S. v. Usama bin Laden et al.*, trial transcript, day 37, 5228.

8. Clarke, *Against All Enemies*, 167–69.

9. Interview with Eric Boswell, November 4, 1998, Foreign Affairs Oral History Collection, Association for Diplomatic Studies and Training, Arlington VA, www.adst.org.

10. *U.S. v. Usama bin Laden et al.*, trial transcript, day 37, 5378.

11. Scheuer, "How Not to Catch a Terrorist."

12. Wright, *Looming Tower*, 265–68.

13. Boswell interview, 1998.

14. *U.S. v. Usama bin Laden et al.*, trial transcript, day 37, 5380.

15. Wright, *Looming Tower*, 266.

16. Omar Abdel Rahman (Blind Sheikh) statement inside prison, http://www .discoverthenetworks.org/individualProfile.asp?indid=1685.

17. Miller and Stone, *The Cell*, 183, 185–92.

18. Miller and Stone, *The Cell*, 214.

19. Mark Morris, "Phone Used in Bin Laden's Dealings Linked to Former Student," Knight-Rider, September 20, 2001.

20. Hamm, *Terrorism as Crime*, 65.

21. Bodansky, *Bin Laden*, 253.

22. Wright, *Looming Tower*, 269.

23. "Al Qaeda's London PR Office Fax Machine Sent Notice of East Africa Bombings," *Seattle-Post Intelligence*, July 13, 1999.

24. Miller and Stone, *The Cell*, 206–7.

25. Clarke, *Against All Enemies*, 184.

26. Wright, *Looming Tower*, 273.

27. Lance, *Tripe Cross*, 296.

28. *U.S. v. Usama bin Laden et al.*, trial transcript, day 14, March 7, 2001.

29. Wright, *Looming Tower*, 278–79.

30. Berntsen and Pezzullo. *Jawbreaker*, 22.

31. Reuters, "Charges Dropped in an Embassy Bombing," *New York Times*, March 20, 2000.

32. Rose, "The Osama File."

33. Gellman, "U.S. Was Foiled."

34. U.S. Congress, Senate, Committee on the Judiciary, statement of Patrick J. Fitzgerald, 108th Cong., October 21, 2003.

35. Nolan, *Tyranny of Consensus*, 93.

36 Government Accountability Office, *Combating Terrorism*, June 16, 1999.

37. Performance of the Intelligence Community, Staff Report #11 of the 9/11

Commission Report: Final Report of the National Commission on Terrorist Attacks upon the United States, July 22, 2004, 12.

38. James Risen, "U.S. Failed to Act upon Warnings in '98 of a Plane Attack," *New York Times*, September 18, 2002.

39. Clarke, *Against All Enemies*, 212.

40. Clarke, *Against All Enemies*, 204.

41. Clarke to Condoleezza Rice, memo, "Presidential Policy/Initiative Review: The al Qaeda Network," National Security Council, January 25, 2001.

42. Barbara Elias, ed., "Bush Administration's First Memo on al-Qaeda," declassified January 25, 2001, Richard Clarke memo, *National Security Archive Electronic Briefing Book*, no. 147, February 10, 2005, original post, updated September 27, 2006, http://www.911independentcommission.org/clarkememo012501.htm.

43. *9/11 Commission Report*, 349.

12. The Outcomes

1. Lance, *Triple Cross* (rev. ed.), 209.

2. Mahle, *Denial and Deception*, 273.

3. Executive summary of "Office of the Inspector General: Report on Central Intelligence Agency Accountability Regarding Findings and Conclusions of the Report of the Joint Inquiry into Intelligence Community Activities before and after September 1, 2001," June 2005.

4. Nolan, *Tyranny of Consensus*, 80.

5. Eric Boswell, interview, 1998.

6. Drucker, *Essential Drucker*.

7. "1994 Rwanda Pullout Driven by Clinton White House, UN Equivocation," *National Security Archive Electronic Briefing Book*, no. 511, April 16, 2015.

8. Bushnell, "One Story. Two Events. Seven Leadership Lessons."

9. Mark Thompson, "The $5 Trillion War on Terror," *Time*, June 29, 2011.

10. Kimberly Amadeo, "War on Terror Facts, Costs, and Timeline: Who Spent More on War? Bush or Obama?" *Balance*, January 17, 2017.

11. Nejad, *Body Count*, 15.

12. Amr and Ferris, "Displacement in the Muslim World."

13. Undersecretary of State Patrick Kennedy testimony to the House Oversight Committee, October 10, 2012.

14. Accountability Review Board, "Report on Benghazi Bombing September 11, 2012," September 19, 2012.

15. House Foreign Affairs Committee, *Benghazi: Where Is the State Department Accountability?*

16. Karen DeYoung, "How the Obama White House Runs Foreign Policy," *Washington Post*, August 4, 2015.

17. Report of the Independent Panel on Best Practices, Washington DC, August 29, 2013. Published to internet by *Aljazeera America*, http://www.ajam.fullreport-final-best-practices-report.

18. David Ignatius, "Can We Close the Power Gap?" *Washington Post*, March 1, 2013.

19. Krishnadev Calamur, "ISIS: An Islamist Group Too Extreme Even for Al-Qaida," June 13, 2014, http://npr.org/sections/thetwo-way/2014/06/13/321665375/isis-an-islamist-group- too extreme-even-for-al-qaida.

20. American Academy of Diplomacy Report, "American Diplomacy at Risk," April 2015, http://www.academyofdiplomacy.org.

21. Diplopundit, "Did We Ship Anyone Off to Timbuktu?"

22. Edward Delman, "Obama Promised to End America's Wars—Has He? The President's Military Record by the Numbers," *Atlantic Monthly,* March 30, 2016.

23. Ian Black, "Report on Syria Conflict Finds 11.5% of Population Killed or Injured," *Guardian,* February 10, 2016.

24. Crawford. *U.S. Costs of 2014.*

25. "Most Victims of Terrorist Attacks Are Muslim," VOA News, September 4, 2016.

26. Pew Research Center, "Beyond Distrust: How Americans View Their Government," November 23, 2015.

27. Institute for Economics and Peace, *Global Terrorism Index 2016.*

28. Goepner, "Learning from Today's Wars."

29. "Migrant Crisis: Migration to Europe Explained in Seven Charts," BBC News, March 4, 2017.

30. Spencer Ackerman, "NATO-Caused Civilian Casualties Increasing in Afghanistan," *Washington Independent,* April 16, 2010.

31. Thomas H. Kean and Lee H. Hamilton, 9/11 Commission chairmen, "2016 Terror Threat Worse than 2009," USA *Today,* September 9, 2016.

Epilogue

1. John Wagner and Scott Clement, "Poll Finds Disunited State of America," *Washington Post,* October 29, 2017.

2. Remarks by President Trump to the People of Poland, July 6, 2017, White House Office of the Press Secretary, http://www.whitehouse.gov.

3. David Inserra, "Foiled Virginia Attack Brings Total U.S. Terror Plots to 97 since 9/11," *Daily Signal,* September 7, 2017.

4. Carol Morello, "Security Chiefs: No Need for New War Authorization," *Washington Post,* October 31, 2017.

5. Rashed Mian, "Is There Room for Dissent within the Trump Administration?" *Long Island Press,* February 1, 2017.

6. Jasmine C. Lee and Kevin Quealy, "The 425 People, Places, and Things Donald Trump Has Insulted on Twitter: A Complete List." *New York Times,* January 3, 2018, http://www.nytimes.com/interactive/2016/01/28/upshot/donald-trump-twitter-insults.html.

7. Josh Rogin, "Lindsey Graham: Trump's State Department Budget Could Cause 'a Lot of Benghazis,'" *Washington Post,* May 23, 2017.

8. A. Trevor Thrall and Erik Goepner, "Step Back: Lessons for U.S. Foreign Policy from the Failed War on Terror," Policy Analysis 814, *Cato Institute,* June 26, 2017, https://www.cato.org/publications/policy-analysis/step-back-lessons-us-foreign-policy-failed-war-terror.

9. James A. W. Sarren, "Special Ops Rule in War on Terror," *Daily Beast*, June 28, 2016, https://www.thedailybeast.com/special-ops-rule-in-war-on-terror.

10. Bacevich, *New American Militarism*, 218, 219.

11. Adam Frisk, "Donald Trump Says He's 'Only One That Matters' When It Comes to Policy," *Global News*, November 3, 2017, https://globalnews.ca/news/3842063/donald-trump-only-one-matters-policy/.

12. cnn.com World, "Bin Laden: Goal Is to Bankrupt U.S.; Al-Jazeera Releases Full Transcript of al-Qaeda Leader's Tape," November 1, 2004.

13. Rashmi Singh, "Assessing Success and Failure in Terrorism and Counterterrorism: Development of Metrics on the Global War on Terror and the Global Jihad," *National Consortium for the Study of Terrorism and Responses to Terrorism*, October 2011, http://www.start.umd.edu/research-projects/assessing-success-and-failure-terrorism-and-counterterrorism-development-metrics.

14. Goepner, "Learning from Today's Wars."

15. Goepner, "Learning from Today's Wars."

BIBLIOGRAPHY

The 9/11 Commission Report: Final Report of the National Commission on Terror-ist Attacks upon the United States. New York: Norton, 2004. Academy of Diplo-macy. "A Foreign Affairs Budget for the Future: Fixing the Crisis in Diplomatic Readiness." October 2008. http://www.academyofdiplomacy.org//publications / fab_report_2008.pdf.

———. "American Diplomacy at Risk." April 2015. http://www.academyofdiplo macy.org.

Accountability Review Board. *Bombings of the U.S. Embassies in Nairobi, Kenya, and Dar es Salaam, Tanzania, on August 7, 1998.* January 11, 1999. Available at www/zgram.net/embassybombing.htm.

———. *Report on Benghazi Bombing of September 11, 2012.* December 19, 2012.

Ahmed, Nafeez Mosaddeq. *The War on Freedom: How and Why America Was Attacked on September 11, 2001.* Joshua Tree CA: Tree of Life, 2002.

———. *The War on Truth: 9/11, Disinformation, and the Anatomy of Terrorism.* Northampton MA: Olive Branch Press, 2005.

Albright, Madeleine, with Bill Woodward. *Madam Secretary.* New York: Mira-max Books, 2003.

Alexander, Yonah, and Michael S. Swetnam. *Usama bin Laden's al-Qaida: Profile of a Terrorist Network.* Ardsley NY: Transnational, 2001.

Armstrong, Karen. *Islam: A Short History.* New York: Modern Library, 2000.

Bacevich, Andrew J. *America's War: For the Greater Middle East.* New York: Ran-dom, 2016.

———. *The Limits of Power: The End of American Exceptionalism.* New York: Metropolitan Books, 2008.

———. *The New American Militarism: How Americans Are Seduced by War.* New York: Oxford University Press, 2005.

———. *Washington Rules: America's Path to Permanent War.* New York: Metro-politan Books, 2010.

Baer, Robert. *The Devil We Know: Dealing with the New Iranian Superpower.* New York: Three River Press, 2008.

———. *See No Evil: The True Story of a Ground Soldier in the CIA's War on Terrorism*. New York: Three Rivers Press, 2002.

———. *Sleeping with the Devil: How Washington Sold Our Soul for Saudi Crude*. New York: Crown, 2003.

Bamford, James. *A Pretext for War: 9/11, Iraq, and the Abuse of America's Intelligence Agencies*. New York: Doubleday, 2004.

Baranowsky, Anna B. "Psychological Response to States of Post Trauma Disaster." Traumatology Institute, 2002. http://www.traumaline1.com/.

Benjamin, Daniel, and Steven Simon. *The Age of Sacred Terror*. New York: Random House, 2002.

Bergen, Peter L. *The Osama bin Laden I Know*. New York: Free Press, 2006.

Bergen, Peter, et al. "In-depth Terrorism in America after 9/11." *New America, International Security*. http://www.newamerica.org/in-depth/terrorism -inamerica/what-threat-united-states- today/.

Berntsen, Gary, and Ralph Pezzullo. *Jawbreaker: The Attack on Bin Laden and Al-Qaeda*. New York: Three Rivers Press, 2005.

"Bin Laden: Goal Is to Bankrupt U.S., Al-Jazeera Releases Full Transcript of al-Qaeda Leader's Tape." CNN.com World, November 1, 2004. http://www.cnn .com/2004/world/meast/ 11/01/binladen.tape/.

Bodansky, Yossef. *Bin Laden: The Man Who Declared War on America*. Roseville CA: Prima, 1999.

Brisard, Jean-Charles, and Guillaume Dasquie. *Forbidden Truth: U.S.-Taliban Secret Oil Diplomacy and the Failed Hunt for Bin Laden*. New York: Nation Books, 2002.

Bruno, James. *The Foreign Circus: Why Foreign Policy Should Not Be Left in the Hands of Diplomats, Spies, and Political Hacks*. Canastota NY: Bittersweet House Press, 1964 (paperback, 2014).

Brzezinski, Zbigniew. "How Jimmy Carter and I Started the Mujahideen." *Counterpunch*, January 15, 1998. https://www.counterpunch.org/1998/01/15/how -jimmy-carter-and-i-started-the-mujahideen/.

Bushnell, Prudence. "Leadership at State: The Neglected Dimension." *Foreign Service Journal*, June 1999.

———. "One Story. Two Events. Seven Leadership Lessons." *Foreign Service Journal*, January/February 2017.

———. Unclassified cable to Department of State Officials. Subject: Request You Visit, October 7, 1998.

Calamur, Krishnadev. "ISIS: An Islamist Group Too Extreme Even for Al-Qaida." June 13, 2014. http://npr.org/sections/the-two-way/2014/06/13/321665375 /isis-an-islamist-group- too-extreme-even-for-al-qaida/.

Campbell, John Franklin. *The Foreign Affairs Fudge Factory*. New York: Basic Books, 1971.

Casper, Lawrence E. *Falcon Brigade: Combat and Command in Somalia and Haiti*. Boulder: Lynne Rienner, 2001.

Clarke, Richard A. *Against All Enemies: Inside America's War on Terror.* New York: Free Press, 2004.

———. "Presidential Policy Initiative Review: The al-Qaeda Network." Memorandum to Condoleezza Rice, National Security Council, January 25, 2001. *National Security Archive Electronic Briefing Book No. 147,* February 10, 2005, updated September 27, 2006.

———. *Your Government Failed You: Breaking the Cycle of National Security Disasters.* New York: Harper, 2008.

Cohen, Bonnie R. Statement of undersecretary for management before Senate Task Force on Function 150. Washington DC, September 17, 1998.

Coll, Steve. *Ghost Wars: The Secret History of the CIA, Afghanistan, and Bin Laden, from the Soviet Invasion to September 10, 2001.* New York: Penguin Press, 2004.

Conwill, Kinshasha Holman, ed. *Dream a World Anew: The African American Experience and the Shaping of America.* Washington: Smithsonian Books, 2016.

Cooley, John. *Unholy Wars: Afghanistan, America, and International Terrorism.* New York: Pluto Press, 2002.

Copeland, Thomas E. *Fool Me Twice: Intelligence Failure and Mass Casualty Terrorism.* Leiden: Martinus Nijhoff, 2007.

Crawford, Rita. *U.S. Costs of 2014: $4.4 Trillion and Counting: Summary of Costs for the U.S. Wars in Iraq, Afghanistan, and Pakistan.* Boston: Boston University Press, 2016.

Daalder, Ivo H., and I. M. Destler. *In the Shadow of the Oval Office: Profiles of the National Security Advisors and the Presidents They Served from JFK to George W. Bush.* New York: Simon & Schuster, 2009.

Dahl, Erik J. *Intelligence and Surprise Attack: Failure and Success from Pearl Harbor to 9/11 and Beyond.* Washington DC: Georgetown University Press, 2013.

Danieli, Yael, Danny Brom, and Joe Sills, eds. *The Trauma of Terrorism: Sharing Knowledge and Shared Care.* New York: Haworth Press, 2005.

Delman, Edward. "Obama Promised to End America's Wars—Has He? The President's Military Record by the Numbers." *Atlantic Monthly,* March 2016.

Diamond, John. *The CIA and the Culture of Failure: U.S. Intelligence from the End of the Cold War to the Invasion of Iraq.* Stanford: Stanford University Press, 2008.

Diplopundit. "Did We Ship Anyone Off to Timbuktu? Who at Senior Levels Knew What and When about HRC's Communication?" February 3, 2016. https://diplopundit.net/2016/02/03/did-we-ship-anyone-off-to-timbuktu-who-at-senior-levels-knew-what-and-when-about-hrcs-communications/.

Dreyfuss, Robert. *Devil's Game: How the United States Helped Unleash Fundamentalist Islam.* New York: Metropolitan Books, 2006.

Drucker, Peter. *Essential Drucker: Management, the Individual, and Society.* New York: HarperCollins, 2000.

Executive Summary of "Defeating Terrorists, Not Terrorism: Assessing U. S. Counterterrorism Policy from 9/11 to ISIS Task Force on Terrorism and Ideology." Bipartisan Policy Center, September 2017.

Executive Summary, June 2005. "Office of the Inspector General Report on Central Intelligence Agency Accountability Regarding Findings and Conclusions of the Report of the Joint Inquiry into Intelligence Community Activities before and after September 11, 2001." https://www.cia.gov/library/reports/Executive%20summary_oig%20report.pdf.

Faddis, Charles S. *Beyond Repair: The Decline and Fall of the* CIA. Guilford UK: Lyons Press, 2010.

Farah, Douglas. *Blood from Stones: The Secret Financial Network of Terror.* New York: Broadway Books, 2004.

Fenton, Kevin. *Disconnecting the Dots: How* CIA *and* FBI *Officials Helped Enable 9/11 and Evaded Government Investigations.* Waterville OR: Trine Day, 2011.

Freeh, Louis J. *My* FBI: *Bringing Down the Mafia, Investigating Bill Clinton, and Fighting the War on Terror.* New York: St. Martin's Press, 2007.

Friedman, Robert I. "The CIA's Jihad." *New York Magazine*, March 1995.

Gelb, Leslie H. *Power Rules: How Common Sense Can Rescue American Foreign Policy.* New York: HarperCollins, 2009.

Gertz, Bill. *Breakdown: How America's Intelligence Failures Led to September 11.* Washington DC: Regnery, 2002.

Global Terrorism Index 2016: Measuring and Understanding the Impact of Terrorism. Institute for Economics and Peace. http://economicsandpeace.org/wp-content/uploads/2016/11/Global-Terrorism-Index-2016.2.pdf.

Goepner, Erik W. "Learning from Today's Wars: Measuring the Effectiveness of America's War on Terror." U.S. Army War College, *Quarterly Parameters* 46, no. 1 (Spring 2016).

Goldberg, Jeffery. "The Obama Doctrine." *Atlantic Monthly*, April 2016.

Government Accountability Office. *Combatting Terrorism: Issues to Be Resolved to Improve Counterterrorism Operations.* June 16, 1999.

Gray, John. *Al Qaeda and What It Means to Be Modern.* New York: New Press, 2003.

Gup, Ted. *Nation of Secrets: The Threat to Democracy and the American Way of Life.* New York: Doubleday, 2007.

Hamm, Mark S. *Terrorism as Crime: From Oklahoma City to Al-Qaeda and Beyond.* New York: New York University Press, 2007.

Harris, John F. *The Survivor: Bill Clinton in the White House.* New York: Random House, 2005.

Hoffman, Bruce. *Inside Terrorism.* New York: Columbia University Press, 1998.

Independent Task Force on State Department Reform. *State Department Reform.* Washington DC: Council on Foreign Relations and the Center for Strategic and International Studies, 2001.

Jett, Dennis C. *Why American Foreign Policy Fails: Unsafe at Home and Despised Abroad.* Hampshire UK: Palgrave Macmillan, 2008.

Johnson, Chalmers. *Blowback: The Costs and Consequences of American Empire.* New York: Metropolitan, Henry Holt, 2000.

Jones, Ishmael. *The Human Factor: Inside the* CIA's *Dysfunctional Intelligence Culture.* New York: Encounter Books, 2010.

Jones, Milo, and Philippe Silberzahn. *Constructing Cassandra: Reframing Intelligence Failure at the CIA, 1947–2001*. Stanford: Stanford University Press, 2013.

Kennedy, Patrick F. "Transcript: Foley, Kennedy Brief on Bombings in East Africa." *USIS Washington File*, August 14, 1998.

Kopp, Harry W. *The Voice of the Foreign Service: A History of the American Foreign Services Association*. Washington DC: Foreign Service Books, 2015.

Labeviere, Richard. *Dollars for Terror: The United States and Islam*. New York: Algora, 2000.

Lance, Peter. *1,000 Years for Revenge: International Terrorism and the FBI, the Untold Story*. New York: HarperCollins, 2003.

———. *Triple Cross: How bin Laden's Master Spy Penetrated the CIA, the Green Berets, and the FBI—and Why Patrick Fitzgerald Failed to Stop Him*. New York: HarperCollins, 2006.

———. *Triple Cross: How bin Laden's Master Spy Penetrated the CIA, the Green Berets, and the FBI*. Rev. ed. New York: HarperCollins, 2009.

Leebaert, Derek. *Magic and Mayhem: The Delusions of American Foreign Policy from Korea to Afghanistan*. New York: Simon & Shuster, 2010.

Lewis, David E. *The Politics of Presidential Appointments: Political Control and Bureaucratic Performance*. Princeton: Princeton University Press, 2008.

Lippman, Thomas W. *Madeleine Albright and the New American Diplomacy*. Boulder CO: Perseus, 2004.

Mahle, Melissa Boyle. *Denial and Deception: An Insider's View of the CIA*. New York: Nation Books, 2006.

Mamdani, Mahmood. *Good Muslim, Bad Muslim: America, the Cold War, and the Roots of Terror*. New York: Pantheon Books, 2004.

Mann, Thomas E., and Norman J. Ornstein. *The Broken Branch: How Congress Is Failing America and How to Get It Back on Track*. New York: Oxford University Press, 2006.

Mayer, Jane. "Outsourcing Torture." *New Yorker*, February 8, 2005.

Miller, John. "Greetings, America: My Name Is Osama Bin Laden." *Esquire*, February 1, 1999.

Miller, John, and Michael Stone with Chris Mitchell. *The Cell: Inside the 9/11 Plot and Why the FBI and CIA Failed to Stop It*. New York: Hyperion, 2003.

Miniter, Richard. *Losing Bin Laden: How Bill Clinton's Failures Unleased Global Terror*. Washington DC: Regnery, 2003.

Moynihan, Daniel Patrick. *Secrecy*. New Haven: Yale University Press, 1998.

Nejad, Ali Fathollah. *Body Count: Casualty Figures after 10 Years of the "War on Terror": Iraq, Afghanistan, Pakistan*. Washington DC: Physicians for Social Responsibility, March 2015.

Neumann, Ronald E. "American Diplomacy at Risk." *Foreign Service Journal*, July/August 2015.

Nolan, Janne E. *Diplomacy and Security in the Twenty-First Century*. Washington DC: Georgetown University Institute for the Study of Diplomacy, 2009.

————. *Tyranny of Consensus: Discourse and Dissent in American National Security Policy*. New York: Century Foundation, 2013.

Nolan, Janne E., and Douglas MacEachin with Kristine Tockman. *Discourse, Dissent, and Strategic Surprise: Formulating U.S. Security Policy in an Age of Uncertainty*. Washington DC: Georgetown University Institute for the Study of Diplomacy, 2006.

Northouse, Peter. *Leadership: Theory and Practice*. New York: Sage, 2013.

Persico, Joseph E. *Casey: From OSS to the CIA*. New York: Viking, 1990.

Pope, Laurence. *The Demilitarization of American Diplomacy: Two Cheers for Striped Pants*. Basingstoke: Palgrave Macmillan, 2014.

Posner, Richard A. *Preventing Surprise Attacks: Intelligence Reform in the Wake of 9/11*. Stanford: Stanford University Press, 2005.

Power, Samantha. "Bystander to Genocide." *Atlantic Monthly*, September 2001.

Priest, Dana, and William M. Arkin. *Top Secret America: The Rise of the New American Security State*. New York: Little, Brown, 2011.

Reeve, Simon. *The New Jackals: Ramzi Yousef, Osama bin Laden, and the Future of Terrorism*. Boston: Northeastern University Press, 1999.

Rose, David. "The Osama Files." *Vanity Fair*, January 2004.

Ross, Lee Ann. "Voice: We Are Asked to Do Anything and Everything Except Be Victims." In *The Trauma of Terrorism: Sharing Knowledge and Shared Care*, ed. Yael Danieli, Danny Brom, and Joe Sills. Binghamton NY: Haworth, 2004.

Rothkoph, David. *Running the World: The Inside Story of the National Security Council and the Architects of American Power*. New York: Public Affairs, 2004.

Rovner, Joshua. *Fixing the Facts: National Security and the Politics of Intelligence*. Ithaca: Cornell University Press, 2011.

Sageman, Marc. *Understanding Terror Networks*. Philadelphia: University of Pennsylvania Press, 2004.

Schake, Kori N. *State of Disrepair: Fixing the Culture and Practices of the State Department*. Stanford: Hoover Institution Press, 2012.

Scheuer, Michael. *Imperial Hubris: Why the West Is Losing the War on Terror*. Washington: Potomac Books, 2004.

————. *Through Our Enemies' Eyes: Osama bin Laden, Radical Islam, and the Future of America*. Washington: Potomac Books, 2007.

————. *Marching towards Hell: America and Islam after Iraq*. New York: Free Press, 2008.

————. "How Not to Catch a Terrorist." *Atlantic Monthly*, December 2, 2004.

Scott, Peter Dale. *The Road to 9/11: Wealth, Empire, and the Future of America*. Berkeley: University of California Press, 2007.

Shenon, Philip. *The Commission: The Uncensored History of the 9/11 Investigation*. New York: Twelve, 2008.

Sick, Gary. *All Fall Down: America's Tragic Encounter with Iran*. New York: Random, 1985.

Singh, Rashmi. "Assessing Success and Failure in Terrorism and Counterterrorism: Development of Metric on the Global War on Terror and the Global

Jihad." National Consortium for the Study of Terrorism and Responses to Terrorism. http://www.start.umd.edu/research-projects/assessing-success - and-failure-terrorism- and-counterterrorism-development-metrics/.

Soufan, Ali. *The Black Banners: The Inside Story of 9/11 and the War against al-Qaeda*. New York: Norton, 2011.

Special Report of the Independent Panel on Best Practices, submitted to Department of State senior officials on August 29, 2013.

Tarpley, Webster Griffin. *9/11 Synthetic Terror: Made in USA*. Joshua Tree CA: Progressive Press, 2006.

Tenet, George. *At the Center of the Storm: My Years at the CIA*. New York: HarperCollins, 2007.

Thrall, Trevor A., and Erik Goepner. *Step Back: Lessons for U.S. Foreign Policy from the Failed War on Terror*. Policy Analysis 814. Cato Institute, June 26, 2017.

Trento, Joseph J. *Prelude to Terror: The Rogue CIA and the Legacy of America's Private Intelligence Network*. New York: Carroll & Graf, 2005.

United States Agency for International Development (USAID). "Up from the Ashes: Lessons Learned from the Bombing of the United States Embassy, Nairobi, Kenya." Nairobi, 2001. http://pdf.usaid.gov/pdf_docs/Pnacn621.pdf.

United States State Department, Office of the Coordinator for Counterterrorism. *Patterns of Global Terrorism*, introduction, April 1996.

Ursano, Robert J., Carol S. Fullerton, and Ann E. Norwood, eds. *Terrorism and Disaster: Individual and Community Mental Health Interventions*. Cambridge: Cambridge University Press, 2003.

USA v. Usama bin Laden et al. "U.S. Grand Jury Indictment against Usama bin Laden and Others." *USIS Washington File*, November 6, 1998.

———. *Jamal Ahmed Al-Fadl testimony*. Trial transcript, day 2, February 6, 2001, 265–68.

———. George Mimba testimony. Trial transcript, day 14, March 7, 2001, 1896–1908.

———. Government's closing argument. Trial transcript, day 37, May 1, 2001, 5347–58, 5378–80.

———. Government's closing argument. Trial transcript, day 39, May 3, 2001, 5554–5609.

Vandenbroucke, Lucien S. "Nairobi: Remembering the Sacrifice." *State Department Magazine*, April 1999.

———. "Eyewitness to Terror: Nairobi's Day of Infamy." *Foreign Service Journal*, June 2000.

Waugh, Billy, with Tim Heown. *Hunting the Jackal: A Special Forces and CIA Ground Soldier's Fifty-Year Career Hunting America's Enemies*. New York: HarperCollins, 2004.

Weiner, Eric. *Geography of Genius*. New York: Simon & Schuster, 2016.

Weiner, Tim. *Legacy of Ashes: The History of the CIA*. New York: Anchor Books, 2008.

Wright, Lawrence. *The Looming Tower: Al-Qaeda and the Road to 9/11*. New York: Knopf, 2006.

Yusufzai, Rahimullah. "Wrath of God." *Time*, November 9, 1999.

Zegart, Amy B. *Flawed by Design: The Evolution of the CIA, JCS, and NSC*. Stanford: Stanford University Press, 1999.

————. *Spying Blind: The CIA, the FBI, and the Origins of 9/11*. Princeton: Princeton University Press, 2007.

Zeman, Ned, David Wise, David Rose, and Bryan Burrough. "The Path to 9/11: Lost Warnings and Fatal Errors." *Vanity Fair*, November 2004.

Zinni, Tony, and Tony Koltz. *The Battle for Peace: A Frontline Vision of America's Power and Purpose*. New York: Palgrave Macmillan, 2006.

————. *Leading the Charge: Leadership Lessons from the Battlefield to the Boardroom*. New York: Palgrave Macmillan, 2009.

INDEX

Bomer, Ellen, 77

Boswell, Eric, 172, 175, 191, 201

Briehl, Daniel, 73, 102

Brzezinski, Zbigniew, 117, 118

Buckley, Richard, 7, 28, 29; as CLO, 33; in Guatemala, F21, 93–95; in Bailey's Crossroads, 106; at Marine Corps Ball, F27; in Nairobi, 40–41, 43, 48, 56, 58, 74–75, 78; networks formed by, 66–67; at New York trial, 101, 103, 152; in Senegal, 31–32, 122, 134, 136; television appearance by, 52; in U.S., 158; with USAID, 32; as a volunteer, 41, 160

budget cuts, 23, 70, 137

Bush, George H.W., 127, 130–31, 133–34, 218

Bush, George W., 96, 189

Bushnell, Bernice Dufie, F7, 21; in Cooperstown, 29; death of, 113; in France, F3, 23–24; in Germany, 19–21; visit to Nairobi, 80

Bushnell, Gerry, F7, 21; in Berlin, 19; death of, 113; and foreign service, 22; in France, F3; retirement of, 29–31; visit to Dakar by, 36; visit to Nairobi, 80

Bushnell, Prudence: articles written by, 193, 202; as bilingual secretary, 27–28; birthday celebrations, 217; in Bombay, 33–34; cake-cutting ceremony, F8; called to testify, 100; childhood of, F7, F26, 19–21, 22–26; in Dallas, 29; as DAS, 37–38, 141; as DCM, 35–36; as dean, 106; demonstrations against, 97–98, 104; as director, 121; embassy management, 178–80; EMDR practiced by, 114; enters Foreign Service, 30–31, 119; first job of, 26; gift for, F19, 75, 89; goodbye event for, 89; in Guatemala, F20, 93–94; in her garden, F15; holding Ka-Bar knife, F13; in Kenya, F23, F24, F25; with Jesse Jackson, F22; and knitting, 114, 207; laying wreath at bomb site, F11; and leadership issues, 122, 193–94, 199; with Madeleine Albright, F12; and management training and skills, 28, 32, 34; at Marine Corps Ball, F8, F27; and media, 89; in Nairobi, 40–41; at NASA, 29–30; in New York, 29; parents of, F3, F7; performance appraisal of, 72, 174–

76; with President Moi, F28; promotion of, 32, 33; and Reiki treatments, 68; resentment issue, 22, 61, 65; retirement of, 109; with Riz Khaliq, F2; in Senegal, 31–32, 129–36; with sister, F4, F5, F6; speaking and training, 113, 192–93, 203–4; and Susan Rice, F18, 61; views on terrorists, 146–47; as a volunteer, 192; in Washington, DC, 38–40; wildlife sightseeing by, 83; and William Crowe, 69–70; and William Daley, F14

Bushnell, Susan, F7, 20–23, 26

Carney, Timothy, 154

Carter, Jimmy, 28, 30, 115, 117, 118, 119

Casey, William, 120, 121

Cato Institute, 220–21

Central Intelligence Agency (CIA), 81, 119–20, 230n3; CIA-FBI team, 70, 81, 163, 179

chancery building, 5–7, 10–11, 15, 41, 72, 179

chemical weapons, 73, 101

civilian casualties, 199, 212, 218

civil rights, 27, 103, 211

Clarke, Richard, 39, 139, 153, 154, 162, 230n42

Clinton, Bill, 14, 40, 134, 137, 142–43, 159; administration, 67, 96, 140, 154, 203

Clinton, Hillary, 114, 198, 202, 203; and email server issue, 204, 206, 210

Cohen, Bonnie, 12, 62, 66, 72, 175

Cold War, 20, 94, 117, 133, 134, 142

communism, 22, 23, 119, 216

Comprehensive Employment and Training Assistance Act, 29

conflict resolution strategies, 147–48

Cooperative Bank Building, 3, 44, 86, 103, 199

counterterrorism operations, 142, 148, 151, 184, 191, 213

Counterterrorism Security Group (CSG), 142, 143, 146, 153, 171

coup d'état, 8, 26, 36, 94, 115

Crowe, William J., 69, 73, 82, 184

Crusaders, 121, 134, 170, 176

Dakar, Senegal, 132–36

Daley, William, F14, 77, 78, 178–80

Dallaire, Roméo, 207, 208

Pakistan, transfer to, 23–25
Peace Accords, 94, 95
Peace Corps volunteers, 8, 57, 224
Pickering, Tom, 53, 66, 200, 203
polygamy, 124, 135
Portillo, Alfonso, 95, 105
post-bombing actions, 59, 78
post-traumatic stress disorder (PTSD), 93, 98, 113–14, 192, 205
Powell, Colin, 107, 108, 197
presidential daily briefing (PDB), 184
presidential elections, 173, 195
proxy war, 113–25, 211
public resentment, 78, 79, 194

al-Qaeda, 43, 59; attack on U.S. military personnel, 73; cells operated by, 70, 101, 151; formation of, 125; mission and passion of, 124; office in Nairobi, 70; purpose of, 124; revelations about, 155–56; and USS *Cole*, 100, 185. *See also* bin Laden, Osama

radical Islam, 170, 216, 220
radio jamming, 39
radio net broadcasts, 14, 16, 161
RAD method, 68
Reagan, Ronald, 30, 119, 120
refugee camps, 37, 39, 179
Reiki treatments, 68
Remembrance and Recognition Ceremony, 84–85
rendition program, 162, 172
Reno, Janet, 143, 151
Rice, Condoleezza, 109, 185, 197
Rice, Susan, 11, 12; and author, F18, 61; cable sent to, 66; and NSC, 201–2; at Remembrance and Recognition Ceremony, 84
rule of law, 27, 94
Russia, 30, 118–19
Rwanda genocide, 38, 113, 193–96

Sand, Leonard, 101, 102
Saudi government, 114, 138, 145, 153
Scheuer, Michael, 134, 139, 150, 155, 172, 185
search and rescue teams, 10, 14, 47, 48, 55
security issues, 12, 33, 53, 72, 166–67, 170
security threats, 59, 64, 72, 186, 220
September 11, 2001, attacks, 104–5; and

9/11 Commission, 154, 184, 186, 190, 213, 223
shah of Iran, 30, 115, 116, 117
Shia Muslims, 115, 116
Shirley, Katherine, 35, 36, 130
Smart, Annie, 28
social entrepreneurship, 206
Somalia, 134, 139, 140
Soviet Union, 115, 119, 123, 134
Special Operations Command (SOCOM), 221
Statue of Liberty tour, 103
Stephens, Chris, 199, 200
Stevenson, Barbara, 219
Sudan: and al-Turabi, 117; bin Laden's move to, 131, 132; intelligence sharing in, 170–71; and Louis Freeh, 59; as sponsor of terrorism, 138, 144
Sunni Islam, 24, 25, 27, 115, 211
Swift, Ann, 116, 117

Taylor, Charles, 40, 146
Tehran, 25–26, 30
Tenet, George, 140, 158, 162, 172, 181, 184
terrorist attacks, 11; on Benghazi compound, 199; at CIA headquarters, 137; at Federal building, 149; homegrown, 223; increase in, 145–46, 211–12; medium risk of, 12, 64; on U.S. embassies, 11, 30, 160; on U.S. military, 73, 101, 144; at World Trade Center, 104–5. *See also* bombing, Nairobi; bombings
Tillerson, Rex, 220, 221
Top Spouse. *See* Buckley, Richard
transnational issues, 7, 37, 141
truck bomb, 12, 60, 71, 137, 149, 170
Trump, Donald, 207, 212, 213, 215–17, 220
al-Turabi, Hassan, 117, 131
TWA Flight 800 explosion, 157

Ufundi House, F1, 10, 15, 44, 86, 88
Union Carbide plant, 34
United Fruit Company, 94
U.S. Agency for International Development (USAID), 8, 11, 13, 45, 46, 141
US v. Usama bin Laden, 100
U.S. Department of Defense: budget issues, 210, 215; flight screw up by, 46–47; impact of, 218; and "preventive defense," 142; and radio jamming, 39

American Ambassadors: The Past, Present, and Future of America's Diplomats
Dennis C. Jett

Echoes of a Distant Clarion: Recollections of a Diplomat and Soldier
John G. Kormann

The Architecture of Diplomacy: Building America's Embassies
Jane C. Loeffler

Escape with Honor: My Last Hours in Vietnam
Terry McNamara, with Adrian Hill

American Diplomats: The Foreign Service at Work
William Morgan and C. Stuart Kennedy

The Other War: Winning and Losing in Afghanistan
Ronald C. Neumann

Witness to a Changing World
David D. Newsom

The Craft of PoliticalAnalysis for Diplomats
Raymond F. Smith

In Those Days: A Diplomat Remembers
James W. Spain

Losing the Golden Hour: An Insider's View of Iraq's Reconstruction
James Stephenson

African Wars: A Defense Intelligence Perspective
William G. Thom

Abroad for Her Country: Tales of a Pioneer Woman Ambassador in the U.S. Foreign Service
Jean Wilkowski

For a complete list of series titles, visit adst.org/publications.